DANGEROUS WOMEN

DANGEROUS WOMEN

Fifty reflections on women, power and identity

Edited by
Jo Shaw, Ben Fletcher-Watson and Abrisham Ahmadzadeh

First published in 2022

Unbound
Level 1, Devonshire House, One Mayfair Place, London W1J 8AJ
www.unbound.com

Text design by PDQ Digital Media Solutions Ltd.

A CIP record for this book is available from the British Library

ISBN 978-1-80018-064-2 (paperback)
ISBN 978-1-80018-065-9 (ebook)

Printed and bound in Great Britain by Clays Ltd, Elcograf S.p.A.

1 3 5 7 9 8 6 4 2

Contents

Introduction

The Dangerous Women Project is an initiative of the Institute for Advanced Studies in the Humanities (IASH) at the University of Edinburgh. It was founded in 2016 by Dr Peta Freestone and Professor Jo Shaw, with Peta as editor.

The Project asks: what does it mean to be a 'dangerous woman'?

The idea that women are dangerous individually or collectively permeates many historical periods, cultures and areas of contemporary life (despite, and in some instances in response to, explicitly feminist movements).

We may take lightly the label attached by mainstream media outlets to women such as Shami Chakrabarti, formerly of Liberty, or Scotland's First Minister Nicola Sturgeon as being 'the most dangerous woman in the UK'. But behind this label lies a serious set of questions about the dynamics, conflicts, identities and power relations with which women live today.

The Dangerous Women Project curated more than 365 responses to those questions from all over the world between International Women's Day 2016 and International Women's Day 2017, gathered together on our website at dangerouswomenproject.org. Many of these essays have been updated since first published on the Dangerous Women Project website.

Each Dangerous Women Project essay explores, examines or critiques the 'dangerous women' theme by inviting reflections from women of diverse backgrounds and identities, including poets, playwrights and other creative writers, academics, journalists, commentators, artists, performers and opinion formers, and indeed anyone of any gender with an angle on the theme. All views expressed in the Dangerous Women Project's articles are therefore the views of the individual author, not of IASH or the University of Edinburgh.

When We Are 'Dangerous', We Can Change the World

Nicola Sturgeon

Scottish First Minister Nicola Sturgeon MSP explains what being labelled a 'dangerous woman' means for her.

In the lead-up to the 2015 UK general election, I was given the title of 'Dangerous Woman' by the *Sun* and *Daily Mail* newspapers. It was, I believe, based on the supposition that my party's prospective success in that election would have a number of significant effects on the existing political power balance.

However, my advocacy of feminism was also used as an indication as to my so-called hazardous nature. My appointment of a gender-balanced Cabinet and my public commitment to use my time as Scotland's First Minister to improve the lives of women across our country were highlighted as evidence of this nature.

As a result, although the term was meant to give pause to those who might have been considering voting for the Scottish National Party (SNP) in the general election, it could also be viewed as yet another pejorative term used to minimise women's achievements. Terms like 'dangerous' can belittle the positions of women in power by implying that we should be feared. I am extremely concerned that women can be collectively branded in a way that men are simply not subjected to. Despite this, I took great pride in being termed 'dangerous' when I considered those with whom I shared the title, such as Liberty director Shami Chakrabarti and German Chancellor Angela Merkel.

To be counted among those women felt like a validation of my challenge to the status quo. When I look at the women who inspired me to take on a political career and ultimately leadership responsibilities, my role models include the strong women who played an important part in shaping the SNP, Margo MacDonald and Winnie Ewing, who helped the party become the social democratic force for change we are today.

I am sure they too were seen as threatening to the political establishment of the day, as they challenged the perceived order in Scotland. Their work did so much to encourage women like me and showed us that there could be a place for us in politics.

Winnie Ewing's election victory in 1967 was a significant by-election in Scottish political history and began a surge of support for the SNP. She said at the time of her election, 'Stop the world, Scotland wants to get on', and her presence at Westminster proved to be a real focus for the SNP, with a significant rise in membership as a result. Many feel it was as a result of her victory that the Government established the Kilbrandon Commission to look into the establishment of a devolved Scottish Assembly.

Margo MacDonald's victory in 1973 in the Glasgow Govan by-election, until then a Labour stronghold, was another landmark result for the SNP. She faced blatant sexism and harassment, as all women MPs suffered at that time, and dealt with this in her own inimitable way, as she would in her battle with Parkinson's disease towards the end of her life. She and Winnie helped pave the way for all of the amazing female SNP MSPs and MPs that we have today here and at Westminster.

Their great legacy of political engagement is something I am proud to see continue in the women of Scotland, particularly in the grassroots campaigns of the Scottish Referendum. I will work hard to ensure that the next generation of 'dangerous women' flourish in Scotland. Whether that be in politics, the arts, science and technology, business or sport – I want young girls to know that they should always aspire to be their best and challenge the status quo. When we are 'dangerous', we can change the world and our place in it.

Rt Hon. Nicola Sturgeon MSP
First Minister of Scotland

Crime and Punishment in Love

Laura Elizabeth Woollett

Laura Elizabeth Woollett is the Melbourne-based author of a short story collection, The Love of a Bad Man *(Scribe, 2016), and two novels,* Beautiful Revolutionary *(Scribe, 2018) and* The Newcomer *(Scribe, 2021).* The Love of a Bad Man *was shortlisted for the Victorian Premier's Literary Award for Fiction and the Ned Kelly Award for Best First Fiction.* Beautiful Revolutionary *was shortlisted for the 2019 Prime Minister's Literary Award for Fiction and the Australian Literature Society Gold Medal.*

Sixteen was the age I wanted my own Raskolnikov. The handsome, brilliant, impoverished law student at the centre of Dostoevsky's *Crime and Punishment*, who attempts to distinguish himself from the rabble by taking an axe to his landlady's head in an act of 'perfect murder' – to my sixteen-year-old mind, he was far more fascinating than the boys at my high school. I liked his melancholy dark eyes; his shiny chestnut hair; his tall, slim, well-built body. I liked the holes in his clothes and the cold places he dwelled in. Most of all, I liked his hunger for the extraordinary, the way he was willing to cast morality aside to prove his extraordinariness.

The convulsions of guilt that follow Raskolnikov's crime interested me less. His confession and conversion to Christianity didn't interest me at all. I hoped the extraordinarily handsome law student would pull himself together, evade justice forever, and be a very successful lawyer *and* criminal. At sixteen, it goes without saying, I made an art of missing the point.

Sixteen was also the age I read about Myra Hindley and Ian Brady, the Manchester serial-killing duo better known as the Moors Murderers. Like thousands of moody, gloomy teens the world over, I was a fan of The Smiths. Entombed in my turquoise-and-lilac bedroom, I listened to 'Suffer Little Children', Morrissey's downbeat crooning about the moors.

I didn't know what a moor was, but I liked the song enough to look it up. I followed the online threads to Myra Hindley and Ian Brady. I read about Myra, the eighteen-year-old secretary who fell in love at first sight with a tall, slim, sullen twenty-three-year-old office clerk. How he was rude to her for a whole year before asking her out. How they had sex on their first date, in the front room of the row house where Myra lived with her gran. How she changed her appearance for him, dyed her hair blitzkrieg blonde and dressed in sexy mod fashions: go-go boots, miniskirts. How she hopped on the back of his motorcycle and let him take her to the wilds beyond town, those moors where they'd later kill and bury four children.

How he gave her books to read.

Crime and Punishment was the first of those books. It wasn't an accident. In the year before they committed their first murder, they discussed murder in a philosophical sense; what it would take to succeed where Raskolnikov failed, to transcend the ordinary world and commit the perfect crime.

My dad was ten, the same age as the Moors Murderers' youngest victim, when his family left Newcastle upon Tyne for a sunny new life in Western Australia. It was 1970, four years after the trial that saw Myra and Ian sentenced for life, all of England – most especially the working-class North – calling for a return of the rope. When I mention Myra Hindley to my dad, there's a sarcastic snort, a decades-old shudder, the words 'nasty stuff'. He was a child in Myra's England, a place of coal mines and steelworks, chain-smoking women with Dusty Springfield hairdos. A place where little boys were told only to beware of strange men, but never women.

I grew up a world away from that England. Hard blue skies and white sand beaches. Too much space rather than too little. A room of my own with dollhouse colours I chose and the certainty of a university education. I chose *Crime and Punishment* too, the dog-eared copy from Mum's bookshelf. Which is to say, it wasn't given to me by a boy.

But all this seems circumstantial, compared with that other thing – the dreamy drumbeat inside our bodies and outside our neighbourhoods; our hunger for the extraordinary.

There's something dangerous about the hunger of girls, young women. Because, detached from experience, it's philosophical. Because it's shapeless, can take many shapes. Because it wants to prove itself. Because it doesn't just want a man; it wants the world.

Eight years after first hearing of the Moors Murderers, I read *The Gates of Janus*, an analysis of serial killing written by Ian Brady. By its 2001 publication, he and Myra had been on the outs for decades, far longer than they were ever a couple. Ian's references to Myra in the book are snide, oblique; she is the 'pupil' to his 'master', the weaker party who, once caught, blames the stronger for her criminal actions. But mostly, it reads as a quasi-academic manifesto of moral relativism. Chapters are headed with quotes by Dostoevsky, de Sade, Shakespeare, Wilde, Wordsworth. The tone is detached, pompous and – knowing the horrific crimes behind it – odious in a way Raskolnikov's musings on the same subject never were to me, at sixteen.

What it takes to bridge the gap between the philosophical lure of crime and the reality of it is something few people ever confront. Looking back, my own teenage 'crimes' were banal: ditching school, raiding the liquor shelf, a handful of hookups with regrettable boys. None of these crimes interfered with my education, my reputation. Certainly, none had the lifelong consequences of Myra's infatuation with Ian Brady. Yet, though I was without doubt a very different girl from Myra, there are ifs that keep me wondering. If I had my own Raskolnikov. If he spoke to me of extraordinary things beyond my turquoise-and-lilac walls. If he showed me how my ordinary self might be cast off. If all those things – the question isn't so much *would* I have followed, but *how far*?

Women in Organised Crime

Liz Campbell

Liz Campbell is the inaugural Francine McNiff Chair in Criminal Jurisprudence at Monash University's Faculty of Law, Melbourne, having worked previously at Durham Law School, Edinburgh Law School and Aberdeen Law School. Her main research interest lies in the politics of definition in the criminal law. She has used this lens to analyse the legal responses to organised crime, corruption, DNA databases and the presumption of innocence.

Mention 'organised crime' in casual conversation and most of us will think of guns, drugs, Mexican cartels and Italian godfathers. Claiming that it also covers LIBOR rigging or police corruption might raise a few eyebrows. That aside, the term is now part of popular parlance, despite much controversy, academic and otherwise, as to its meaning. And further debate centres on the role of women within it. The common depiction is rarely one of a truly autonomous and thus dangerous woman, but rather of the supporting and wilfully blind partner – think of Carmela in earlier seasons of *The Sopranos*, or Margaret in *Boardwalk Empire*. Both characters grapple with their complicity in their male partners' actions and their failure to resist and reject these criminal benefits.

Besides these fictional accounts, there is limited but growing consideration of the roles that women adopt and play in the context of organised crime. This knowledge gap is especially evident in the UK. Some of the literature suggests that our more active participation in the paid legal workforce is linked to a parallel increase in criminality. In this vein, we might recall Freda Adler's 1975 book *Sisters in Crime*, focusing on the 'dark side of emancipation', where the drive for equal opportunity in the legitimate sphere is mirrored by a growing involvement in serious crime. Increased labour opportunities, coupled with the changing role of women in the family and society, can impact previously demarcated gender roles in organised crime networks and groups.

Much of the existing academic literature focuses on certain *types* of organised criminality, such as human trafficking and, to a lesser extent, drug dealing. Research indicates that women's involvement in human trafficking in particular seems to be due to some existing connection to the crime, either as a former victim or through partnership with men already involved. Rose Broad's work – specifically her 2015 article in the *British Journal of Criminology*, '"A Vile and Violent Thing": Female Traffickers and the Criminal Justice System Response' – flags up the implicit suggestion that women's involvement is rarely through pure greed or personal choice, as is presumed in relation to men, but rather that their roles are determined by past experience and relationships. Sheldon Zhang, Ko-Lin Chin and Jody Miller have called these 'gendered markets' in their work on transnational human smuggling. Women are more prevalent in such markets because of the relatively low role of violence, the importance of interpersonal networks in facilitating such operations, and presumptions about care-giving to the exploited individuals.

In other words, human trafficking, which often involves sexual exploitation or forced domestic labour, intersects with the conventional interpretation of the 'world of women.' As for drug dealing, in a 2014 paper in the *European Journal of Criminology* titled 'Keeping out of trouble: Female crack cocaine dealers in England', Jennifer Fleetwood notes that the female crack cocaine dealers she interviewed used and performed 'respectable femininity' as a key strategy for keeping their dealing hidden and themselves out of trouble. They hid and subverted their gendered dangerousness in a reflexive way.

Beyond these studies, there is relatively little in the way of research in the UK on the role of women as quintessential 'organised criminals' like drug traffickers and money launderers, and professional facilitators like lawyers and accountants. Are women more or less likely to be involved in certain crimes or echelons of a group or network, and if so, why? Do their styles of leadership and enforcement differ from that of their male colleagues in organised crime? Are professional women averse or immune to the temptations of corrupt payments from organised crime groups, or is a lack of opportunity stymieing involvement in this form of crime?

As well as the limited consideration of women as dangerous organised criminals themselves, no attention has been paid to the impact that counter-organised crime laws have on women in particular. To take Scotland as an example, the main piece of legislation is the Criminal Justice and Licensing (Scotland) Act 2010, which introduced a number of offences such as directing serious organised crime. The Act also makes it an offence to fail to report to the police your knowledge or suspicion that another person is involved in or directs serious organised crime. This is what's called a crime of omission; in other words, it is your failure to act or to prevent harm, rather than a positive action, which is the 'external' element of this offence. Your knowledge or suspicion must come from information obtained through your employment, or as a result of a close personal relationship if you have benefited materially from the other person's commission of serious organised crime. The latter component is significant here, as it means that family members/partners of criminal actors must report under this section, for fear of prosecution and conviction. Nonetheless, the requirement of what's called 'material benefit' is to mitigate the potential harshness of this provision on family members/partners of persons suspected of involvement in serious organised crime who become aware of matters inadvertently.

In Scotland, the majority of those involved in organised crime are men – 89 per cent of persons identified through the Scottish Serious Organised Crime Group Mapping Project were male, according to a 2010 preliminary findings report on the scale and extent of serious organised crime by the Scottish Government. Furthermore, a July 2016 Freedom of Information request revealed that 637 persons have been reported to the procurator fiscal since the relevant sections of the 2010 Act came into force, and of those, 98 were women. Given this gender disparity, the burden of reporting falls on their partners (the majority of whom will be women). Thinking in terms of human rights law, I suggest that this offence encroaches in a disproportionate way on private and family life (which is protected by Article 8 of the European Convention on Human Rights) and places an unjustifiable and dangerous burden on partners, spouses and children.

That said, there is a defence for a person charged with this offence to prove that she had a 'reasonable excuse' for not making the disclosure. Surely her age, the nature of the relationship between the parties, and any potential imbalance of power would be taken into account at this juncture. As there does not appear to have been a reported case involving the section, it remains to be seen how it is applied by the courts. The Crown Office and Procurator Fiscal Service has reported that to date eleven women have been charged under this section, but no information regarding the outcome of these cases was available, according to the same July 2016 Freedom of Information request. Moreover, it's difficult to measure the effect of a law which prompts people to come forward with information when previously they would not have done so.

Of course, it would be preferable for people to report any suspicions and knowledge regarding serious organised crime to the police – but while we might agree that there is a civic responsibility and moral duty to assist the police, this shouldn't be translated into a legal requirement punishable by imprisonment. Interestingly, 81 per cent of people living in Scotland say that they would report someone whom they suspected of being involved in organised crime, and this figure rises to 85 per cent among women, according to a 2013 Scottish government report on public perceptions of organised crime. It's questionable whether this sentiment would also cover reporting on one's partner. Overall, this provision overlooks the dynamics of intimate relationships, and the possible intimidation and danger experienced by female partners in particular.

Thinking about women's involvement in organised crime, the critical question here hinges on whether women's roles are shaped and determined by their individual characteristics, or by the opportunities for crime. As women reach further into leadership roles in various sectors, will this growth in power be mirrored in the illegitimate context? And simultaneously, we must ask whether women are or should be a feminising, and thus civilising, force who will compromise their safety and personal relationships to adhere to the requirements of the criminal law in reporting serious organised crime.

Motorbike Murderers and Femmes Fatales: The Rise of the Female Assassin in Colombia

Pascale Baker and Catalina Jaramillo

Dr Pascale Baker is a lecturer in Latin American Studies at University College Dublin. Previously, she taught at the Universities of Sheffield and Edinburgh in the Departments of Hispanic Studies. Her teaching has centred on Latin American literature and culture of the nineteenth and twentieth centuries. Her specialist area of research is on banditry in Latin America, with a particular focus on Mexico. Her monograph, Revolutionaries, Rebels and Robbers: The Golden Age of Banditry in Mexico, Latin America and the Chicano American Southwest, 1850–1950, *was published in November 2015 by the University of Wales Press.*

Dr Catalina Jaramillo is originally from Medellín, Colombia but moved to Dublin and received an MSc in Architecture from the University of Ulster, Belfast. She was recently awarded a PhD in Architecture at the University of Edinburgh. The title of her thesis is 'Narco-Baroque: Intertextuality and Magic in the Architecture and Visual

Culture of Pablo Escobar'. In her PhD, she explores the narco-baroque, which is the interaction of Pablo Escobar's visual and 'illegal' representations in the media and urbanism as another way of gathering knowledge. Her published articles include 'How Savagism of the Narco Motorbike Has Shaped the Contemporary City' for the 22nd International Conference on Urban Transport and the Environment, and 'Pablo Escobar: Zoomania in the narco imperium and the glorification of the cocaine network' for The Design Journal.

Colombia, a country conjured up in the evocative magical realist writings of Gabriel García Márquez, is also known as the place that occupied the centre of the illegal drugs trade from the late 1970s until the early 1990s, as the number one producer and transporter of cocaine to the USA and Europe. This murderous trade spawned the rise of the drugs barons and their powerful cartels, the likes of which had never been seen before. Pablo Escobar was the premier narco, becoming a legend, both prior to and following his death in 1993, despite the terror and violence that he unleashed on Colombia. Traditionally the drug trade in Colombia, as elsewhere, has been associated with powerful men, but women have always played their part, rising up through the ranks via family connections or the patronage of influential political figures.

It was Griselda Blanco – known by her nicknames 'the Godmother', 'the Black Widow' and 'La Dama de la Mafia' – who became one of the most dangerous women to ever grace the drugs business. She made it to the top by aggressively expanding her cocaine-trafficking operation from Colombia into

New York and then Florida in the 1970s and early 80s. Blanco, who was herself gunned down in 2012, has been held largely responsible for fostering a culture of brutality in Miami during those years, and her organisation Los Pistoleros are infamous for pioneering the murder-on-a-motorbike style of killing. This was also adopted and technically perfected by Escobar to despatch victims in Medellín and Bogotá with maximum efficiency at the height of the Colombian drug wars; this is discussed further by David Ovalle in the *Miami Herald*, Candace Amos in the *New York Daily News*, Fabio Castillo in his 1987 *Los jinetes de la Cocaína*, and Dominic Streatfeild in *Cocaine: An Unauthorized Biography*. As Jhon Jairo Velásquez (alias Popeye), one of Pablo Escobar's leading henchmen and now a celebrity, commented in an interview in 2018, discipline, in terms of the exact, military-style planning of the crime, was a key part of Escobar's success. A (probably fictional) meeting between Escobar and Blanco, the two drug bosses, is relayed for dramatic effect in the 2012 Colombian drama *El Patrón del Mal* [*Pablo Escobar: The Drug Lord*]. The motorcycle murderers have generally been assumed to be male, with the bike and the gun adopted as macho tools of the trade; however, there is a current cultural appetite in Colombia for portraying women in these roles, in particular in the ever-popular telenovelas, or soap operas, reflecting the dark reality of *sicarias*, or female assassins, operating inside the cartels.

One of the best-known Colombian novels to portray a female assassin is Jorge Franco's 1999 *Rosario Tijeras*, adapted in 2005 into a film of the same name and also inspiring a song composed and sung by Colombian pop star Juanes. The continued interest in the Rosario Tijeras story led to a 2010 television drama series. Rosario is a beautiful young woman, described through the filter of her besotted middle-class admirer Antonio in the novel and in the film. Trapped in a web of poverty and childhood sexual abuse, she decides to execute justice through the gun and escapes the slums of Medellín to join the cartel as a prostitute and assassin. Rosario appears to gain a measure of power and wealth as a killer and seductress. However, despite the myth that builds up around this mysterious character, who murders her victims with a kiss and a bullet, it becomes clear that Rosario is at the whim of the cartel bosses, who hire her out for sexual favours and can withdraw her luxurious lifestyle at any time. She is a bandit, yes, and a dangerous woman, but in this world of male cartel bosses she wields no real power. In both the novel and the film, Rosario never kills on a motorbike. She blesses her brother Johnefe and former lover Ferney before they embark on their motorised killing sprees, and it is clear that they are considered to be the most skilled assassins by the bosses. Rosario's modus operandi is to lull her victims into a false sense of security through her beauty and charm, as a traditional femme fatale. The overt sexualisation of Rosario in the novel and particularly the film is reflected by other Colombian stars famous for their sultry appeal in contemporary popular visual culture, such as Shakira and Sofia Vergara, although their allure is not nearly so deadly. In the 2010 television adaptation, the story is modernised, as Rosario herself learns how to ride a motorbike, although she does not yet make the transition to becoming a motor assassin. However, the motorbike is no longer an exclusively male preserve in cartel land.

The female assassin's mastery of the motorbike as a killing machine is intensified in another popular Colombian soap series from 2009–10, *El Capo* [*The Boss*]. In one episode, the character known as 'La Perrys', who will become the big boss Pedro Pablo's right-hand woman, demonstrates her absolute skill as a biker hitwoman as she outdoes her rivals in a practice assassination on the motorbike, deftly killing a rabbit and a dog in the process. The Colombian TV company RTN that made the series describes La Perrys on their website as '*una mujer fría, cruel, calculadora y asesina por naturaleza*' [by nature a cold, cruel, calculating assassin] who is an '*excelente motociclista y el mejor sicario del país*' [an excellent biker and the best hitman in the country]. *El Capo* is a fictionalised account, but the events and characters it represents are mirrored by the real-life female assassins who appear periodically in the Colombian press. In 2011 one such character, a seventeen-year-old girl, made headlines for her ability to recruit and train other youngsters to become assassins for the local cartel in the Aburrá Valley near Medellín. Such was her hard-headed skill in this task that she became known locally as La Perrys after the soap-opera killer, wrote Yeison Gualdrón in a 6 August 2011 article in *El Tiempo*. In fact, the fictional La Perrys from *El Capo* seems to have provided the prototype for the cruel but efficient female criminal in present-day Colombia. On 14 January 2016, *El Espectador* reported the arrest of another narco in Medellín, Patricia de Jesús Montoya Montoya, a 'La Perrys' figure who specialised in kidnapping, extortion and torture.

Quite apart from the association of the motorbike with criminals in Colombia, it would seem that as an economic and easy mode of transport, the *moto* is peerless. This is underlined by the fact that in 2013, 8 million Colombians were using one daily, and that in the year 2012–13, 25 per cent of motorcycle buyers were women, according to *Semana* magazine. As the magazine reports, '*se les ha quitado el miedo [y] cada vez son más arriesgadas*' [these women are losing their fear and are becoming ever keener to take risks], an analogy that could be drawn with the rise of the female motorbike assassin in Colombia, too. According to the ANDI (*Asociación Nacional de Empresarios de Colombia/National Business Association of Colombia)*, in 2016 the percentage of female motorbike buyers had risen to 31.6 per cent. In some regions/towns, such as Pereira in the coffee-growing region, the statistics showed that women accounted for as much as 51.22 per cent of motorbike buyers.

It seems that in Colombian life, as well as on film, the rise of the female assassin, criminal and underworld figure is unstoppable. Unlike Rosario Tijeras, a sexual object for the narcos, or Catalina, the main character from another Colombian soap opera *Sin tetas no hay paraíso* [*Without Breasts There is No Paradise*, 2006], who moulds her body to the drug bosses' requirements, many of the women characters appearing in these new soaps are not simply prostitutes or gangsters' molls. They are trained assassins and members of the criminal underworld, carefully plotting their way up the cartel hierarchy to grasp power, either through their family links to influential narcos or on their own terms. As well as La Perrys, the motorcycle assassin from *El Capo*, there are the women from the soap opera *Las muñecas de la mafia* [*The Mafia Dolls*, 2009], who are the wives, girlfriends and daughters of prominent capos and are heavily involved in the drug-trafficking business. Then there is the character Alicia Benitez, nicknamed 'La Mariposa' [The Butterfly], from the 2012 cartel drama of the same name. This 'Butterfly' is a high-class money launderer, and she runs a successful business which is highly sought after by the drug traffickers to hide the true criminal origin of their wealth. In addition, in the 2016 version of *Sin tetas no hay paraíso*, Catalina's friend and rival, Yésica Beltrán, alias 'La Diabla' [The She-Devil], transforms into a notorious drug lord and madam, having escaped from an American prison. She is an ambitious, cruel and clever woman, perhaps reflecting the trajectory of Griselda Blanco. A real-life and influential *sicaria*, Yuri Patricia Sánchez, only twenty-two years old, also appeared in Latin American newsfeeds in 2016. Popularly known as 'La Diabla' and described as '*una temible sicaria colombiana*' [a fearsome Colombian hitwoman], she was accused of involvement in the assassinations of fourteen people, including seven policemen, *Clarín* reports on 8 June 2016.

The current Colombian fascination for the era of powerful cartels is a natural development, according to former trafficker turned author Andrés López López, who has penned many of the most successful recent cartel novels and television dramas, including *Las muñecas de la mafia*. In a 2013 interview with *Latin Times*, he claims of his countrymen that:

> we're becoming one of the most mature Latin American societies, but we need to hear about things that are happening in our country. It's important for our society to know what really happened [during the years of the cartels' dominance] so that we can go forward, so we can understand ourselves. They have to be understood so that society can grow stronger.

That understanding of the past, and indeed the present, includes an acceptance and uncovering of women's role in the cartels, not just as sexual partners and prostitutes to the bosses, but as potential bosses, leaders and skilled assassins themselves, who are becoming ever more daring and dangerous.

Wikipedia's Women Problem

Melissa Highton

Melissa Highton is Director of Learning, Teaching and Web Services and Assistant Principal for Online Learning at the University of Edinburgh. Melissa has lead responsibility for the university's online learning platforms, media production, digital skills development, classroom technologies and web applications. In her spare time, she edits Wikipedia. She blogs at thinking.is.ed.ac.uk/melissa and tweets as: @HoneybHighton.

Wikipedia has a women problem. Less than 20 per cent of the people who regularly edit Wikipedia are women. The lack of women writers in itself is a problem, as articles may become biased or skewed, and some topics – particularly those relating to women's history and achievement – are poorly covered.

Everyone is free to edit Wikipedia. The content only gets there because someone has made that effort. The technology is neutral, and Wikipedia, when it began nearly twenty years ago, was supposed to transform the ways in which information was collected, contributed and shared. It was supposed to offer new ways of democratising participation, overturning old structures, and yet it has become a place where women do not choose to contribute and do not choose to spend time. What has gone wrong?

In the context of Wikipedia, what does it mean to be a dangerous woman? As we see in many of the contributions to this project, a dangerous woman is one who shines a light on an inequality and tries to fix it. Dangerous women create accounts in Wikipedia and start editing. Dangerous women run Wikipedia edit-a-thons and support each other to improve and create Wikipedia articles which describe the experiences of women. Dangerous women understand how information is created, controlled and contested. Dangerous women encourage their colleagues and friends to become editors too.

The University of Edinburgh hosts a Wikimedian in residence as part of our partnership with Wikimedia UK. Our resident Wikimedian is tasked to identify ways in which the University of Edinburgh, as a knowledge creation organisation, can participate, as a community, more fully in the open knowledge projects which are part of Wikimedia worldwide. He was also tasked, by me, to engage more women in editing and encourage sustained engagement with Wikipedia from within our academic schools through curriculum projects. His residency has been an enormous success. Wikipedia edit-a-thons are events at which groups of people come together to edit Wikipedia in a social setting. Edit-a-thons often focus on a theme or topic, and editors are supported by experts and librarians to research appropriate sources. We aim to improve the quality of articles and increase the spread of coverage. Members of the University have participated in edit-a-thons around the history of women in science and Scottish history, history of medicine, history of veterinary medicine, history of nursing, women in espionage, women's suffrage, women in religion, literature, art and feminism, women in STEM, reproductive biology, mental health, Gothic literature and celebrations of Ada Lovelace Day.

We have trained hundreds of new editors and trained new trainers to run their own events. At each event, we discuss how the information in Wikipedia is contributed, shared and contested online, and we learn how to contribute to an open knowledge community. Each new editor contributes to the quality of knowledge shared.

For anyone who does not think they have the time or content or confidence to contribute, I ask: if not you, then who?

Dangerous Is Not Safe: A Poem

Dorcas Agbogun

Dorcas Agbogun was born and raised in Nigeria. As a creative writer since she was five years old, her works have spanned many genres, from fiction to screenwriting and poetry – a huge part of her output explores issues that affect women and the girl child. She currently works as a creative writer with a digital agency based in Lagos, Nigeria and is working on her debut novel, Bruised Begonias. *You can keep up with some of her work at thewritingazelle.wordpress.com and follow her on Twitter @KassieOsesie.*

Our world continues to be governed by a macho system which presents itself as natural, therefore unquestionable and invariably a just process. To thrive, this system depends on sustaining the popularity of its ideology.

A dangerous woman is one who reneges on loyalty to the standards and expectations of the patriarchal society, becoming a threat and danger to the existing system.

Dangerous Is Not Safe

Be Safe; be weak
You'll do just fine!
Be the fancy; the prim
Well, that's mine!
Draw the curtains; lock the doors
Stay in!

But what am I?
Evil? No good?
What is to fear?
Myself?

A thousand pictures
Distorted images
Slivers off a shattered mirror
What you are? Or what you're told to be?

An iron curtain
But *around* her mind
Chains
But inside her head
The Macho
He's Mr Jailer
He's the Jury
The sentence
The gaol term
He's the charges made.

He said:
She's evil

She's no good
She's to be feared
Even by herself.

Like a scolded child
Face to the wall
The curtains drawn
Door locked
Stayed-in
Now, she's safe.

A voice calls
Someone's at the door
I can't open, it's locked
– Of course you can; you locked it yourself
But I'm safe this way
– Who said you're meant to be safe?

Back and forth
And back and forth
To heed the stranger?
Or hide from danger?

For the first time
She pulls open the door
The illusions defragment
Like pieces of a jigsaw.

Be safe? No.
Dangerous is who she truly is
Trojan to the Macho organism

Threat to its system
Untamed by its customs
Nor existing on its terms.

What the Kitchen Witch Said

Claire Askew

Claire Askew's debut poetry collection, This changes things, *was published by Bloodaxe in 2016 and shortlisted for a variety of accolades including an Edwin Morgan Award and the Saltire First Book Award. Claire is also the author of the novels* All The Hidden Truths *(2018),* What You Pay For *(2019) and* Cover Your Tracks *(2020), published by Hodder & Stoughton.* All The Hidden Truths *won the 2019 Bloody Scotland Crime Debut Prize, and Claire's novels have been twice shortlisted for the CWA Gold Dagger.*

What the Kitchen Witch Said

Begin at the tips: the tops
of stems erecting
their cities in the blue spring.
Things have to be clipped
at the seed-head, at the bud:
like witches,
plants must be kept down.
Correct the bolt,
unpick the stalk –
parch it to a wand

on the hot sill –
twist off the stamen,
wash its peppery stain
from your hands.
Save the blooms.

If you're not on your knees,
you should be: level
with deadhead and bee-path
in the garden's stained-glass
nave. See how the earth
made you; the way
it laid fat tears of rain
in the Lady's Mantle.
Everything damp: cut
any plant and it will bleed.
Your lungs are like two
charmed hands, open
to the stink of sage,
of dill, the clean
bright peal of mint.

To seal the charm, you dig.
First a seed dib, then a pothole,
soon a pit. This
is the part where you get
what you want:
the things you've wasted,
lost. First, roots,
their shapes like tongues
and hands cut off.

The small, brown teeth
of seed. Keep
going: pull back
the curtains of soil,
put down the strong,
white ladders of your hands.

Hit the shocked
mirror of water,
and go on.
Hit bedrock, break it,
get buried alive.
It's there alright:
a land that has
yet to be mapped,
a darkness unlit,
a nation not yet brought
before your good,
clean God.
Keep going. I know
that if anyone can take it,
it is you.

Neema Namadamu

Gillian Mellor

Gillian Mellor stays in Moffat in Dumfries and Galloway, where she helps to run The Moffat Bookshop. She has poetry published in Gutter, Poetry Scotland, Pushing Out the Boat *and online with The Stove Network in Dumfries as part of their 'Homegrown' project put together during the Covid-19 lockdown. She is one of the authors of* Compass Points, *a pamphlet of poetry published with funding from the Wigtown Book Festival Company.*

Neema Namadamu is from the Democratic Republic of Congo (DRC). I knew little of her country's civil wars or the unspeakable brutality of men towards women there that seems to be commonplace. This changed one morning when I read her piece on the women-led social network World Pulse, shocked into it by a friend's share on Facebook which included a grim photograph at its head. My friend, Jane, said it was a difficult share, not knowing what else to do to highlight the problem. The poems included here are in response to Neema's article and its photograph.

Neema raises awareness of the situation in the DRC through her writing and visits to the international community to fundraise for the Maman Shujaa Media Centre, which she founded to empower women to tell their stories.

Neema's own story unfolds with contracting polio aged two, which left her with disabilities. Too poor to afford crutches, Neema's mother would carry her on her back to school when road conditions were bad. Neema was the first disabled woman from her ethnic group to graduate from university in DRC. She has since represented her province in Parliament and been technical advisor for the DRC Minister of Gender and Family.

The population of North East Congo is one of the most war-torn and disadvantaged in the world. They have had to deal with the crimes of war, outbreaks of Ebola virus and now Covid-19. Neema works with women and girls in practical ways to improve their lives. She tells girls they are equal, that they need to be in school. Her charity provides the means to make sanitary kits so girls can attend school every day once they have reached puberty and brings taboos out into the open. They have been making their own soap and facemasks to improve hygiene during the current pandemic. Less than 4 per cent of the population have access to the internet, and few of this number are women, so provision of technical training to enable women to become digital activists is vitally important. There are plans underway for the provision of clean water, the improvement of farming and to address climate change. There is positivity, love, pride and determination to change things from the grassroots up. There is much to admire.

You can read more about Neema and her work at www.herowomenrising.org

From a Photo Taken August 18th, 2016
Béni, North Kivu, Congo

(I)

After I averted my eyes
I googled *machete*, found it
was essentially a tool for survival.
I tried to equate this with the image
I'd just seen. Female shoulders
sliced open to reveal the meat
beneath, a survivor from the 100
or so killed just this week.
The women stay to protect
the children. The ones that aren't
butchered are raped. I'm sorry
we've all been silenced.

(II)

Was she standing when he cut her, were her
arms around her head? Was she bound, had
he raped her, were the children still around?
Was she on her knees before him, did she
ask death to finally come, did her sisters
watch her suffer, were they lying still
before her, was she the last one in the line?
Did she scream out loud to stop him,
did she silently bear pain? How long
before they found her? Who is she?

Pink Sceptics: Dangerous Women and the 'Pink Ribbon' Culture

Adela Briansó

Adela Briansó was born and raised in Spain. In 2021, she finished her MSc in Global Health at the University of Copenhagen, following her education in Social Anthropology and Politics at the University of Edinburgh. In 2016–17 she carried out an ethnographic research project on the experience of breast cancer in Spain. Through this project, Adela explored health and illness and became interested in the intersections between gender, power and public health. She would like to pursue a career in climate change and health with a focus on social justice, and she remains interested in issues of sexual, reproductive and menstrual health and rights.

Wondering why pink ribbons flood the city? Unsure about the effects of turning public buildings pink or printing pink ribbons on cereal boxes? So am I. Let me introduce you to the dangerous women who question the pink ribbons.

I first met Maria two years ago. She is a Spanish nurse and has a twenty-six-year-old daughter. A few years ago, Maria had a double mastectomy because of breast cancer. Now, she is a dangerous woman who disagrees with the pink ribbon culture: 'I'm fed up of pink ribbons everywhere,' she announced. Initially, I was a little shocked. I had never questioned the good intentions behind the symbol. 'It makes me feel like I'm just one more, another woman with breast cancer,' Maria continued.

Breast cancer is a disease that affects one in eight women in Spain, with similar rates in the UK. Although this cancer has one of the highest survival rates, it still causes thousands of deaths every year. Over 95 per cent of breast cancer patients are women. Audre Lorde, an iconic feminist who had breast cancer, spoke against narrowing the disease to a single account, affirming that there are 'so many silences to be broken' in her 1980 book *The Cancer Journals*. The truth is, a lot has been written on breast cancer. But most of it speaks of one particular kind of experience. I would like to contribute to Lorde's plea by introducing you to the pink-sceptic women.

Early detection has a major impact on increasing the chances for survival, making breast cancer prevention crucial in lowering mortality. But Maria got me thinking: what is the symbol of lung cancer? Or liver, or throat, or skin cancer? Or the icon of other tough, chronic pathologies like diabetes or Crohn's disease? Why is breast cancer's pink ribbon overwhelmingly more visible than any other symbol?

Breast cancer campaigns are normatively feminine and preach optimistic messages of support. All year round, pink floods the city, from cereal boxes to pink-awareness 5k races. It was an American woman, Charlotte Haley, who created the symbol in 1990, although hers was peach, not pink. Soon adopted by *Self* magazine, the pink ribbon campaign spread globally, achieving undeniable benefits in raising awareness and funds. But the pink ribbon culture has also become a business – a veiled, profitable and marketable one. Women like Maria disagree with the hypocrisy behind *pinkification*. When I met Maria two years after our first encounter in order to revisit her opinion, she was even more convinced: 'I do not identify with the symbol. Pink ribbons objectify breast cancer, which for me is a very private experience.'

The first issue is secretive profits. Often, the final destination of big fundraising campaigns is unclear. Prominent pink ribbons decorate products while less than 1 per cent of profits are dedicated to research. Massive corporations use and abuse the harmless, feminine look of the pink ribbons. At the end of the day, who would say no to increasing hope in the fight against breast cancer? However, a worrying number of the companies embracing pink awareness sell products that are suspected to be carcinogenic, yet they dare to festoon their products with pink ribbons as a marketing strategy. Make-up, deodorants, body creams… the list goes on. Women like Maria question the immaculate pink. They are an obstacle to the maximisation of profit.

The second issue is social media. Changing one's profile picture to a pink ribbon may be well intentioned. But for those who have been through cancer, or who have mourned someone's death to the disease, being digitally bombarded with pink ribbons can be difficult. It might be a 'first-world problem', but it affects real women. 'It annoys me so much when all my contacts set pink ribbons as their [profile] picture. What is the purpose?' Maria explains. The purpose, of course, is awareness, but the real-world effects that Facebook likes might have are questionable.

Third, massification. The massification of the pink ribbon has informed thousands of people about breast cancer, no doubt.

'Unfortunately, the pink ribbon has lost part of its meaning on the way,' Maria believes. This process has simplified a complex and individual experience to a single narrative: a pink universe of hope and heroism. Pink ribbons invite everyone to 'fight against' cancer, personifying breast cancer like a single evil enemy. While de-stigmatising breast cancer is a positive thing, the pink ribbons are often overused, so much so that their impact has been diluted. 'Perhaps I would wear a peach ribbon now. But not a pink one,' she reflects.

Dressing in pink to raise funds is dangerous to cancer as a disease. But so is the choice of those who prefer to manage their illness in private. Those who cringe with every pink ribbon, and who refuse to buy carcinogenic cosmetics. They are already speaking up, and they are doing so loudly. They are the pink-sceptic women.

Exposing Trauma: The Post-Surgery Selfie

Lizzy Rose

Lizzy Rose is an artist with a diverse practice spanning writing, video, photography, ceramics and curation. She currently lives and works in Margate in Kent. She was Assistant Curator at LIMBO arts, an artist-led space in Margate, from 2012 to 2015, and she is now part of the programming team at CRATE, an artist-led studio space and project space also in Margate.

I want to write about myself and other women who expose their body over the internet. I don't mean pornography; I mean women who post photos of their surgery scars and stoma bags.

Crohn's disease is an illness that typically affects teenagers and stays throughout your life. Every Crohn's patient is unique, because several years after being diagnosed, it can affect you in such a multitude of ways that you end up sharing very little in common with anyone else other than a few key phrases: sickness, pain, surgery and, the winner, diarrhoea.

There is a whole movement in the Crohn's disease community of sharing photographs of surgery scars. I belong to countless forums and groups for people diagnosed with Crohn's disease, and people post these photographs daily.

I can describe the typical photograph: the frame of the shot is taken up entirely by flesh, usually with a row of staples and blood stretching across the middle of the frame; or a beautiful woman, standing in her pants in her bedroom, in front of a mirror, with a stoma bag neatly tucked to one side.

Being dangerous is a relative term, and one that I think links closely to bravery. For me, I see these women as dangerous. I see them as putting themselves in danger. Speaking out about your illness is dangerous for anyone – it is revealing a weakness to others – but these women do it nevertheless because they know how important it is to talk about illness and that it is not done enough.

Of course, the reasons why people share photographs of their surgery are complex, and I don't want to attempt to read people's minds; but I have a few theories from my own time of being sick.

Crohn's disease is truly a hidden disease. Sometimes doctors even have trouble measuring it. It can be buried somewhere down in your small intestine, unreachable by cameras and scans. But you can feel it all the time. Every time you eat you feel something, and sometimes even when you don't. On the one hand, this can be very useful. If I get very unwell, I can pretend there is nothing wrong for as long as I can keep it together to escape the situation. There is no tell-tale hair loss or terrible rash, no shortness of breath or seizures. It can be frustrating in the long term, as you start to wonder if it is all in your head. I was half convinced just before I had my last surgery (which took over eight hours) that they would go in and find nothing. Scars of surgery are one of the few outward signs that there is anything untoward going on. They are often the only indication of an invisible illness. These scars do not tell the whole story, but they are at least proof that, yes, I am not imagining it.

The conventional rationale for the selfie-taker seems to be to upload an idealised version of one's life. Essentially positive marketing for how great your life is. However, this theory does not account for the post-surgical selfie. You are not presenting an idealised version of your life; you are presenting a harsh reality, one you are uncomfortable with. In his book *Understanding Media,* Marshall McLuhan describes the selfie as a form of self-amputation or self-numbing. The selfie is either a way of finding a reassuring image of yourself in a world of turmoil and stress, or it is removing a part of yourself that you find troubling. He describes how the body does this as a reaction to physical trauma: 'In the physical stress of superstimulation of various kinds, the central nervous system acts to protect itself by a strategy of amputation or isolation of the offending organ, sense, or function.' He suggests that the selfie is a digital extension of this act of the body. The stress that the body is under in the case of post-surgery selfies is evident. In this case, perhaps the selfie is a way of managing the stress and trauma of surgery, by removing the offending body part with a smartphone photograph.

The internet has transformed the experience of being chronically ill. In the past, you would have to belong to a support group to find a common ally in your illness, but these days you can search a hashtag and find countless people who are experiencing a similar reality to you. Having said this, being sick is lonely in real life. I do not think I know anyone with Crohn's disease whom I have come across socially after thirteen years of living with it. Every sick person is painfully aware of how uncomfortable we can make people just by talking about being unwell. You really have to pick the right person and the right time to talk about your disease. This can be very lonely, as for you, a trip to the hospital is as normal as someone else's trip to the pub. Yet you cannot tell people about it for fear of being seen as negative. This develops into a cycle of keeping whole swathes of your life a secret. And sometimes, I think you just snap and need to tell people about your reality.

One of the most famous illness-awareness campaigns has been #getyourbellyout. People with inflammatory bowel disease (IBD) were invited to share photographs of their bellies on social media to raise awareness and money for IBD charities. It was set up in response to the #nomakeupselfie, which raised lots of money for charity. The women leading the campaign are confident in the positive impact sharing these photographs can have. Sahara Fleetwood-Beresford, one of the founders of #getyourbellyout, said in an article for the charity Crohn's and Colitis UK: 'What started out as a campaign to raise awareness of an invisible illness that so many people suffer with in silence has turned in to a campaign of INSPIRATION and UNITY!'

However, one of the side effects of sharing these photographs is that they may get picked up by the national news, as happened to Bethany Townsend, and more recently, Aimee Rouski. Both young women with Crohn's disease posted photographs of their surgery scars and stoma bags on social media, which were then published by national news agencies. These young women were thrust into the media spotlight with the full horror of comment sections and public notoriety. The danger for them is very real in this situation. However, I see this selfie sharing almost as an act of protest. It shows a defiance to not conform with society's vision of the perfect body and to challenge people's perceptions of illness, whatever the dangers to the sharer's personal life.

I have never actually been brave enough to share a photograph of my surgery scars, although I have many. The alternative to the photograph being picked up by national newspapers is something much more horrifying in many ways. What if no one responds at all? What if your act of personal defiance and bravery goes completely unnoticed? What if after sharing this intimate secret, it simply disappears into the swirling void of rolling updates, remaining forever searchable but instantly forgotten?

As Crohn's disease typically first appears in young people, this may be why the surgery selfie has taken off in our community. Many of us have grown up with the internet, and perhaps we are seeing the birth of a phenomenon that will eventually become commonplace for the generation termed as 'digital natives'. The internet will continue to transform the lives of people living with long-term illnesses in unexpected ways. I believe the women who share these post-surgery selfies are advocating for a more realistic version of our digital self. By putting themselves in danger, they are spearheading the way forward, as our digital lives grow to be an ever-larger part of our reality.

Lies: On the Danger Inherent in Postnatal Depression

Teresa Sweeney

Teresa Sweeney is from Galway, Ireland and has an MA in Writing. Her collection of short stories is titled Stars in the Ground *and is available on Amazon UK. She has been published in journals including* The Blue Nib, Roadside Fiction, Number Eleven Magazine *and* Boyne Berries, *and she read at Cúirt International Festival of Literature in 2015. Teresa was shortlisted for Over the Edge New Writer of the Year in 2014 and 2017 and was commended in 2018.*

This is the story of a woman. She is a dangerous woman because she has lost control. She is lonely, but not alone. She is isolated and cannot explain the feelings she has of despair and the inability to cope. This should be a happy time, the happiest of her life. Her baby cries from the other room. She cannot cope.

She has postnatal depression.

> Postnatal depression (also known as postpartum depression) is a battle that many women face. It is a fierce, oppressing illness that is often fought alone. If you, or someone you know, may be battling this illness, it is not a battle to be fought without support.

If you would like to understand more about what postnatal depression is, or if you are worried about yourself or a loved one, you may find the following resources useful:

- The Association for Post Natal Illness (www.apni.org) is a registered charity in the UK offering information and support.
- The NHS in the UK (www.nhs.uk) and the Mayo Clinic in the US (www.mayoclinic.org) provide information on postnatal depression.
- The *Guardian* has a collection of articles on postnatal depression (www.theguardian.com/society/postnatal-depression).

Lies

There are different kinds of lies. Some lies are for ourselves, made to save us time and bother and explanations. Others are made to protect someone. Lies are as easy to tell as the time of day. And easier to tell than the truth.

I tell lies all the time.

First thing in the morning, before I get out of bed, my lies start. I lie to me.

You can do it; today will be better. I know it is a lie. Today is never better. Usually it is worse.

The next lie will be to my husband.

When he thanks me for making him a cup of tea before he leaves for work at 6.30 in the morning, Monday to Friday.

It's no problem, I say.

My words are a lie, my smile is a lie, my kiss is a lie. I would rather stay in bed, or drown myself in the bath.

The biggest lies I tell are to our daughter.

I pick her up and rock her, and tell her it's OK, when she cries. That is a lie.

Some lies I tell are small. People say, *how are you?* I say, *I'm fine.* That lie is for their sake. I'm not fine. But they don't ask me because they want to know, or because they care. Mostly they ask me while looking out the window, at their shoes, or at our daughter's face.

Me and our daughter are alone together all day. Just me and her in this house moving from room to room. I carry her on my hip as I try to clean the kitchen. I leave her lying down on her soft play mat as I run upstairs to get clothes for washing.

She screams.

This is our routine, our daughter and me, me and our daughter.

I leave her down, she cries. I pick her up, she cries. Maybe she will stop, maybe not.

Yesterday I didn't go back downstairs. I stood there at the door of our daughter's room, a bundle of her soiled and smelly clothes in my arms.

Her screams pierced through my ears into my brain and ripped the wallpaper off my wits. It felt like fine thin strings were being pulled too tightly, already splintering and ready to pop, pop, pop.

I moved slowly, crept into the room I share with her father, my husband. I closed our bedroom door carefully, silently. I heard the lock click. I watched the light and her screams sneak in from under the door.

Dulled slightly, but she did not stop.

I climbed onto our bed, the same place that my husband, her father, and I used to have sex in.

I cried.

I curled up, still holding the dirty clothes that she wore. They had her smell: vomit, cream and that smell that people call *the baby smell.* They say they love it. But it makes me feel like I can't breathe.

I turned my back on the bundle and covered my ears. Pressed them hard so that my arms ached and my ears felt crushed. Then I screamed with her.

I screamed like she screams.

I screamed louder than her.

That was yesterday.

Today, I had told myself, *will be better.*

My daughter waits for me to release her from the barred cot put together for her by my husband, her father. I watched him do it, an eight-month swell from my middle erupting out in front of me, my feet sore, my legs sore, my back sore, my whole self sore.

He cursed that cot.

Who the fuck is meant to follow these instructions?

He knew nothing but wanted to prove something.

And he did too. He finished making that fucking cot for her, our daughter, weeks too early. Weeks before she would rip me open and force herself out, ignoring my screams of agony, and screaming louder.

She was all he talked about as my belly grew and grew. Something like a monster swelling up in there, waiting to attack. I thought, *Maybe he will remember me after she comes out and this body is no longer savaged by her.*

But he didn't.

He got worse.

I saw how his face lit up at the sight of her drool and her vomit and her shit. He loves her more than he loves me. She is worth more to him. I don't need to ask him. I know the lies he would tell. *It is a different kind of love,* he would say.

Me and her, her and me, we fight for his love and affection every day. I fight by fucking him, making him tea, cleaning his house and his clothes and his daughter. She fights by wailing and shitting and pissing.

And she wins every time.

Maybe it is her helplessness, her innocence, her unending and relentless neediness that makes him love her more.

Or maybe it is because she has his eyes.

Yesterday, when my screams went dry and my head throbbed to its own vicious beat, I went down to her.

She was cruel. Unnerving and cruel.

I picked her up. Gave her a long drink of Calpol and gave me four of the strongest painkillers I could find in the press. They would help us both sleep.

And we did. Her in my arms as we lay on the bed her father and I fucked in. Her in my arms smelling just like the bundle of clothes I had held earlier. As dirty and intoxicating as a load of filthy washing.

We only woke when her father, my husband, came home.

How peaceful and beautiful she looks, he said and stroked her head when he finally found us there. He only glanced at me with a smile. I knew that later he would want stroking too.

When we first moved in, we had barricaded ourselves in that house. We locked windows and doors and stayed on the couch. We laughed at nothing and didn't bother to get dressed. We drank vodka on Saturday mornings and spent those whole days in a mad drunken kind of love. We turned off our phones and turned up MTV.

Now she has barricaded us in with her screams and her needs and her wailing. She locks doors and windows with her eternal demands.

She was quiet last night. And when her father, my husband, came home she smiled with that same little pink mouth that had tormented and tortured me all day.

Was she good for you today? he asked me.

Some lies are said to protect ourselves from others' judgements. So I said, *yes.*

He is worried, my husband, her father, that I can't manage. He has said he has concerns.

I'm concerned. Concerned that this is too much for you.

That is a lie, from him to me.

He is concerned, my husband, her father, that I will not make a good mother for our daughter. He is concerned that I will not feed her my milk or clean up her shit. He is concerned that he has picked the wrong woman to fuck, to marry, to have his child.

But he does not see her, our daughter, when she looks up at me and screams rage. He does not see her when she closes her pink mouth tight against my breast.

He sees smiles and a little hand curl up over his finger.

The same hands that grab chunks of my hair and pull and pull until I scream her screams.

He will be home soon, her father, my husband. He will be home soon and then I can give him his angel, this bundle of red raw screams with shit in her nappy. I can give him her and I can go into the shower and let steaming, scalding water burn and wash away the smell of her.

Maybe somewhere inside me is that mother us women are all meant to be. At the flick of a switch, with a virus in our bellies. Off goes sexuality, on goes earthly mothering.

I lay her down on the changing mat. Silent at last, a break from the razors she slices inside my head. I open a nappy, clean and fresh, and wonder how long this time until she pisses again.

This is the insult that was once my own body's produce.

I smile at her and tickle her chin, pick her up and kiss her cheek. She giggles that laugh that her father, my husband, loves so much.

I hold her close.

But my tenderness is a lie.

I feel her tiny heart beat against my shoulder. Her little face hidden, talking to me in a language I will never understand. Her whole little self weighs too heavy in my arms.

We go to the front door, waiting.

He is due home, her father, my husband. Any minute now that door will open. I think of how he will light up at the sight of us, of her. Our daughter in my arms, quiet. Me loving her as I am supposed to.

His face will light up and he will go to her first. He loves her more.

It is me he loves, I whisper in her tiny ear.

She speaks back in her language, laughing. Mocking me.

We wait there.

He is never late.

But tonight he is late.

Our daughter starts to wiggle in my arms, cry boredom, hunger and tears for her father. I hold her tighter.

I want him to see the lie of us together. I want him to see the lie of me, being the mother us women are supposed to be.

Tradition, Sexuality and Power: Questioning the Motivations Behind FGM

Jean Rafferty

Jean Rafferty is a writer of fiction and an award-winning journalist. Her first two works of fiction were both nominated for literary prizes. Her third, Foul Deeds Will Rise, *about Satanist ritual abuse, was published in June 2019 by independent publisher Wild Wolf Publishing. Rafferty was formerly an award-winning journalist with a wide range. She worked for a variety of both broadsheet and tabloid publications, from the* Sunday Times Magazine *to the* Sunday People, *as well as writing light-hearted comment for daily newspapers. Rafferty was twice shortlisted in the UK Press Awards, an unusual honour for a freelancer, and has also won awards for medical writing, travel writing and comment. In 2003 she won a Joseph Rowntree Foundation journalist's fellowship for her work on prostitution.*

It's 2003, a hot classroom in Sierra Leone, West Africa, after the end of the eleven-year civil war. The local newspaper has an article about the secret societies that inflict female genital mutilation (FGM) on young women, their members sometimes forcibly holding the girls down as they sew up the entrance to their vaginas in the name of tradition.

'How would we research this?' I ask the group.

'You couldn't,' says one. 'They might do this to you.'

My blood runs cold, despite the heat of the day. There's a sly humour in the way it's said, but the malice of a broader cultural attitude towards women is behind it. I may be the teacher here in this Thomson Foundation project for the training of Sierra Leone's journalists, but I'm also a woman and the object of some curiosity for the mostly male group.

The secret societies that carry out this practice, that maim their own daughters and nieces and granddaughters, are, it turns out, all made up of women. They believe that the Bondo rituals of FGM mark a girl's passage into womanhood and drive away evil spirits from the community – a strangely surreal notion, as if the spirits become trapped in the profound depths of a woman's vagina so must not gain entrance.

We discuss the journalistic elements we'd need for telling this story more fully and then I ask the basic question: 'Why would you do this to women?' The young man who answers is stunningly handsome, not someone you'd expect to be threatened by women's power. 'To tame them,' he says.

'More fool you,' I say. 'You'd have much more fun if you didn't.'

We all laugh and the tension in the room is broken, but the question remains.

Why? Why would you condemn the women you love to a lifetime of pain and discomfort?

In infibulation, the entrance to the vagina is almost completely sewn up, leaving the narrowest of passages for urine and menstrual blood. It causes infection, pain, an inability to enjoy lovemaking – and in extreme cases, death. Similar problems arise with other forms of FGM, such as type 2, where the inner labia are cut; they often fuse together during the healing process. With both methods, the whole process may have to be reversed when a woman gives birth, which can lead to a fistula, and faeces and urine leaking into the vagina. The woman loses her baby, is left incontinent and then is shunned because not only has she failed as a woman by not delivering a healthy child, but she stinks of excrement.

If you're shivering reading this, you're probably female and deeply aware of your own physical vulnerability. You're right to shiver. There is no mercy for women who oppose the prevailing norms. In 2009, four women journalists were marched naked through the streets of a Sierra Leone city because they'd criticised FGM in radio broadcasts.

But it's not just Sierra Leone. In 2011, American broadcast journalist Lara Logan was stripped, beaten and sexually assaulted in Cairo's Tahrir Square during Arab Spring celebrations at the resignation of President Hosni Mubarak.

An aberration? High spirits gone wrong? Not exactly. Logan was simply the most famous victim – British, French and Dutch journalists have been attacked, as well as hundreds of Egyptian women. And as we now know, in Cologne and other cities across Europe, there have been mass rapes by groups of men when crowds gather for what should be joyous celebrations. Closer to home, over 139 women were killed by male partners in the UK in one year, according to the 2018 Femicide Census published by Women's Aid. That's more than two women every week.

In 42 per cent of those murders, the violence used was completely disproportionate, far more than was needed to kill the woman. One victim was stabbed 175 times. Another was bludgeoned 40 times with an axe. 'Overkilling', they call it, as if mere killing is not enough.

Our physicality disturbs men. Women mostly think of themselves as powerless, but to men all women are dangerous.

From the very beginning of his life, a woman – his mother – is the most powerful figure in a man's world. But when he reaches adulthood, another form of female power has him in thrall. Desire takes away men's power, their image of themselves as being in control, which is why they go to such extreme lengths to contain women's sexuality.

But at least in some Muslim and Asian cultures, the drive to 'tame' one's partner is an acceptance that sexuality is central to women's lives. Ancient tantric thought said that a woman, once awakened, has higher levels of eroticism than a man. Hence the need to control her by mutilating her body – her nature is so wildly wanton, she'll be off sleeping with your best mate if you can't satisfy her, or you could end up bringing up his child without even knowing.

In Judeo-Christian culture, female sexuality is regarded as aberrant, a sin, something only bad women do. A woman is a receptacle for men's desire but has none of her own. She's empty, a hollow doll, but as terrifying as Chucky if she suddenly starts moving and feeling. No wonder almost military tactics are needed to curb her – women are brainwashed into believing they should be chaste, and then battered when they prove not to be. Their children are taken away from them or they're exposed to public shame or they're just plain battered.

We've been fighting inequality in the West for many years, but now, in our supposedly equal times, modern refinements have been added – slut-shaming, top-sharking (where a woman's top is pulled up in public to reveal her breasts), and inevitably, the recording of such events on mobile phones.

I was shocked in 2010 when a class of journalism students referred to someone as a 'slut'. 'I suppose you mean sexually active?' I said, but they looked at me like I was a dinosaur. It was accepted by both the young men and the young women in the group that it was acceptable to label women sluts. The women had internalised the deeply misogynistic idea that their sexuality was shameful. Not surprising – they're always being told that what they wear is immodest and incendiary and it's their own fault if they get raped.

Like the *soweis* in Sierra Leone, the senior women who carry out FGM – like most of us – my students found it hard to break free of the attitudes of the society around them. Even if we believe fervently in our own equality, we might not feel it; we are often not sure of ourselves sexually or physically – because women's bodies are the battleground. If you want to win hearts and minds, first subdue the body.

In the last fifty years of feminism, since women started burning their bras and seeking freedom from the stultifying standards imposed upon them, body fascism has exploded to the extent that, according to the 2017 Dove Global Girls Beauty and Confidence Report, 80 per cent of women in the UK are dissatisfied with their bodies. As ordinary women have become taller and heavier, the images they're surrounded with have become ever leaner. Only 2 per cent of American women are as thin as the models they see, but probably zero per cent of the models are as thin as their own pictures, thanks to the ubiquitous photoshopping and airbrushing that goes on in the media. You don't have to have an eating disorder to be undermined by it, you just have to be around.

It's another form of taming women, a way to rob them of the power that men know and many women doubt they have. The *soweis* in Sierra Leone too have power: not the power of sex, but political and economic power. They're trusted with training the next generation of women and are paid in cash and food for their services. It's no coincidence that the training they offer is in domestic skills, women's traditional area of control, though I pity the poor girls recovering from such a procedure and having to stay in the forest, learning bloody housework.

'We teach the girls that when you marry you need to do the laundry, sweep and cook. You must get on with the new mother-in-law and the father-in-law; all the small brothers, you need to treat them properly. So that is why we put them in Bondo,' village *sowei* Baromie Kamara told Lisa O'Carroll of the *Guardian* in 2015. 'If the girls come back into town and can't do these things it will cause the *sowei* problems. They will always curse us.'

It's easy to demonise the *soweis* as women who collude with male oppression. They do, but why? Women I discussed it with at the 2016 IASH/Scottish PEN 'Dangerous Women' symposium at the University of Edinburgh thought they were either venal or jealous of the younger generation of women. I wonder if perhaps it started out as a kindness, protection for their girls as otherwise the male elders of the village would perform the cutting. Can you imagine the sense of violation in young women if men inflicted such a mutilation on them?

Whatever the truth, it's unlikely that this practice will disappear any time soon. Women are too poor, too disadvantaged in Sierra Leone (where a 2018 Thomson Reuters Foundation report shows almost 90 per cent of women are cut) for the *soweis* to willingly give up the power of the knife. And in the Middle East, Asia and many other African countries, traditional ideas about women's modesty and fidelity mean that FGM is routinely carried out on young girls. The World Health Organization has been battling against the practice for decades, but it goes on and on. There are an estimated 200 million women living in the world today who have been mutilated in this way. UNICEF predicts that if the practice is not reduced, the numbers will grow from 3.6 million annually in 2013 to 6.6 million in 2050.

We can all imagine what FGM does to women: the terror and humiliation of the ceremony, the shock. Lifelong pain can follow, and lifelong health risks, both physical and mental – infections, menstrual and sexual problems, the need for later surgery. And how do you deal with the sense of having had part of you taken away?

But I also think about that handsome young man in the journalism group and wonder what it has done to his life. Can his wife welcome his lovemaking if she dreads the discomfort it will cause her? Can she love a man who wants to restrain and rule over her? Can there be any warmth in their lives together?

Dangerous women, the *soweis*, damaging their daughters and granddaughters, brutalising themselves in the name of power. But dangerous too to the lives of men, taking away the freedom and fun of a truly equal relationship with women.

More information about female genital cutting can be found at Orchid Project: orchidproject.org

Mental Health and Becoming a Danger to Yourself

Irenosen Okojie

Irenosen Okojie is a Nigerian British writer. Her debut novel Butterfly Fish *won a Betty Trask award and was shortlisted for an Edinburgh International First Book Award. Her work has been featured in the* New York Times, *the* Observer, *the* Guardian, *the* BBC *and the* Huffington Post *among other publications. Her short stories have been published internationally including* Salt's Best British Short Stories 2017 *and* 2020, Kwani? *and* The Year's Best Weird Fiction. *She featured in the* Evening Standard Magazine *as one of London's exciting new authors. Her short story collection* Speak Gigantular, *published by Jacaranda Books, was shortlisted for the Edge Hill Short Story Prize, the Jhalak Prize, the Saboteur Awards and nominated for a Shirley Jackson Award. She is a fellow of the Royal Society of Literature. Her latest collection of stories,* Nudibranch, *published by Little, Brown's Dialogue Books in 2019, was longlisted for the Jhalak Prize. She is the winner of the 2020 AKO Caine Prize for African Writing for her story 'Grace Jones.' Irenosen was awarded an MBE for Services to Literature in 2021. www.irenosenokojie.com / Twitter: @IrenosenOkojie*

When my friend Rosa told me that a spy had been attempting to steal memories from her brain, we were sitting in a hospital waiting room, creating false lives for every interesting-looking person that walked in. Rosa had struggled with severe depression since she was randomly, viciously attacked in public a few years before, beaten and left bleeding on the pavement. Her attacker, another woman, was never charged, but Rosa was left to contend with the aftermath from that incident: panic attacks, the feeling of drowning intermittently, insomnia. Some days, she found herself shaking uncontrollably, scared to go out, to know other people. Understandably, other days she seethed with a blinding rage that left a metallic taste in her mouth, twisting her naturally bubbly personality into something she didn't recognise. Following a bout of psychosis, other entities entered her life. She confessed that these figures chose to create accidents in her world, telling her *you will collapse in the supermarket today, on your way to that job interview you really want; you will suddenly have a punctured lung; you will be unable to explain how it happened at the A&E reception desk. Outside your house, there's a man sitting in a dark blue Ford Mondeo, he's holding your passport and a blueprint to another life; after you collect them from him, call the police.* Each time her body followed suit, caught in an all-consuming terror that held her limbs hostage and made her hyper-alert. These occurrences weren't isolated; they continued. Days became bleak passages of time to get through.

Tormented for several months, she eventually visited a local shop, stared at the row of knives in the centre aisle, positioned above frying pans guaranteed to produce the perfect omelette or pancake. She bought one with a small handle her hand would grip steadily. The voices kept talking, telling her it would be better for everybody if she just ended the misery. She remembered it being so hot that day in July her T-shirt clung to her skin. She remembered the jangle of house keys in her pocket, the recorder at the bottom of her bag she'd taken to leaving voice diaries on to ease the pressure in her head; she remembered she'd run out of space. By the time she hit the high street, the noise had become one clear instruction playing on loop. Her head felt ready to split open. The weight of living inside it had become unbearable. If she listened to the instruction, that dark, omnivorous throbbing would stop. She walked to the park, sat down in an isolated area and began to cut herself. It was only after she arrived home, after the wounds talked too, that she started screaming in her kitchen.

I was devastated when she shared this with me some time later. I couldn't get over the fact that she'd kept it to herself for such a long period for fear of appearing weak and incapable of functioning properly. I felt sad and frustrated. Despite how close we were, she hadn't come to me early on. A feeling of helplessness lingered. I vowed to myself I'd do something to help. I wrote my novel *Butterfly Fish*, which centres on a woman struggling to maintain her grip on reality following a traumatic loss, partly to combat this feeling, but also partly because we don't talk enough about mental health issues in communities of colour. It is a silent, tangled thing amongst us. In Britain, African and Caribbean people are far more likely to be diagnosed with mental health problems than their white counterparts. They also face high levels of discrimination in the quality of treatment and care they receive, forced to deal with prejudice on two levels.

It can be difficult getting someone struggling to cope to seek professional help. They can become untrusting of others and increasingly remote. We need to have spaces where we can talk about these issues in supportive environments. When a young woman becomes a danger to herself through no fault of her own, she needs to not feel ashamed. We have to remove the stigma from mental health and consider alternative therapies to help people on their way to recovery. In addition, people who support loved ones with mental health issues often get left out of the equation. It is a thankless, seemingly unending situation. There should be places we can go to for help and groups we can join with people in similar positions. It's encouraging to see the growth of organisations like Black Mental Health UK, The Black, African and Asian Therapy Network, Time to Change, as well as Mind and Samaritans.

A few weeks ago, I went to visit Rosa. After some time in hospital, she was better, back home on a course of cognitive behavioural therapy which was helping. She beat me mercilessly at table football. It was amazing to see the light in her eyes again, that zest for life I'd always admired slowly coming back. She told me she still had her difficult days, still wrestled with anxiety. There are no neat resolutions, but she was slowly learning to manage more, to reach out when she needed to. She told me that the man in the dark blue Ford Mondeo watching outside her house had disappeared, that he no longer held onto her passport. And this, at least, was good news.

More Information

The Black, African and Asian Therapy Network
www.baatn.org.uk

Time to Change www.time-to-change.org.uk

Mind www.mind.org.uk

Samaritans www.samaritans.org

Unsexing Fulvia: A Dangerously Undomesticated Roman Wife

Suzanne Dixon

Suzanne Dixon is a feminist activist and scholar, now retired from her position as Reader in Classics & Ancient History at the University of Queensland, but still writing and agitating from her idyllic island home off the east coast of Australia. She has edited and written several books and innumerable articles about women, especially Roman women (and other things, including changing representations of motherhood, the history of the European family and marriage, and debt and gift exchange). While not as energetic as Fulvia, she is proud that her achievements include active promotion of interdisciplinary women's studies, childcare and rape law reform in Australia and the founding of a rape crisis centre and a university childcare collective.

In the wake of Labour MP Jo Cox's 2016 murder, *Guardian* journalist Emine Saner highlighted the violent online abuse of women politicians: '"If I could kill you I would" was one of the many online threats [Labour MP Tulip Siddiq] has received… Labour MP Jess Phillips said she received more than 600 threats of rape in one night on Twitter in May.'

Women who step out of line must be punished. A woman who intrudes on the male public sphere is fair game. Her appearance, sexuality and fertility will be mocked. She will probably face violence and the threat of violence.

Because women are ALL intrinsically dangerous, but they can – like rivers or wild animals – be contained. There is an uneasy truce while they conform to the male rules of propriety. But once the river overflows or the elephant tramples the stockade, all bets are off.

Fulvia was a political woman born into a well-connected political family in Republican Rome. The Roman political elite was divided – like Whigs and Tories – between the reforming Popularis tradition and the more traditional Optimate cause, which favoured senatorial legislation over the less predictable proposals of plebeian tribunes in the popular assembly. Fulvia's birth family and her three husbands – Clodius, Curio and Marcus Antonius ('Mark Antony') – were all Populares, their cause generally vilified by the conservative tradition of Roman chroniclers. Her life was short by modern standards (*c.*78–40 BCE), but she left her mark on history. In a position of great power following the assassination of Caesar in 44 BCE, she was ultimately on the wrong side of the civil war which ended, some years after her death, with the triumph at Actium in 31 BCE of Caesar's youthful great-nephew Octavian over her husband Mark Antony. As 'Augustus', founder of a new regime, Octavian reigned supreme. Victors' spoils include the archives. The hostile tradition against Fulvia has endured for two millennia, replete with reactionary dislike of the Popularis cause and vicious misogynistic stereotypes. Only since the late twentieth century has this hostile image been tempered, especially by feminist scholars such as Judy Hallett.

Why was Fulvia dangerous?

Not only did she plunge openly into politics and public demonstrations – albeit in the role of supportive wife – but she also collected, led and addressed armies in the Italian peninsula to ensure her husband's support base.

Politics and the military: two bastions of masculine exclusivity.

Her body, her marriages, her sex appeal were all subject to abuse. And it served her right.

Obviously.

By the second century CE, the hostile tradition was well established. In his *Life of Antony* (Perrin's Loeb translation), the biographer Plutarch, source of so many of Shakespeare's influential images of these personalities, wrote of Fulvia:

> She was a woman who took no thought for spinning or housekeeping, nor would she deign to bear sway over a man of private station, but she wished to rule a ruler and command a commander. Therefore, Cleopatra was indebted to Fulvia for teaching Antony to endure a woman's sway (*gynocracy*), since she took him over quite tamed, and schooled at the outset to obey women.

What could be worse? Clearly a very dangerous woman.

Paradoxically, Fulvia's transgressive intrusion into male politics and warfare has guaranteed her more exposure – in every sense – in the historiographic tradition, which focused on these Boy's Own activities. Her treatment constitutes a warning for women contemplating public life. The resemblance to warnings meted out by misogynist trolls towards her modern equivalents is often chilling. In a 1991 collection of essays, *Stereotypes of Women in Power*, several of us contributors showed the repetitious character of attacks on political women in different cultures and historical periods, sexualising the women and painting their power as illegitimate and devious – scheming concubines and domineering dowagers.

By the second century BCE, the power of Rome extended throughout the Mediterranean, but from the late second century BCE onwards, its internal politics were characterised by upheaval, instability and terrible civil wars. By 43 BCE, the Republican constitution was a façade. Once its self-styled (Optimate) defenders, assassins of Julius Caesar, had been decisively defeated by Caesar's Populares heirs and supporters, the state was ruled in practice by the Second Triumvirate of Antony, Octavian and Lepidus. In the fashion which had become horrifically normal throughout that terrible century, the triumvirs confiscated land to give to their supporters, including their soldiers. They drew up lists of 'proscribed' enemies, whose lives and estates were forfeit. Their heads, brought to Rome as proof of their murder, would elicit rewards.

Inevitably, the head of the orator Cicero, a bitter enemy of Antony, was brought to Rome. Other sources record Antony's satisfaction, but only the much later author, Cassius Dio, adds a detail of Fulvia's response:

> Antony uttered many bitter reproaches against it and then ordered it to be exposed on the rostra more prominently than the rest, in order that it might be seen in the very place where Cicero had so often been heard declaiming against him, together with his right hand, just as it had been cut off. And Fulvia took the head into her hands before it was removed,

> and after abusing it spitefully and spitting upon it, set it on her knees, opened the mouth, and pulled out the tongue, which she pierced with the pins that she used for her hair, at the same time uttering many brutal jests.

What a bitch! In a narrative filled with cruelty and violence, this scene is designed to showcase Fulvia's savagery, executed with a particularly feminine weapon.

When Mark Antony left Italy to pursue Roman affairs in the Eastern Mediterranean, his position seemed assured. He had loyal generals, senatorial supporters and soldiers on his side in Italy. His younger brother, Lucius Antonius, was one of the two consuls for 41 BCE. Fulvia, says Dio, was effectively the other consul.

Trouble soon developed between Lucius Antonius and the triumvir Octavian, who schemed to win over Antony's supporters. Fulvia was immensely active throughout 41 BCE, travelling around the country to ensure that Antony's former soldiers knew that their land grants and other benefits came from him, not Octavian. She took Antony's children with her – a form of display which was to become familiar under the imperial dynasties of the future. The appearance of a loyal wife and young children before the troops was a very direct kind of appeal.

Initially, Fulvia attempted to make peace with Octavian and to temper Lucius's provocative behaviour throughout this period. Until, says the Civil War chronicler Appian, Antony's agent Manius made mischief:

> Antony's soldiers, and Octavian also, blamed [Lucius Antonius] for working against Antony's interests, and Fulvia blamed him for stirring up war at an inopportune time, until Manius

> maliciously changed her mind by telling her that as long as Italy remained at peace Antony would stay with Cleopatra, but that if war should break out there he would come back speedily. Then Fulvia, moved by a woman's jealousy, incited Lucius to discord.

So Fulvia started a war to get her husband to leave the foreign mistress and return to Italy! Rather at odds with her astute political actions.

So womanish.

Once open warfare broke out, Lucius Antonius ensconced himself in Perugia in the north with his troops, while Fulvia was based closer to Rome in Praeneste (modern Palestrina), taking advice from high-ranking supporters before dispatching orders to the various Italian regions. Dio predictably damns her usurpation of masculine prerogative. 'And why,' he asks rhetorically, 'should anyone be surprised at this, when she would wear a sword around her waist, give out the password to the watch and even address the troops directly on occasion?'

So unfeminine.

The tone was set by contemporaries and orchestrated by Octavian. His own jingle, cited by the satirist Martial, as translated by Amy Richlin in 1983, taunts Fulvia for Antony's infidelity with the foreign queen Glaphyra:

> Because Antony fucks Glaphyra, Fulvia has set
> this penalty for me, that I fuck her in turn...
> 'Either fuck me, or let us fight,' she says. What if my prick
> is dearer to me than my life? Let the trumpets sound!

A rather different way of blaming her for the armed conflict.

A generation later, Velleius Paterculus (19 BCE–18 CE), also blaming her for the war, denounced her unwomanly behaviour: 'Fulvia, the wife of Antony, who had nothing of the woman in her except her sex, was creating general confusion by armed violence.'

Fulvia marshalled Antony's legions to bring reinforcements to her brother-in-law, besieged by Octavian's troops in Umbria, as Appian relates in his *Civil Wars*. Inscriptions on surviving missiles from the siege of Perugia in 41–40 BCE link Fulvia and her brother-in-law as equal targets, urging them to present their arseholes to the bullets catapulted into the town.

Eventually, the Antonine forces were starved out and Perugia was taken and sacked by Octavian's soldiery. In the ensuing slaughter, Lucius, Fulvia and many of their high-ranking supporters were spared and allowed by Octavian to leave Italy. Fulvia, her children and the core of Antonine loyalists went east to meet up with Antony.

And then, suddenly, she died in Greece.

Strange to relate, a new pact was forged between the warring triumvirs, this time reinforced by Antony's marriage to Octavian's sister Octavia. Plutarch tells us in his *Life of Antony* that it suited both men to lay the blame on the dead Fulvia for the deterioration of their triumviral solidarity.

A poor return for her loyalty.

The attacks on Fulvia are not unique. Roman political invective was vigorous and virulent in the Republican era, when crowds turned out to hear great orators like Cicero or Antony's grandfather lambast their enemies (and even their friends) mercilessly in the forum and the law courts. Prominent men's sex lives, appearance and pedigree were routinely held up to ridicule in Catullus's political lampoons and the chants, graffiti and songs of the masses.

In the years between Fulvia's death and Antony's final military defeat in 31 BCE, Octavian successfully depicted Antony to the Roman public as the emasculated slave of a scheming foreign queen, Cleopatra VII, and Plutarch duly credited the domineering Fulvia with grooming him for this subservience. Plutarch could as well have cited Antony's mother Julia, also a forceful political actor, the type of woman credited by Roman authors with their famous sons' successes, a process I detailed in my 1988 book *The Roman Mother*. But then, as now, uninhibited attacks were a sign that a woman was being taken seriously in public life, particularly as an opponent. Both Fulvia's political clout and Cleopatra's famous statecraft were trivialised, reduced to laughable womanish defects.

The moral of the story?

Even strong women can become political pawns. With rare exceptions, the media tend to harden their judgement of those who have gone beyond the pale. Fulvia's record as a dedicated Popularis, an extraordinarily supportive wife and prolific mother, reveals a woman in the tradition of exemplary Roman matrons like Cornelia, revered mother of the Gracchi brothers. Fulvia's energy almost to the moment she died was monumental. Yet her legacy is a cluster of stock 'bad woman' epithets – overbearing, jealous, nagging, unfeminine, unfuckable. A true warrior – literally – for the Popularis cause and for her husband Antony, she was vilified in her lifetime. And – the final insult – betrayed and blamed in her death by Antony himself to suit his immediate political convenience.

She was, indeed, dangerous: a harbinger of the imperial women who would appear on the coins of the new dynasties, embodying the womanly virtues, if they were 'good'. Or, conversely, condemned, like Octavian's/Augustus's disgraced daughter Julia and the executed empress Messalina, to perpetual satiric and historiographic abuse as a sexual joke, a dangerous woman properly exiled from the masculine portals of power.

Josephine Butler: A Dangerous Woman?

Leigh Denton

Leigh Denton studied English Literature and Fine Art before becoming a litigation lawyer in Sydney, Australia. She maintains an interest in Victorian and Edwardian social history and blogs on this subject at downstairscook.blogspot.com. She currently lives in a coastal region north of Sydney and divides her time between writing, lawyering, travelling and beachgoing.

Could a woman born into an upper-class family in the mid-nineteenth century, schooled at home and raised to be devoutly religious, be dangerous? If that woman's name was Josephine Butler, the answer is definitely 'yes.'

The danger with Josephine was that she was not afraid to call a spade a spade and that she was forthright and vocal on a subject which many men of her time did not want to hear about publicly: their sexual lives.

Speaking out thus, in pamphlets and public lectures where she did not shy away from outlining the procedures employed by police and doctors under the Contagious Diseases Acts of 1864–1869 in shocking and graphic detail, earned her odium and disapprobation. But she continued doing so until these Acts were finally repealed in 1886.

Josephine Butler was born in 1828 to a father who treated all his children equally and a mother who gave her a strong Christian faith. Hers was an affluent family with connections to prominent figures such as the reformist Prime Minister Lord Grey, her father's cousin, and William Wilberforce, with whom her grandfather worked on the campaign for the abolition of the slave trade. She was schooled at home and developed a political and social conscience early in life before marrying George Butler, a fellow libertarian who supported her later reform work.

Josephine first threatened the social order in Great Britain by joining forces with Elizabeth Wolstenholme to form the Married Women's Property Committee, which sought reform of the law of coverture which gave a married man full control over all property his wife owned at the time of their marriage. Their campaign led eventually to the enacting of the Married Women's Property Act in 1882.

But it was Josephine's strident and thunderous condemnation of the criminal acts sanctioned by the Contagious Diseases Acts that really earned her widespread opposition from men. She considered prostitution to be abuse or exploitation of one sex by the other, and she was fearless in describing the barbaric practices employed by doctors and policemen under this legislation in forcibly examining women internally whom they merely suspected of engaging in prostitution. Men were not examined.

The Contagious Diseases Acts were introduced in an attempt to halt the spread of venereal disease in the army and navy, and groups of plain-clothed policemen regularly hauled in women they deemed to fit the definition of 'common prostitute', which under the legislation was broad and vague.

The examinations were brutal and could not be more harrowing than in the case of 'Nancy', a thirteen-year-old girl whose widowed mother took in washing from the navy garrison in Southampton to make ends meet. Nancy collected and delivered the washing and one day was arrested by a policeman who had observed her going to and fro and, upon searching her pockets, found threepence. She was marched into a police cell while a doctor was summoned. He quickly came and asked if she could write her name. When she said she could, he thrust a piece of paper and said, 'Write it here.' She did so, unknowingly giving consent to be examined. She was forcibly restrained on an examination table by the policeman pulling her skirts up over her head and tying them underneath, effectively binding and gagging her. Her feet were placed in stirrups. The doctor began his examination for signs of venereal disease by repeatedly thrusting a metal speculum into her vagina, and then a long-handled forceps in order to grab hold of her cervix so it could be examined. The examination took forty-five minutes, when it should have taken only two or three, and amounted to nothing less than instrumental torture and surgical rape.

Nancy, when she was first bound and gagged, had thrashed around in confusion and terror, managing to throw the upper half of her body off the table. Hanging by her legs, one of her lower vertebrae was crushed against the metal edge of the table, an injury from which she never recovered.

She was found to be clean and issued with a certificate to this effect. Her distraught mother, knowing it was futile to complain to the police about the incident, as the men had acted entirely within the law, wrote to the Ladies National Association for the Repeal of the Contagious Diseases Acts, also founded by Josephine and Elizabeth Wolstenholme, and received a visit from Josephine herself.

She advised that Nancy needed to leave Southampton at once, as she was at risk of being seized and re-examined. Josephine promised to find a position for her and so Nancy became lady's maid to the daughter of a baronet who later became a nun: the nun referred to as Sister Monica Joan by Jennifer Worth in her memoir *Farewell to the East End.* Nancy's back was severely injured; she was cringing and traumatised. She worked for the future Sister until she was twenty-four, when she died of tuberculosis of the spine.

Josephine, in her continued campaign to have the right to perform these examinations overthrown, wrote letters to all and sundry containing detailed accounts women had given her of the horrors to which they had been subjected. One such letter containing the following account (written in capitals) was sent to Dr J.J. Garth Wilkinson, a Swedenborgian and homeopathist with a practice in London:

> THE ATTITUDE THEY PUSH US INTO FIRST IS DISGUSTING AND SO PAINFUL, AND THEN THESE MONSTROUS INSTRUMENTS – OFTEN THEY USE SEVERAL. THEY SEEM TO TEAR THE PASSAGE OPEN FIRST WITH THEIR HANDS, AND EXAMINE US, AND THEN THEY THRUST IN INSTRUMENTS, AND THEY PULL THEM OUT AND PUSH THEM IN AND TWIST THEM ABOUT AND IF YOU CRY OUT THEY STIFLE YOU WITH A TOWEL OVER YOUR FACE.

Dr Wilkinson annexed Josephine's letter to the pamphlet he published in 1870 entitled 'Forcible Introspection of Women for the Army and Navy by the Oligarchy, Considered Physically', and Josephine was no less sparing in detail when she addressed public meetings called to raise support for the reform of a law which she saw as benefiting men while victimising women.

And Josephine, despite being described by a journalist as 'an indecent maenad, a shrieking sister, frenzied, unsexed, utterly without shame', was effective. By 1871 an MP said to her: 'Your manifesto has shaken us very badly in the House of Commons: a leading man in the House remarked to me, "We know how to manage any other opposition in the House or in the country, but this is very awkward for us, this revolt of women."'

Awkward indeed. Josephine had struck at the core of the double standard that said men could only satisfy their sexual desires with a prostitute rather than with the woman characterised by Coventry Patmore as *The Angel in the House* in his eponymous 1854 poem, who tended their home and children. The same double standard said prostitutes preyed on men for financial gain, with hapless males as their victims, as these morally corrupt women both aroused and gratified desire.

Josephine was nothing if not persistent. Her initial attempts to have the Contagious Diseases Acts repealed came to naught, but in 1883 the forcible examinations were suspended. Three years later, the Acts were repealed.

Josephine did not stop there, however. In 1885 she persuaded W.T. Stead, the editor of the *Pall Mall Gazette*, to help her expose child prostitution and its associated trade of young girls to brothels on the Continent. He obliged by purchasing a thirteen-year-old girl for five pounds from her mother in a slum in Marylebone and took her with him to France. A few days after the publication of an article in Stead's newspaper detailing this escapade and exposing the extent of child prostitution in London, Josephine gave a speech calling for increased child protection and the raising of the age of consent. The next month, Parliament passed the Criminal Law Amendment Act 1885, which raised the age of consent from thirteen to sixteen and made it a criminal offence both to procure young girls for prostitution by fraud, intimidation or drugs, and to abduct girls aged under eighteen for the purpose of carnal knowledge. Josephine showed again that she was a force to be reckoned with.

Was this middle-aged genteel lady, wife of a schoolmaster and clergyman, dangerous? She was an agent of progress, certainly. She was also a threat to the established order, as she dared to tell men they needed to change in the male-dominated society of mid-nineteenth century Britain.

A dangerous woman – by any stretch of the imagination.

R.A. Kartini and the 'Clover Leaf'

Annee Lawrence

Annee Lawrence's debut novel, The Colour of Things Unseen, *is set in Sydney, Yogyakarta and Central Java (Aurora Metro, 2019). Annee lives in Sydney and has a PhD in creative writing from the Writing and Society Research Centre, Western Sydney University. She was awarded the inaugural Asialink Tulis Australian-Indonesian Writing Exchange Residency at Komunitas Salihara, Jakarta in 2018, and has published in* Griffith Review, New Writing: The International Journal for the Practice and Theory of Creative Writing, Cultural Studies Review *and* Hecate.

Dangerous woman? A danger
To whom? To what? She writes her
way to critique, to consciousness raising
through traces of anger, shame and grief.
Unmasks inequality, injustice, oppression.
If societies are made by humans, they can
be changed. She works for that change, her
emotions keep her moving, she puts her body
on the line, speaks truth to exoticism, tradition

and colonial power, stays true to
her chosen value, her chosen path of reform.

Raden Ajeng Kartini (1879–1904) remains a dangerous woman, and perhaps that is why hardly anyone outside Indonesia has even heard of her, let alone read the collection of letters she wrote in Dutch between 1899 and 1904. Today, the revolutionary richness of emotion, experience and intelligence expressed in her correspondence confounds any stereotype of what might have been on the mind of a young Javanese woman at that place and time. But perhaps there were many just like her, then and now, who were silenced or not heard because of the threat they posed to vested self-interests in their respective societies.

Kartini's powerful feminist, intellectual and nationalist legacy was created between 25 May 1899 and 14 September 1904 when she wrote to more than ten Dutch socialists, feminists and educationalists. After her untimely death in childbirth in 1904, the letters were collected and published in the Netherlands in 1911, and in English in 1920. Within them, she speaks to and exposes the social relations of power within the Javanese aristocracy and the Netherlands East Indies (NEI) colonial system, and presses the case for: Javanese education (for girls especially); an end to polygamy; greater agency for women in choosing a career and/or marriage; the training of more Javanese teachers, midwives and doctors; and the cessation of colonial injustice and exploitation.

While Kartini did not live to benefit from or achieve many of the changes she dreamed of and set in motion, her four younger sisters – Roekmini (1880–1951), Kardinah (1881–1971), Kartinah (1883–?) and Soematri (1888–1963) – became active proponents of the change they collectively sought. And, arguably, the dream of freedom for the Javanese, which began as a trickle in her letters, developed into a flow by the 1920s and 1930s, and became an unstoppable torrent after the Japanese surrendered on 15 August 1945, finally ending the Second World War.

Kartini was born in Jepara on the north coast of Central Java on 21 April 1879 and, as the title Raden Ajeng indicates, she was part of an aristocratic Javanese family that was integral to the Dutch colonial administration. Her father, the Regent of Jepara, was educated by a Dutch tutor in the 1860s, spoke Dutch fluently and was widely read in Western literature. When Kartini turned six, she and her two younger sisters were sent to a Dutch elementary school where they became sensitised to the cultural freedom expressed by their Dutch schoolgirl friends' expectations of one day having a career. This discovery inspired a dream in the sisters that if Java's women were granted vocational training and meaningful paid work, they could assume an active role in the country's social and economic development.

The bond between the three older sisters – Kartini, Kardinah and Roekmini – was expressed in the name they gave to themselves: the 'Clover Leaf'. From the age of twelve, this bond grew even stronger after they were made to leave school and follow the Javanese aristocratic custom of seclusion for young girls until their marriage was arranged. In the four painful years that followed, the sisters read, studied and made the acquaintance of the influential Dutch women and men with whom Kartini, as the main letter writer, maintained contact.

Their main interlocutors included Mevrouw Ovink-Soer – a socialist and feminist and wife of the NEI Assistant Resident who wrote for the Dutch women's magazine *De Hollandsche Lelie*. After taking out a subscription to the magazine, Kartini placed an advert for a penfriend which led to her correspondence with the radical Dutch feminist Stella Zeehandelaar. A year later, in 1900, she met and began corresponding with J. H. Abendanon, the Director of Education, Industry and Religion in Java (1900–1905), and his Spanish wife, Rosita Abendanon-Mandri.

For Kartini, letter writing was a means of creative expression that linked her to a cosmopolitan world of books and philosophical ideas and helped her to make meaning in relation to the embodied experiences of the family's everyday lives. In the opening lines of her first letter to Stella Zeehandelaar, dated 25 May 1899, Kartini, who had just turned twenty, articulated her passionate desire to embrace modernity:

> I have so longed to make the acquaintance of a 'modern girl', the proud, independent girl whom I so much admire; who confidently steps through life, cheerfully and in high spirits, full of enthusiasm and commitment, working not just for her own benefit and happiness alone but also offering herself to the wider society, working for the good of her fellow human beings. I am burning with excitement about this new era and yes, I can say that, even though I will not experience it in the Indies, as regards my thoughts and feelings, I am not part of today's Indies, but completely share those of my progressive white sisters in the far-off West.

Kartini describes to Zeehandelaar how, when she turned sixteen, the family finally broke with tradition and allowed the three sisters out in public so they could attend the festivities for the investiture of Queen Wilhelmina of the Netherlands. While her parents' unconventional move did not pass unnoticed in society at the time, for Kartini, the concession did not go nearly far enough:

> No, attending festivities or amusements were not what I had yearned for … I longed to be free to be able to be independent, to be able to make myself independent, not to have to be dependent on anyone, [and] … never to have to marry.

The painful reality for the sisters was that tradition required that they marry and, as well as being denied the right to choose or even meet their husband beforehand, there was also the Javanese aristocratic norm of polygamy, which she deplores in a letter to Zeehandelaar on 6 November 1899:

> And who does not do this? And why would they not do so? It is no crime, nor is it a scandal … And can you imagine what hellish pain a woman must experience when her husband comes home with another whom she has to recognise as his lawful wife, her rival? He can torment her to death, mistreat her as much as he likes for as long as he chooses not to give her her freedom again; she can whistle to the wind for her rights! Everything for the man and nothing for the woman is our law and general belief.

Although not revealed to Zeehandelaar, the Clover Leaf knew first-hand the suffering within families due to the polygamous marriage arrangement because their own father had two wives: the woman Kartini called 'mother' was her stepmother and the official first wife (*Raden Ayu*); her biological mother was the second wife (*selir*).

Kartini's ethical stance in her letters brings the collision between the public and private into focus when it becomes clear, as her translator Joost Coté says, that 'not only was there a real sense in which Kartini had to change the world to free herself, but that also personal autonomy had no moral meaning for Kartini if it were not projected as a universal right and ideal'. As Coté argues, Kartini strove to choose her own path, to assert her autonomy, and it is this 'chosen value' that 'launches her into the uncertain ground of modernity'. Coté cites Ágnes Heller's 1992 definition of a chosen value as one 'conceived of as superior, essential, real and rational', and which stands in contrast to 'the accepted values of traditional society'.

Kartini's letters were first collected and edited by J. H. Abendanon and published in the Netherlands in 1911 as *Door Duisternis Tot Licht* (Through Darkness to Light). An English language version followed in 1920 under the (unfortunate) title, *Letters of a Javanese Princess*, and translations were later released in Malay (1922), Arabic (1926), Sundanese (1930), Javanese (1938), Indonesian (1938) and Japanese (1955). While this initial collection to ten interlocutors was edited (even censored) to protect the sensitivities of her close family, unabridged collections of Kartini's letters (as well as those of her four younger sisters) have been translated into English by Joost Coté in recent decades. They include a collection of her letters to Rosita Abendanon-Mandri, *Letters from Kartini: An Indonesian Feminist, 1900–1904* (1992); *On Feminism and Nationalism: Kartini's Letters to Stella Zeehandelaar 1899–1903* (2005); *Realizing the Dream of R. A. Kartini: Her Sisters' Letters from Colonial Java* (2008); and *Kartini: The Complete Writings 1898–1904* (2015).

The letters map a period of growing emotional maturity, difficult choices and insightful reflection, alongside awareness of an emerging more enlightened colonial policy – the Ethical Policy – that supported greater education and a (limited) governing role for Indonesians, as well as the implementation of agricultural improvements and development of an indigenous handicraft export industry.

Kartini's access to Western education and absorption of the Enlightenment ideals of social equality and freedom led her to the conclusion that changes had to be made in Javanese society, particularly in regard to colonisation. In a letter to Zeehandelaar, dated 13 January 1900, perhaps in response to questions from Zeehandelaar on the topic, she writes:

> I am very, very fond of the Dutch people, and I am grateful for much that we enjoy from them and because of them. Many, very many, of them we can call our best friends, but there are also very, very many who are hostile towards us for no other reason than that we dared to compete with them in terms of education and culture. They make this clear to us in very painful ways. 'I am European, you are Javanese' or, in other words, 'I am the conqueror, you are the conquered'. Not just once, but several times, we are spoken to in broken Malay even though the person knew very well that we could speak the Dutch language ...
>
> Why is it that so many Hollanders find it unpleasant to converse with us in their own language? Oh, now I know, Dutch is too beautiful to be uttered by a brown mouth.

In the same letter, Kartini expresses outrage at the inequalities and discrimination imposed by the system of apartheid that both exploited and humiliated, and which, at the same time, relied on the Javanese aristocracy to maintain power.

> Oh! Stella, I have had the opportunity to observe all kinds of situations in the Indies society, and as a matter of course I have looked behind the conventions of the world of public officials. There are ravines there so deep, Stella, that the very sight of

> them would make you dizzy! Oh God! The world is so full of misdeeds, full of such horrible atrocities!

By 1900, Kartini was articulating a view that change for the Javanese would come with education, for 'when the Javanese is educated, he will no longer say "yes" and "amen" to everything that his superior chooses to impose on him'. In order to explain the need for eventual emancipation, she makes a direct comparison between Javanese resistance to colonial domination and feminist resistance to patriarchal oppression in Europe:

> Here it is just as with the women's movement with you, the Javanese are emancipating themselves. And in the same way that your women and girls are being opposed by those who have been their masters for centuries, here the Javanese are being hindered in their development by their superiors.
>
> Here it is only just beginning. ... The battle will be fierce: the fighters will not only have to cope with their opponents but also the indifference of their own compatriots for whom they are taking up arms. And when the battle for emancipation of our men is in full flight, then the women will rise up. Poor men, what a lot you will have to put up with.
>
> Oh! How wonderful that we happen to be living in these times! In this period of transition from the old to the new.

While Kartini valued her Dutch friends, and recognised that they held different and more enlightened views than many of their countrymen and women on the colonial project, Hildred Geertz observes in her 1963 introduction to *Letters of a Javanese Princess* that she became increasingly keen to affirm the unique value of Java's ancient and rich civilisation as something that 'should not be abandoned for a shallow modernity'.

At the same time that the utopian promise of modernity pushes Kartini to embrace its spirit, this entails great personal cost and considerable pain within her family as her search for 'a viable personal life' exposes her to the contradictions between the political and philosophical implications of modernity and the traditions of Javanese society. In so doing, Geertz argues, she courageously and publicly puts at risk her own self-esteem and quest for identity:

> The confrontation between Western and Eastern cultures is a continuous, unending process of great difficulty and momentous significance. It is all the more painful because neither the Western nor the Oriental outlooks are single, consistent philosophies – both comprise within themselves conflicting, even warring, points of view. Within both ... there are numerous alternative moral doctrines.

Kartini was not naïve as to the backlash that might incur as the reformist paths she and her sisters sought became more widely known. By the time of her death, however, the Clover Leaf had already been shattered by two events that brought great emotional turmoil and suffering. These were the arranged marriage of Kardinah, and two years later in 1901, that of Kartini herself to the Regent of Rembang, a widower with six children and three other wives still living.

While the letters from her Dutch correspondents have not survived, what is remarkable in Kartini's is their high degree of reflexivity and open critical analysis as, again and again, she engages the cross-cultural gap to enrich her political thinking and practice. The letters offer a snapshot of the interdependence of the Dutch colonisers and Java's gentry as well as Kartini and Roekmini's ongoing campaign to secure their own further education and training. Although almost succeeding in achieving this (first in the Netherlands, and then in Batavia), a combination of powerful forces triggers a situation that highlights innumerable risks in going ahead with their plan.

The emotionality of the texts highlights the embodied materiality of family and daily life, Javanese cultural practices and politics, and the impacts of recurrent physical and emotional ill health within the family. Time and again, Kartini reflects on the stratification of Javanese society under Dutch colonisation as well as her growing sense of an urgent need for Java to modernise, and for the colonial administration and the Javanese aristocracy to advance this. Kartini's letters – especially those written to Rosita Abendanon-Mandri, which are the most intimate – express joy, pain, pleasure, love, despair, suffering, anguish and confusion in response to the twists and turns of their lives. In the aftermath of her death, her surviving four younger sisters assumed the task of realising the dream of educational reform and social and cultural change. For example, as Coté observes, while Roekmini was successful in arranging her own marriage, the two youngest sisters, who were three and eight years younger than her, 'already reflect a different age':

> They benefited from the pioneers, assumed attending school as a right, enjoyed extra post-elementary classes, and gaily flaunted their learning of languages and geography without feeling, as their older sisters did, the heavy weight of the privilege and of the battle between tradition and modernity [the older sisters] had fought. In particular ... Soematri seems to represent the

> modern age ... [as her correspondence extends to] just a few years before the end of colonialism.

After Kartini's death, her four surviving sisters' own letters – to some of the same interlocutors – link to and reflect the 'much broader narrative of cultural change' that was to come during the first half of the twentieth century. This involved an era of emerging nationalism and significant cultural and social upheaval up to and including the surrender by the Dutch after the Japanese invasion in 1942, the Japanese occupation, and then the struggle that followed the declaration of Indonesian independence by the nationalist leaders, Soekarno and Hatta, on 17 August 1945.

In just four years, Kartini showed that emotions are dangerous. Emotions generated the critical thinking that moved her forward in her advocacy of education for the Javanese, and for women especially. Emotions – anger, shame, humiliation, grief and despair – must be felt and faced, and when that was done, she was able to move beyond decrying injustice to finding new pathways for the Javanese to modernise. This is why her passion and activism, clarity and perception still resonate because, as Sara Ahmed argues in *The Cultural Politics of Emotion*, 'The emotional struggles against injustice are... about how we are moved by feelings into a different relation to the norms that we wish to contest, or the wounds we wish to heal.'

Kartini's expressions of emotion to her friends and mentors arose out of layers of lived experience and the witness of colonial, class and gendered injustice and inequality. They led her to a consciousness of what needed to be done and set in motion the steps to its accomplishment. Her European interlocutors encouraged her dreams and offered a community of belief and moral and practical support. The most direct and measurable achievement of her legacy was the setting up of a string of schools for girls.

It is because Kartini's letters have survived and remained in circulation that her voice as one of Indonesia's first feminists continues to speak to the present. Kartini and the Clover Leaf and their two younger sisters had an active role in educating and inspiring later generations of feminists and nationalists. Her voice and their actions helped lay a foundation for the emergence of the Indonesian Women's Movement (Gerwani) in the early 1950s, which grew to an estimated 3 million members by 1965.

Shockingly, Gerwani would be decimated after the 1965 coup that deposed President Soekarno and launched thirty-two years of dictatorship under President Suharto. In the violence that followed the coup, more than 500,000 progressive Indonesians – including feminists, writers, journalists, farmers, university teachers and doctors – were massacred, tortured and imprisoned. The United States CIA provided weapons and names, and the Indonesian military and local militias carried out the deeds. The world stood by and said and did nothing (as they would years later in Chile, Uruguay, Argentina and elsewhere in South and Central America).

In 1964 Kartini was recognised by President Soekarno as a national hero (*pahlawan nasional*) and every year on her birthday – 21 April – Indonesia celebrates Kartini Day. Like all dangerous women, however, while her legacy has been pored over – debated, contested, neglected, reinvented and even co-opted – it remains a powerful reminder that society can change. It may take time, it may be fast or slow and involve personal and political struggle and sacrifice, but it is possible.

Partizanke: Their Dangerous Legacy in the Post-Yugoslav Space

Chiara Bonfiglioli

Chiara Bonfiglioli is a lecturer in Gender & Women's Studies at University College Cork, Ireland. She has published and researched on gender history in Yugoslavia and post-Yugoslav states, as well as on transnational women's and feminist movements during the Cold War. She is the author of Women and Industry in the Balkans: The Rise and Fall of the Yugoslav Textile Sector *(I.B. Tauris, 2019). www.chiarabonfiglioli.net*

The contribution of *partizanke,* or female partisan fighters, to the Yugoslav liberation war was unprecedented in occupied Europe: official statistics of the socialist period report 100,000 women fighting as partisans and two million participating in various ways to support the National Liberation Movement. Approximately 25,000 women died in battle, 40,000 were wounded and 2,000 of them acquired officer rank, while 92 women were designated as national heroes.

Women of all nationalities and ages performed a variety of tasks, particularly as fighters and nurses in the army, but also as couriers, cooks and typists, as highlighted by historian Barbara Jancar-Webster in her 1990 book *Women & Revolution in Yugoslavia, 1941–1945*. Women also played a very important role away from the front, working in agriculture, bringing supplies to the troops and taking care of the wounded and the orphans, especially within the framework of the Antifascist Women's Front (AFŽ).

The Antifascist Women's Front was founded in an attempt to mobilise large masses of women in the struggle against the occupation. Since the majority of the population at the time lived in rural areas, the National Liberation Movement strived to gain consensus among peasant women. The support of the female population in the villages became crucial for partisans' victory, as demonstrated by historian Jelena Batinić in her 2015 volume *Women and Yugoslav Partisans: A History of World War II Resistance*.

The first generation of AFŽ leaders – who were also former partisans and communist party members – included many outstanding women from all over Yugoslavia, generally highly educated and from families with a tradition of leftist engagement. They took part in illegal revolutionary activities in the interwar Kingdom of Yugoslavia, after the banning of the communist party in 1921. They often joined legal women's and youth organisations, spreading socialist and antifascist ideas.

Women in the communist leadership embodied a radically different femininity than the majority of peasant women living in Yugoslavia at the time, as made evident by a well-known photograph of Judita Alargić, Mitra Mitrović and Vera Zogović, resting and sunbathing in swimsuits between battles in summer 1944 on the Adriatic island of Vis, where the headquarters of the Yugoslav Army had been located after the capitulation of Italy.*

During the Second World War, partisan women were dangerous primarily for their enemies, namely Nazi and Fascist troops and local collaborationist forces, whom they fought with incredible courage and sacrifice, incurring torture, deportation to concentration camps, loss of loved ones and death. They were portrayed as ugly, dirty and promiscuous by enemy propaganda, which saw women's participation in the liberation struggle as something that went against the natural gender order. Partisan women were indeed dangerous for existing patriarchal gender norms. Their participation in the struggle carved new subjectivities for women, whose political, social and economic rights were recognised for the first time in the Yugoslav constitution of 1946.

Through the local and national activities of the AFŽ, moreover, antifascist leaders reached out to the most underdeveloped territories of the Federation, promoting women's literacy and education, healthcare for mothers and children, as well as women's equal engagement in the processes of post-war reconstruction and industrialisation. Their activities on the ground met the frequent opposition of men and local authorities, including party members, as well as women's reticence to abandon their traditional customs.

At times, prominent female partisans became dangerous for the socialist system they had contributed to create, especially in the aftermath of the Soviet–Yugoslav split of 1948, when alleged pro-Stalin supporters, including women, were subjected to political

* A recent re-appropriation of the image was circulated by the Manonija designers' collective under the title *Rest is Resistance*: www.manonija.com/blog/odmor-je-otpor/#more-2379

repression, prison camps and political ousting. Anthropologist Renata Jambrešić-Kirin documented the extent of such repression in her 2009 book *Dom i Svijet* (Home and the World). Of the female leaders portrayed in the well-known photograph on Vis, only Judita Alargić continued to have a relevant political career in socialist institutions, while translator Vera Zogović suffered the consequences of political repression together with her husband, poet Radovan Zogović. Mitra Mitrović was also ousted from politics because of her closeness to Yugoslavia's most famous dissident, her ex-husband Milovan Đilas.

Cold War times were complex and dangerous, as exemplified by Želimir Žilnik's 2011 documentary *One Woman One Century*. Dragica Vitolović Srzentić (1912–2015), former partisan, first Yugoslav BBC reporter and diplomat at the Ministry of Foreign Affairs, was the one who brought Tito's letter of insubordination to Stalin in 1948, only to be incarcerated for Stalinism together with her husband three years later. As the film shows, however, she never regretted her leftist choice nor denied socialism's progressive tenets.

And here is a dangerous element of the *partizanke*'s legacy: the complexity of their engagement and of their life trajectories, or, in other words, their irreducible agency during the Second World War and its aftermath. While many scholars are keen to study women's participation in the antifascist resistance, very few are ready to recognise women's agency in socialist Europe, or the importance of women's state socialist organisations such as the Antifascist Women's Front. These organisations and their leaders, in fact, are often seen as too dependent on party politics or the socialist state.

The very idea of women's agency during socialism seems indeed dangerous for some feminist scholars, since it challenges their ingrained representation of state socialism as inherently totalitarian and patriarchal, as well as the liberal equation between feminism and women's autonomy from the state. This is perfectly exemplified by the 2014 article by philosopher Nanette Funk, 'A very tangled knot: Official state socialist women's organisations, women's agency and feminism in Eastern European state socialism', published in the *European Journal of Women's Studies*. As other feminist scholars have shown, however, it is time to question pre-existing historical interpretations influenced by long-standing Cold War paradigms, which risk reducing women to the mere victims of state socialism, without understanding their actual political contribution in such complex and dangerous times. On this issue, see notably the two Forums published in the journal *Aspasia*, edited by historian Francisca de Haan: 'Is "Communist Feminism" a Contradictio in Terminis?' (2007) and 'Ten Years After: Communism and Feminism Revisited' (2016).

To silence the legacy of women's participation in the antifascist resistance, and their engagements in socialist times, would mean undermining the struggles against patriarchy that were waged through state socialist women's organisations, as well as the progressive legacy of such struggles in the contemporary post-Yugoslav space. As historian Lydia Sklevicky wrote in her pioneering study of the Antifascist Women's Front, *Konji, Žene, Ratovi* (Horses, Women, Wars): 'Listening today to the voices of women from the past, one sees not only the mistaken choices which should not be repeated, but also the unspent reserves of utopian energy'. And then she added, quoting Walter Benjamin's Fifth Thesis on the Concept of History, 'For it is an irretrievable picture of the past, which threatens to disappear with every present, which does not recognise itself as meant in it.'

In the contemporary post-Yugoslav space, young activist women recognise themselves in antifascist women's struggles for women's rights and emancipation, particularly now that many of the social and economic rights gained during socialist times have been deteriorating due to the Yugoslav wars and the post-socialist privatisation process, which led to widespread deindustrialisation and unemployment. In 2010, for instance, architect and curator Ana Džokić recalled the story of her grandparents, Rajka and Vukašin Borojević, two former partisans and social entrepreneurs who founded a juice factory in Banja Luka, as well as a cooperative of women weavers in the village of Donji Dubac. The project was significantly titled *Taking Common Matter into Your Own Hands* as homage to the socialist legacy of collective solidarity and workers' self-management.

The figure of Rajka Borojević is exemplary of the idealist spirit carried by partisan women well into the Cold War. A teacher and partisan of Serbian ethnicity from Herzegovina, she took shelter with her two children in rural Serbia during the war and felt indebted to the local peasant population. She moved to the village of Donji Dubac in the early 1950s, and started her first workshops with peasant women in 1954, teaching basic hygiene, nutrition, housekeeping and sex education, and overcoming many difficulties, including the mistrust of male villagers, as recounted in her 1964 autobiography *Iz Dubca u svet* (From Dubac to the World). Later, she founded the Dragačevo weavers' cooperative, which employed 420 women in the early 1960s. Women's position in the village gradually improved, and in 1967, the newly founded House of Culture even hosted the finals of the 'best husband' competition. The building itself had been funded with self-organised 'best husband' parties in the surrounding villages.

Young activists, archivists and scholars are putting renewed efforts into preserving the dangerous legacy of partisan women across the former Yugoslavia. The legacy of workers' self-management, inter-ethnic solidarity and women's struggles for emancipation has been taken up as a form of counter-memory by local activists in different post-Yugoslav states, against new hegemonic national narratives centred on ethnic homogeneity and based on the rehabilitation of anti-communist collaborationist forces. Such counter-memories are also serving as a repertoire against the post-socialist re-traditionalisation of gender relations and workers' gradual loss of social rights, as I describe in my 2019 book *Women and Industry in the Balkans: The Rise and Fall of the Yugoslav Textile Sector*.

The reaffirmation of antifascist values happens through archiving, exhibitions and activist initiatives. Two recent examples of such efforts are the digitalisation of the existing archive of the Antifascist Women's Front located in Sarajevo by the CRVENA feminist collective (www.afzarhiv.org); and an exhibition on the AFŽ recently organised in the National and University Library of Republika Srpska, in Banja Luka, which featured former partisan Branka Bjelajac as a guest, and which was titled 'Re-establishing a Lost Relationship: the AFŽ in the Bosnian Krajina'.

Another example is the Zagreb Anti-Fascist Network (*Mreža antifašistkinja Zagreb*, MAZ), founded in 2007, which organises antifascist parties, commemorations and solidarity marches (www.maz.hr). The subversive legacy of workers' solidarity, women's struggles and antifascism is also revived by a number of antifascist, feminist and queer choirs across the region, such as Kombinat in Slovenia, Horkestar in Serbia, and Le Zbor and Zbor Praksa in Croatia, as reported in the 2015 book *Glasba, politika, afekt: novo življenje partizanskih pesmi v Sloveniji* (Music, Politics, Affect: New Lives of Partisan Songs in Slovenia) by ethnomusicologist and anthropologist Ana Hofman. Such choirs have been performing different local partisan songs, together with other international protest songs ('The Internationale', 'Bella Ciao', 'Bread and Roses'), as a way of protest against current neo-liberal and neo-conservative politics, for instance in support of workers of bankrupted factories, or as part of Pride marches for LGBTQI+ rights.

The 'unspent reserves of utopian energy' contained in the antifascist heritage are thus re-appropriated and re-signified, in multiple dangerous ways, by the nieces and nephews of *partizanke*, seventy years after the end of the Second World War.

Marie de Guise

Amy Blakeway

Amy Blakeway is a lecturer in Scottish History at the University of St Andrews. She is interested in the power and politics of sixteenth-century Scotland, including the many intelligent and tenacious women who shaped this history, and is the author of Regency in Sixteenth-Century Scotland *(Boydell Press, 2015).*

On 12 April 1554, Marie de Guise, widow of James V of Scotland and mother of Mary, Queen of Scots, walked into the Scottish Parliament. After gracious ceremonies and serious formalities, when Marie left the building later that day to shouts of acclaim, she had been transformed from a dowager queen to Regent of Scotland. To symbolise this change in status from widow of the king to ruler of the country, as Marie left Parliament the crown jewels, known as the honours, were carried before her. These precious items included gifts from popes and, above all, the monarch's crown, refashioned by her dead husband to assert his status, and that of his country, to the whole world. Having these objects carried before her symbolised the fact that it was now Guise who held her daughter's royal power.

Describing this ceremony around fifteen or twenty years later, Marie's arch-rival the Protestant Reformer John Knox placed a different spin on events. Knox claimed that Marie had been so power-hungry that the crown jewels weren't just carried before her, but that she actually had the crown – reserved only for Scotland's anointed hereditary monarch – placed upon her own head. Worse still, Knox howled, this action wasn't performed by a Scot but by the French ambassador. Sneering that seeing Marie crowned in this way was 'as seemly a sight (if men had eyes) as to place a saddle on the back of an unruly cow', Knox turned the story into a powerful (and gendered) attack on a woman who, he claimed, sought to hand control of Scotland over to the French, dissembled her way through her regency, and, crucially for Knox, fought to keep Scotland Catholic in the face of his push for religious reform.

As the ultimate victor in their struggle, Knox wrote history – quite literally: hundreds of pages of the stuff, all fashioned to discredit Marie, her daughter, and those who supported their vision of an alternative future for Scotland – aligned with Catholic France, against his hopes for a Protestant alliance with England. For centuries, historians have accepted Knox's claim that Marie was crowned, even those who have challenged his claims about her cruelty and ambition. But, when we look closer, alarm bells should start ringing. This story only emerges in accounts critical of Marie written after her death: sources from 1554 or her subsequent regency make no mention of the crowning incident. This might seem like a technical point, but Knox's story had been designed to signal Guise's dangerous ambition and thus that she was dangerously unsuitable to rule. By accepting this version of events, we buy into his broader narrative about Marie de Guise and her daughter, Mary, Queen of Scots, and that, generally, seeing women in power was 'repugnant to nature, contumely to God, a thing most contrarious to his revealed will and approved ordinance; and, finally, it is the subversion of good order, of all equity and justice'.

To challenge Knox, we need to hold ourselves to a higher standard of history writing than he has been held to, and we can make a start on this by placing Marie in her proper context as a regent. This is important because, for over half the sixteenth century, Scotland was ruled by children. In an age when the monarch's will was the axis upon which political life turned and his or her authority was the source of all justice, periods without an adult ruler, known as royal minorities, were dangerous times indeed. Contemporaries said that regents 'bore the person of the monarch' – that is, they were the monarch for the time. This total control over royal power meant it was essential to get the right man, or, occasionally, woman, for the job.

Usually, regents were men: six out of eight in the sixteenth century. This was because, given a choice, the Scots, like most nations, sought to appoint the dead king's closest adult male relative to act as caretaker for the new child monarch. However, if a monarch chose and planned properly, they could make alternative arrangements. Alternatively, if a monarch was living abroad and needed to delegate their power during their absence, she or he could take their pick. This is what happened in 1554: Mary, Queen of Scots, was living in France and, since she was betrothed to the French heir to the throne, would remain abroad for the foreseeable future. Claiming that (aged just over eleven) she was now an adult, Mary nominated her mother, Marie de Guise, to replace her cousin and heir, James Hamilton, Earl of Arran, who had ruled on her behalf since her father's death.

As regent, Marie de Guise therefore followed in the footsteps of other Stewart wives and mothers in the previous century, such as Joan Beaufort, mother of James II, and Mary of Guelders, mother of James III. Between 1513 and 1515, Margaret Tudor, Henry VIII of England's older sister and the widow of James IV, was regent for her son James V – she lost power when she remarried. Since a woman passed into the legal control of her new husband on remarriage, the law reckoned she acquired new duties and loyalties: so women forfeited any rights to care for her first husband's children or manage their property. But, despite their great power, all these female regents, and, indeed, the men who held the job, were only ever temporary rulers who would eventually lose power – if not by remarriage or in a coup then when their child came of age. Marie de Guise was different. As her daughter would remain in France with her husband, Marie was a new kind of regent, a permanent ruler on behalf of a perpetually absent monarch.

Despite these challenges in retaining and keeping power, there was one strong argument in favour of a dowager queen becoming regent, and that was her love for her children. Shakespeare's *Richard III* told the story of a man who was second in line to the throne and who, overcome by ambition, brutally murdered the nephews he had been appointed to protect. This was effective drama precisely because it reflected contemporary fears. By contrast, it was assumed a mother would protect her children – and female regents manipulated that rhetoric to their own advantage, perhaps none more skilfully than a woman Marie knew personally, Catherine de Medici, regent for her young son Charles IX of France. Ironically, therefore, gender was both the central argument against women becoming regents (seeing a woman in power was 'contumely to God'), and the cornerstone of their defence (mothers had, as one French defender of Catherine's regency put it, the most 'tender and loving' hearts towards their children and would defend their welfare tirelessly).

However, queen mothers were not only defined by their gender. Their nationality posed problems for their candidacy as regent. Catherine de Medici was an Italian ruling France. In Scotland, Margaret Tudor was English, and Marie de Guise herself was French. Could a foreign-born woman really have Scotland's interests at heart? We have already seen that, in Knox's eyes, the mixture of gender and nationality, combined with the extra-flammable ingredient of religious tension, formed a lethal cocktail.

In 1554, however, Marie seemed a good choice of regent. She was well known to the Scots, having arrived in Scotland in 1538. As queen consort she brought considerable cultural capital to Scotland, corresponding with relatives in France to arrange for craftsmen to come over and remodel the royal palaces, and securing technical know-how for the Scottish mining projects. She also fulfilled her main job as queen consort: to get pregnant and produce (preferably) male children, although sadly the two boys she bore in 1540 and 1541 lived only a short time.

In other words, Marie de Guise was a model queen consort, but there is no evidence to suggest that she sought political influence. After James V died in 1542, no one suggested that his widow should become regent: Marie de Guise's job was to bring up the new queen. This poses an interesting question: how did Guise move from being an apparently apolitical royal spouse in 1542 to becoming regent and ruling Scotland?

The process had begun by 1544, when she and a group of the nobility, dissatisfied with the regent Arran, proposed a scheme that she should share power with him. Unsurprisingly, he rejected this, and for a few months Marie de Guise tried to head up an alternative government. However, this failed – even the English, with whom the Scots were at war, were reluctant to negotiate with her. She and Arran made it up by the autumn and seem to have managed a working relationship of sorts until she took power in 1554.

Even when Guise was part of Arran's regime, she was powerful – the fact that she controlled a third of the crown lands made her a rival source of patronage who had the potential to eat away at his support. She also enjoyed the trust of the King of France; given that the Scots were at war against the English, this was crucial. This was even more important after 1548, when the Treaty of Haddington between France and Scotland promised French support for the war effort and arranged for the marriage of Mary, Queen of Scots, to the Dauphin, François. This planned marriage meant that Mary would be permanently absent from Scotland and so it created the circumstances which eventually developed into Guise becoming regent.

Building his story about Marie de Guise's ambition, Knox, and others who supported his version of events, claimed that Marie's desire for power consumed her so much that from August 1550 until November 1551 she took a group of Scottish nobles to France in order to brainwash them into supporting her. Guise did go to France and certainly played a central role in French court life during this period, negotiating continued French support for Scotland. What is less clear, however, is whether these negotiations included the possibility that she herself would become regent, and, if so, whether Guise herself entertained this idea before she got to France. Again, Knox took the messy reality of complicated power politics and reduced it to a whistle-call narrative about a dangerously ambitious woman.

In the end, Marie became regent because another woman had taken power. In 1553 Edward VI of England died, and the accession of his older sister, Mary Tudor, to the throne had European ramifications. History would call this new queen

'Bloody Mary', but at first her ascent to power had international importance by strengthening her mother, Catherine of Aragon's, family – the Habsburg rulers of Spain and the Holy Roman Empire. Seeing their great rivals gain influence in the British Isles prompted the French to take action. Scotland needed to be bound more securely to France, and following months of intense negotiations, Arran agreed to resign the regency to Marie.

For the six years of her regency, Marie took her duties seriously. For example, she held numerous justice ayres – peripatetic justice courts which moved around Scotland. Despite Knox's claims that a female ruler was against all justice and equity, Marie dispensed justice with aplomb.

No ruler, however, is perfect, and Marie of course had her opponents. In 1555 Parliament passed an act complaining that many Scots had been 'speiking aganis the quenis grace [Marie de Guise] and sawing evill brute anent [spreading evil rumours about] the Maist Christin King of Frances subjectis send in this realme for the commoun weill' and laying down heavy penalties for those who opposed it. In October 1557 the nobility refused Guise's orders to invade England – they claimed that this was not in the best interests of Scotland. John Knox reported that Guise was furious and this marked the beginning of the end for her power, but other evidence shows she and the nobility did manage to rebuild relations and remained on friendly terms for another year.

From September 1558 onwards, the growing Protestant party in Scotland became increasingly vocal. But it was only in May 1559 that this spilled over into violent rebellion. Knox explained this shift in terms of religious fervour on the part of the nobility, combined with a gradual realisation that Marie de Guise had been duplicitous with them. For instance, he claimed that she cunningly persuaded his allies to agree to Mary's marriage to the dauphin. Once they had agreed, and her own power was secured, she 'began to spew furthe and disclose the latent venom of her dowble harte.'

When the Scottish nobility finally did desert her, explaining to the public in Scotland and potential allies abroad why they were resisting their lawfully appointed regent, the nobles cited their religious concerns but, more importantly, their fear of French rule overturning Scottish laws and an eventual French conquest of Scotland. They gained more and more support, and when Marie de Guise died in June 1560, she had been deserted by many of her former supporters and had retreated to Edinburgh Castle for safety in the face of military defeat. God's will, her detractors cried, had been done.

And yet... the fact that many deserted Guise only at the last minute, and that an intense propaganda campaign was required to win them away from her, shows that her defeat was far from inevitable. Was there any truth in these propagandistic claims she was selling Scotland out to France? Marie always denied it. However, she had appointed trusted French officials to major roles in Scotland. She also at times viewed Scotland as a country which needed to be changed, and once wrote to her brother, 'God knows... what a life I lead. It is no small matter to bring a young nation to a state of perfection.'

This is the clearest statement we have of what Marie thought she was doing as regent, and, as with all rulers of her time, on occasion the end justified some fairly unpleasant means. Marie's tragedy was that her view of 'perfection' was only imperfectly shared by those she ruled over – and it was those malcontents who were left to tell her story. But, faced with proper historical scrutiny, Knox's cries that Marie's downfall was divinely ordained and inevitable ring hollow.

Marie de Guise was dangerous not because of an ambitious lust for power, but because she was intelligent, persuasive and had stood a good chance of winning.

Florence's Prostitutes: Dangerous Women Serving the City

Gillian Jack

Gillian Jack wrote her PhD thesis (University of St Andrews, 2018) on civic authorities' involvement with a monastery for repentant prostitutes in Florence between 1329 and 1627. Her main research interests are late medieval and early modern prostitution, religious women, female criminality and poor relief in Catholic Europe. She has taught early modern history, historiography and world history at the University of St Andrews and the Open University. She is currently an Honorary Associate and Associate Lecturer with the Open University.

In August 2016, as one of his twelve Fridays of Mercy, Pope Francis spent an hour talking to twenty former sex workers in a Rome safe house – a refuge run by a Catholic charity. In 2019, he met Elise Lindqvist, the 'Mother Teresa of Prostitution', and thanked her for her work supporting sex workers in Sweden. Like other nations, Italy has a long, imperfect and little-known history of civic response to prostitution. Whether these women were in danger, or dangerous in their own right, remains a bone of contention to this day.

Medieval thinkers tended to follow St Augustine, who described prostitution as a necessary evil, a sin which prevented the greater sin of the corruption of 'good' women by men's insatiable sexual appetites. A follower of St Thomas Aquinas likened prostitution to a palace sewer – necessary to remove the filth from society, but deeply unpleasant and offensive nonetheless. By the twelfth and thirteenth centuries, European cities had mostly stopped trying to expel prostitutes and accepted the inevitability of their presence. In French and German cities, for example, municipal brothels were common and governed by rules set by local authorities.

The late medieval period proved to be something of a turning point in the Italian states' approaches to prostitution. This was nowhere more apparent than Florence. Pope Francis's medieval predecessor Pius II (1458–64) joked that Florence was less a city of merchants (*mercatrice*) and more a city of prostitutes (*meretrice*). In 1328 the government had ordered a brothel to be built outside the walls, at a place called Campoluccio. This was a characteristic policy of the Florentine government – facilitating but also hiding – and one they applied to other groups they found problematic, such as lepers and Jews. It ensured that the service the prostitutes provided was accessible, but out of sight. The women were only permitted to enter the sacred zone protected by the city walls on Mondays. They were expected to behave 'honestly' and were under no circumstances to conduct their business in the city.

This type of regulation should not be mistaken for acceptance. The city governors also sought to ensure that prostitutes were readily identifiable. Sumptuary legislation, restricting displays of wealth, particularly over clothing, sought to preserve the distinctions between social classes. A statute of 1384 banned prostitutes from wearing fashionable high-heeled slippers and required them to wear gloves and bells on their heads. Women suspected of being prostitutes could be hauled before the courts for failing to wear these items. It was imperative to authorities that there was no danger of a prostitute being mistaken for a 'good' woman. They were to be visually and audibly distinguished, and so segregated.

However, in the late fourteenth century there was a more pressing problem. The Florentine population had not recovered from the ravages of the Black Death as quickly as other cities. The city government believed that men were reluctant to marry because women's tastes in clothing and jewellery were too extravagant, and men were turning to one another for sex. The authorities believed that this was having a negative effect on population growth, as well as bringing the city into disrepute. It was, for instance, common parlance in Germany to refer to a 'sodomite' as a Florenzer, so widespread had this reputation become. To resolve this situation, a raft of new moral legislation was introduced to limit displays of wealth in clothing and jewellery and against male sodomy. In 1403 the city also legalised prostitution. It built a civic brothel in the centre of town and charged the women to work there. The authorities hoped that the presence of sexually available women would provide an alternative sexual outlet for young men and remind them of the pleasures of heterosexual sex. In turn, they would choose to marry and would have legitimate children to increase the population.

Despite their new legitimacy, the city's prostitutes found themselves in an ambiguous position. Their profession served the city, but it also contributed to the moral pollution other pieces of new legislation sought to curb. The city governors aimed to ensure that no one unwittingly spoke to a prostitute, mistaking her for a decent woman, and that women were not tempted to follow a richly dressed prostitute into her shameful profession. The city government put in place new legislation to curb prostitutes' conspicuous displays of wealth, banning them from wearing gold and pearls, and later, when it became fashionable to do so, from riding in carriages. In practice, only a very small number of prostitutes could afford such luxuries.

As well as ensuring prostitutes' visual distinction, authorities once again attempted to physically segregate them. At first, they were only to live within the central brothel district. Later, the authorised zone was extended to certain additional streets across the city, but the women had to live and work in the same location. Their homes could not have windows looking out onto streets not authorised for prostitution, and they could not be close to religious buildings. The latter requirement was particularly difficult to fulfil in a city full of churches, monasteries and convents. Although the women served the state with their labour, they were still seen as dangerous.

This small group of women (probably no more than 150 of them in a city of 45,000) were exempted from some of the ancient rules established to keep women in their place. They lived beyond the authority of fathers, husbands or brothers. They worked and earned money beyond the control of a man. Those who had a pimp were usually involved in a one-to-one relationship with him, and such men were regularly prosecuted and exiled from the city. The civic authorities, in the form of the Ufficiali dell'Onestà (Officers of Decency), did not tolerate pimping or procuring, even as they allowed prostitution. As part of the Onestà's strategy to control the sexual economy, they offered certain rights to the women who registered and followed the rules. Most significantly, they were allowed to bring legal cases to the Onestà court. This meant that prostitutes had far more legal privileges than other Florentine women, rights which they exercised. Prostitutes appeared before the Onestà court as plaintiffs and defendants; they brought cases against their customers, and against one another, on matters as varied as petty squabbles and physical violence.

In contrast, there were precious few opportunities for 'good' women to exercise any independence. The law treated them as children: they were prevented from managing their own financial affairs, prevented from taking legal action against anyone, and were only reluctantly accepted as witnesses in court. The law required that a male relative or legally trained notary acted on a woman's behalf if she needed to undertake any legal transactions. In theory, a married woman's dowry remained her property, but in practice many husbands did with it as they pleased. Indeed, were she widowed, her father or brothers expected it to be returned, either for their own use or to marry her off again to the family's advantage. Restricting women's legal rights to representation allowed the city to control their behaviour and limit their freedom. 'Good' women were rarely seen – they did not walk about the streets or hang out of windows as portrayed on recent TV shows such as *The Borgias* and *Medici*. Women who behaved in this way marked themselves as wanton and dishonourable.

Prostitutes were able to live, to varying degrees, independently of male authority. They had found a way to circumvent the city's legal system, which treated its female citizens as minors with much-restricted access to representation. After the 1403 legalisation of prostitution, the women gradually pushed the limits of the legislation, taking more and more liberties. The

Onestà had begun to allow them to purchase immunity from some of the restrictions placed on them, and in the sixteenth century the rules on distinctive clothing were abandoned entirely.

The records that survive about the prostitutes of early modern Florence are all written by the men who sought to regulate their activities. We know about them only through the legislation which governed where they were allowed to live and work and what they were allowed to wear. We can read how much money they paid to the city and the records of their court appearances and petitions. We have no diary, no account book, no records in a prostitute's own hand. In a society with relatively high literacy, women, especially the poor women who became prostitutes, were rarely able to read and write. These women's own voices are silent in the archive.

Over the course of three centuries, the prostitutes of Florence ascended from outcasts – tolerated only beyond the walls and wearing bells to distinguish themselves from 'decent' people – to workers in the service of the state. They were able to throw off much oppressive legislation and gain legal rights. These dangerous women became more independent than the 'good' women of the city could be. Their own words may be absent from the records, but their central role in city life is clear.

Margery Kempe: A Medieval Phenomenon

A.C. Clarke

A.C. Clarke is a poet living in Glasgow and a member of Scottish PEN. She is interested in outsiders and obscure historical figures. Her pamphlet War Baby *was a joint winner of the 2017 Cinnamon Poetry Pamphlet Prize;* Drochaid, *a pamphlet in Gaelic, Scots and English, in collaboration with Sheila Templeton and Maggie Rabatski, was published by Tapsalteerie in 2019, her second with these two collaborators. Her most recent publication (2021) is a solo pamphlet,* Wedding Grief, *also with Tapsalteerie.* A Troubling Woman, *centred on the medieval visionary Margery Kempe, the subject of this article, was published by Oversteps Books in 2017.*

'Where shall I find a man to take this woman away from me?' So cried the Archbishop of York, Henry Bowet, confronted with the force of nature that was Margery Kempe. For Bowet, whose predecessor had been executed for treason and then venerated as a martyr by those who opposed the usurping Henry IV, and who was well aware of the additional threat to stability posed by the Lollards, the followers of the reformist (and in the Church's eyes heretical) John Wyclif, Margery must have seemed the last straw.

Here was a woman who, though married, wore white as if she were a virgin, who told the archbishop to his face that she had heard he was a wicked man, and perhaps worst of all, who was given to delivering impromptu homilies just as Lollard women were supposed to do. She was twice brought before Bowet, and it is plain that he had no idea what to do about her. Her vivid presence and unorthodox behaviour certainly made her seem a danger in a diocese already full of political and spiritual unrest, and throughout her life she was a disruptive influence, even though she was dedicated to a life of secular piety.

Margery Kempe (c.1373–1438), the daughter of a mayor of Lynn (now King's Lynn) in Norfolk, was always, by her own account, a woman who called attention to herself. In her youth, before the birth of her first child and the life-changing visions which followed it, she had worn clothes designed to be 'the more starying to men's sight'. On pilgrimage she antagonised fellow pilgrims by refusing to eat meat and suddenly exclaiming in the middle of a meal: 'It is full merry in heaven!' At home in Lynn she was prone to loud and copious weeping during sermons. All this is recorded in the autobiography which she dictated to an amanuensis, probably a local priest, towards the end of her life.

It is almost certainly *because* she was regarded with suspicion, especially by many of her fellow townsfolk, that she elected to tell her story. It is her apologia. While it is possible that her amanuensis may have rephrased some of the sections dealing directly with her visions and meditations, the voice that comes through is unmistakeably her own. The experiences that that voice describes suggest that in any period, including ours, Margery would have presented difficulties to those she came into contact with. In her own time, much of what she did and said was a provocation. What is fascinating about her, to me, is that while some of her adventures might be textbook illustrations of how a male-dominated society reacts to women who refuse to conform, the very beliefs which sustained that society made many wary of dismissing her as a madwoman – though some did – or condemning her as a heretic. Even the 'boistous' Archbishop of York ended up, after she was brought before him a second time, giving her his blessing and a letter of safe conduct. Though, of course, we have only her word for any of it.

Margery was dangerous in two ways: one which would still be comprehended now – her challenging behaviour – and one peculiar to her time – the danger that to ignore or persecute her might be in effect to ignore or persecute God Himself. And there is, for me, a third way in which Margery might be considered dangerous, which I will come to at the end.

To many, Margery must have seemed a woman who went gadding about the country (sometimes with her husband, sometimes not) upbraiding people, especially the clergy, as she often did, for their sinfulness, their blaspheming oaths (a pet topic) and their general worldliness. Even her supporters frequently had their faith in her tried. Aside from her bold reproof of the Archbishop of York, she reprimanded the Archbishop of Canterbury, no less, for the way men in his household swore; when a friar renowned for his sermons came to preach at Lynn, she 'fell in a boistous weeping' which made him ban her from the church because of the disturbance she caused.

On this last occasion, two of the Lynn clergy, including her confessor Robert Spryngolde, went to the friar in question to plead with him to let her back in to his sermons. Spryngolde was one of her staunchest allies, although she did not always heed his advice. Many of the local religious, including the anchoress Julian of Norwich whom she visited for advice, were well disposed to her, as were those pious laypeople who helped to finance her pilgrimages. They all believed that she did indeed speak with God and the Virgin Mary in vision and that the instructions she said she received, however unorthodox (like wearing white clothes), were to be accepted because they were God-given.

Moreover, although Margery's account of her life is unusual in its circumstantial detail, it has many precedents in the lives of female saints in Catholic Europe: indeed, one way of viewing her actions is to see her as having internalised details from the lives of married saints like Katherine of Alexandria and Bridget of Sweden. Likewise, her sometimes feverish expressions of devotion to the 'manhood of Christ' and her lover-like dialogues with Him were within a tradition of English mysticism that her readers would have found entirely acceptable and indeed proof of her piety.

To modern readers accustomed to a blanket view of women in history as oppressed and suppressed, Margery's frank acknowledgement of her sexuality and apparent domination of her husband might mark her out as a dangerous pioneer. She speaks of 'the great delectation' that she and her husband had in love-making; although it is to her discredit, she recounts how a fellow parishioner tempted her to adultery; the second of the two demonic visions she recounts – the temptations of St Margery, one might say – was entirely sexual in nature, with a succession of men showing her 'their bare members'. To a medieval readership, there would have been nothing unusual in the idea that a woman might enjoy sex (for instance Chaucer's *Wife of Bath* and William Dunbar's *Twa Marryit Wemen and the Wedo*), but equally nothing to be deplored in Margery's final renunciation of sex when she got her husband John to agree that they should 'live chaste', chastity being the more perfect life. She did so by agreeing to pay his debts, which casts an interesting light on a relationship in which she clearly considered herself his social superior – 'she came of worthy kindred and he should never have married her', as she cast in his teeth in one of their quarrels. This superior status no doubt allowed her to be unusually independent, something which was definitely perceived as a threat by the mayor of Leicester, who feared she might 'take away our wives and lead them with you', a telling remark.

The whole narrative of Margery's relations with her husband illustrates the danger of trying to superimpose a modern viewpoint on a very different age. Margery was both far less constrained than we might think and far more imbued with the religious doctrines of her time than we may be able to imagine. And here is the third way in which I think Margery – and not only her, but others who may be celebrated as 'dangerous' in a positive sense – is dangerous. She is a dangerous role model and should definitely not be cited as an example of a woman 'ahead of her time'.

Yes, she stood up to male authority, but equally she put herself under obedience to the Church hierarchy and to principles of asceticism that most would now find repugnant. She comes across as remarkably unaware of the feelings of others. When a man she meets in Italy lends her money he has earned for the two of them by begging, she promptly gives it all to the poor. When she goes with her German daughter-in-law to see her off on her return journey, she suddenly decides to go with her and seems surprised that her daughter-in-law is less than enthusiastic. She forces her company on a wealthy woman she meets near Calais, likewise on pilgrimage, and is astonished to find the next day that the woman has got up early and left – plainly to escape her. And one may question the Christian charity of someone who rejoices in being the one person on that return journey from Calais who escapes sea-sickness – all the sufferers, she concludes, are being punished for their behaviour towards her.

The real significance of Margery Kempe, as I see it, is her exuberant individuality, which clearly made an impression for good or ill on everyone who met her. She was not someone to be ignored. And insofar as she was considered dangerous at the time, perhaps that individuality was her true danger. She presents herself as an obedient daughter of the Church, but she is the central character in her dialogues with Christ (it is the other way around in Julian of Norwich's 'Shewings'), and her obedience never gets in the way of her determination to follow her own path. Robert Spryngolde could probably not have coped with another parishioner like her.

Annie S. Swan: Making People Cry

Glenda Norquay

Glenda Norquay is Professor of Scottish Literary Studies at Liverpool John Moores University and heads their Research Institute for Literature and Cultural History. Born in Dundee and educated at the University of Edinburgh, she researches Scottish writing in the nineteenth and twentieth centuries. She has published widely on Scottish women's fiction and on suffrage literature. Her most recent monograph, Robert Louis Stevenson, Literary Networks and Transatlantic Publishing in the 1890s *(Anthem, 2020), was supported by a research fellowship at IASH. You can find her on Twitter @peedieg.*

The Scottish novelist Annie S. Swan was viewed by many as a dangerous woman: a writer whose sentimental fiction spoke to the nostalgia of a Scottish diaspora, evoking a way of life and set of values increasingly outmoded in the modern world. Her fiction, with its wee villages, rural settings, dying mothers, beautiful but timid heroines, and bashful and romantic ploughboys, likewise inculcated in women an unrealistic vision of home, an impossible domestic ideal.

Certainly Margaret Oliphant, one of the most established Scottish novelists and critics of the nineteenth century, worried about the effects Swan's writing might have. Locating Swan's work in the category of 'Kailyard fiction', those popular but parochial novels that dominated the Scottish literary scene at the end of the century, she attacked women novelists whose sentimental and 'silly' novels were pernicious in their imagining of a national consciousness. As she wrote in her August 1889 column in *Blackwood's Magazine*, such writers produced:

> cheap books and perfectly well adapted, with their mild love-stories and abundant marriages, for the simpler classes, especially of women, whose visions are bounded by the parish, who know nothing higher in society than the minister and his wife and believe that all the world lieth in wickedness except Scotland.

Two of Swan's early novels are singled out amongst those that have a particularly detrimental influence on readers who 'are lower in the scale of intelligence and knowledge'. In the early twentieth century, Scottish poet Hugh MacDiarmid was also scathing about Swan, describing in 1926 a series of women writers 'who all derive from Annie Swan, without her "uplift" and genius for banal narrative, though with considerably more conscious, if not always successful, efforts after psychology and style'.

Annie S. Swan seems an unlikely candidate, therefore, for the more positive interpretation of a 'dangerous woman' that dominates the chapters in this book. Yet the figure of Swan both requires revaluation through her own biography and calls into question easy valorisations of 'danger' as expressed in terms of explicit challenge and radicalism. The extent of her appeal and influence demands a more nuanced analysis of the politics of emotion and the gendering of reader response.

While Annie Shepherd Swan (1859–1943), married name Annie Burnett Smith, was seen to offer both a damaging version of Scottish identity and a limiting idea of womanhood, Swan herself was not confined to the domestic sphere. Publishing in the popular and sentimental journal *The People's Friend* for over sixty years, her income supported her husband's medical training and their move from a country village to Edinburgh and then to England and London. Her admirers included Gladstone and J.M. Barrie and feminist writers Winifred Holtby and May Sinclair. Writing under the pseudonym David Lyall, she contributed to the *British Weekly* (a penny newspaper which first appeared in 1886 and enjoyed a six-figure circulation), through many short stories about the Boer War under his name. Her success in popular publishing led William Robertson Nicoll to establish *The Woman at Home* in 1893, which survived until 1919: Swan did not edit, but she was the chief contributor and her name became that most associated with the magazine. The first edition sold out of 100,000 copies immediately. Annie Swan's *Penny Stories* was established in 1897 as an arena for writers of popular fiction.

Her work was consistently on the bestseller lists and dominated fiction sections in public libraries across the country. Many of her stories were serialised in D.C. Thomson's *The People's Friend*. While her considerable commercial success may account for hostility towards her, she has to be considered as a highly professional writer and editor in a world that was still male-dominated. She herself commented: 'I shall never be recommended by the Book Society nor be allowed to consort with the elect within the guarded portals.' Her efficiency, however, was in no doubt. As she wrote in her 1934 autobiography, *My Life*, 'I have scrupulously observed the rules of the game, so far as Editors are concerned. They know they can depend on me to deliver the goods in time.'

Her activities beyond writing again suggest an energetic and public-facing individual. She was a Liberal, unsuccessfully standing as parliamentary candidate for Glasgow Maryhill in 1922. She was a supporter of women's suffrage and published a novel about it: *Margaret Holroyd, or, the Pioneers* in 1910. She was a founding member of the Scottish National Party and an active supporter of the Salvation Army. She enjoyed a spell as Mayoress of Hertford, worked with the YMCA among the troops in France, and travelled to the USA in 1917 and 1918 on food missions. Her financial success allowed her to keep her own bank account throughout her life. Even the more radical literary circles of the Scottish Renaissance expressed a grudging admiration for her. William Power, historian of Scottish literature, campaigner for the Literary Renaissance and leader of the Scottish National Party 1940–42, told her in a letter of 31 October 1936:

> We have to remember that Scotland was lost, really lost, for the space of nearly two generations, and that when she was found again she had to be 'recommended' by degrees to people who had passed through the dreadful fires of the mid-Victorian era. You it was who did most to bring back the real Scotland to the apprehension of the victims of, let us say, a soul-less capitalism – and to bring them back with all their fine qualities of affection, fidelity and patience, to Scotland. It was a marvellous achievement for which you can never get all the credit you deserve.

After meeting her for the first time at a Scottish PEN dinner for Power, the novelist Neil Gunn, a writer who sought to challenge conventional representations of his homeland, wrote to her on 25 December 1938:

> I do not think the name of any Scottish writer is so well known to the folk of our country as your own. It was a household name about as far back as I can remember. What a privilege therefore to meet you – and, if you will permit me, to meet a spirit as full of eternal youth as the youngest at that strange gathering.

How, then, do we reconcile the different perceptions and contradictions of Swan – a dangerous woman in the most negative sense and a dangerous woman as celebrated by many other chapters in this book? Analyst of Scottish culture Christopher Harvie, in *Scotland and Nationalism*, recognises Swan's 'genuine feminism and nationalism' but perceives these as 'smothered in calculated kailyard sentiment'. His acknowledgement of Swan's importance also identifies her two most apparently dangerous elements: an eye to commercial success and sentimentality. To challenge this definition of 'dangerous', we need to think more about these characteristics.

First, let's consider her popularity. While others saw this as a weakness in Swan's fiction, indicating her failure to challenge mass consumption, Swan was a stout defender of her appeal and fought to keep her books at low prices: in *The Land I Love* (1936), she wrote: 'The people who matter in Scotland, the workers by hand and brain, can't afford seven-and-sixpenny books.' Writing retrospectively in response to Oliphant's criticisms of her, she claimed in *My Life*: 'I wrote almost entirely of the life with which I was familiar, and though the judgment of a young girl was necessarily immature, the public had not fault to find with it and asked for more. After all, it is the reading public which passes the final judgment on any book.'

Swan's claim of a close bond with her audience, reiterated in her autobiography through frequent anecdotes of being approached by grateful and involved members of her reading public, is reinforced, rather than threatened, by the cheapness of her fiction. Her fiction, she suggests, provided that public not only with what they desired but what they actively recognised. She speaks of 'the personal tie established so long ago between writer and reader, and maintained to this day,' although – perhaps bearing in mind the relative failure of her more experimental war novel, *The Pendulum* (1926) – she admits in her autobiography: 'The warm bond between me and my readers has affected my work powerfully, and I think has, in a sense, hampered it by its insistence on a certain kind of writing, for which they would accept no substitute.' Nevertheless she emerges as a writer who recognises that emotional engagement, the 'warm bond' created by her words, is central to the author–reader relationship.

This brings us to the issue of sentimentality. Some of Swan's writings on the home may seem hard to take:

> In the heart of almost every woman, there is a house of remembrance, one which she holds specially dear. Perhaps it is only a cottage on a hillside or in some country lane, the house where she was born and lived with her parents perhaps in her careless happy childhood, it may even be only a room in a tenement to which she came as a young wife and where little children have been born. But it is a house she never forgets and to which her heart never grows cold.

Yet this is more than a celebration of domesticity; rather, it is an evocation of desire, of loss and longing. A range of feminist theorists – from Janice Radway writing about women's reading of romantic fiction, to Lauren Berlant discussing 'The Female Complaint,' from Carolyn Steedman remembering her working-class mother's longings for nice things, to Sianne Ngai thinking about the complexity of 'ugly feelings' – have suggested that the workings of emotion and their political operations are far from simple.

Swan, in her 'tearful' and tear-inducing fiction, it can be argued, offered a language for articulating ideas of a woman-centred space in which feelings might flow – in which the mourning for mothers or the expression of disappointment were acceptable. Likewise, her 'sentimental' versions of a Scottish home and homeland create an alternative to what she often represented as the patriarchal and class-dominated spaces of Britishness. Her readers, Swan argues, recognise, are affected by and want more of the worlds and the feelings that her fiction has produced: that desire does not necessarily equate to quiescence, but can also articulate dissatisfaction.

Other Scottish women writers of the early twentieth century, such as Willa Muir, Catherine Carswell or Lorna Moon, became 'dangerous' in their challenges to small-town life and restrictive morality. But their narratives of 'escape' are in their own ways conventional and accessible only to a few. In Swan's fiction, the language of 'hame' does not necessarily translate into a desire for domestic confinement. And, as Swan's own life suggests, the mobilisation of emotion can be powerful as well as dangerous.

Jeanne Baret, Pioneer Botanist

Glynis Ridley

Glynis Ridley is a graduate of the Universities of Edinburgh and Oxford, a former IASH Visiting Fellow, and currently Chair of the Department of English at the University of Louisville, Kentucky. Her publications include Clara's Grand Tour: Travels with a Rhinoceros in Eighteenth-Century Europe *(London: Atlantic Books; New York: Grove, 2004), winner of the Institute for Historical Research Prize, and* The Discovery of Jeanne Baret: A Story of Science, the High Seas, and the First Woman to Circumnavigate the Globe *(New York: Crown, 2010). Publicity surrounding the latter led Ridley to collaborate with field biologist Eric Tepe on naming a new plant species,* Solanum baretiae, *in honour of eighteenth-century botanist Jeanne Baret, and their co-authored paper was published in* PhytoKeys *in January 2012.*

What happens when a woman refuses to conform to male expectations of what she can be and what she can do?

Historically, types of both physical and intellectual labour have been demarcated as either 'man's work' or 'woman's work'. For a woman to show herself capable of thinking and acting in defiance of these allotted roles is to threaten the status quo. Such a woman is dangerous – because her refusal to conform is a very visible demonstration that there is nothing that should be a male-only preserve.

The first woman known to have circumnavigated the globe refused to accept the gendered and social limits placed upon women in her society. In 1766 Jeanne Baret, the daughter of illiterate French peasants, disguised herself as a teenage boy and presented herself for hire as principal assistant to the expedition naturalist on the first French circumnavigation of the globe. For two years, her floating home was the sailing ship *L'Etoile*: a supply ship 102 feet long and 33 feet wide that Baret shared with 115 officers and men. The larger vessel that they accompanied, *La Boudeuse*, brought the expedition complement up to 330, with Baret the only woman among them. French royal ordinances did not allow women on board naval ships, not even if they were the wives of officers, as was permitted in the British navy at the time. But Baret was no one's wife.

Signing on for a projected three years at sea, she was accompanying her lover, the expedition's official naturalist, Philibert Commerson. Working as his assistant, Jean Baret shared his cabin and botanised with him whenever they could be set ashore. The social gulf between them could not have been greater. Her parents signed their parish register with a cross in lieu of their names; his parents had sent him to university to follow in the family tradition of practising medicine. Women of Baret's background were destined, at best, to be the servants of men like Commerson: in the field, she met him as a fellow botanist. Her discovery of the showy vine that would be named Bougainvillea in honour of the expedition commander, Louis Antoine de Bougainville, is today the most visible sign of her botanical skills. Yet Baret has, until recently, been largely overlooked in history books, her achievements glossed over. When Louis Antoine de Bougainville finally acknowledged in his expedition journal on 28–29 May 1768 that a woman had defied all injunctions meant to keep her ashore and in her place, he presented Baret as someone other women would not choose to emulate:

> Baret, with tears in her eyes, admitted that she was a girl, that she had misled her master by appearing before him in men's clothing at Rochefort at the time of boarding ... that moreover when she came on board she knew that it was a question of circumnavigating the world and this voyage had excited her curiosity. *She will be the only one of her sex to do this* and I admire her determination ... The Court will, I think, forgive her for these infractions to the ordinances. *Her example will hardly be contagious.* She is neither ugly nor pretty and is not yet 25. [italics mine]

It is striking that Bougainville assures his readers, not once but twice, that they should not be alarmed at the prospect of more women following Baret's example: she is less a contagion than an aberration. And this is surely one of the occupational hazards of the dangerous woman. If she cannot be contained in life, her life may be marginalised in the written record, presented as too singular to be a model for others.

The matter-of-fact tone and single paragraph that Bougainville devoted to admitting that a woman had managed to get herself aboard his expedition did not encourage any reader to linger on the episode. This was convenient for the expedition's royally appointed naturalist, Philibert Commerson. Sharing a cabin, it was inconceivable that Commerson did not know Baret to be a woman and, indeed, the two had been lovers for at least two years prior to the expedition setting sail in 1766. But the plan to disguise Baret and have her join Commerson is unlikely to have been simply a grandiose romantic gesture; whatever else Baret brought to her relationship with Commerson, she brought knowledge that he valued. What knowledge could an eighteenth-century peasant woman possess that would be of interest to a university-educated doctor? The one known image that purports to be of Baret offers an intriguing clue.

Dating from 1816, the engraving appeared in an Italian edition of James Cook's voyages and shows Baret dressed in striped fabric not popular with sailors until the 1790s. She is pictured wearing the red liberty cap of the French revolutionaries. But despite these anachronistic puzzles (inappropriate for a woman who set sail in 1766), Baret is shown with a sheaf of flowering plants in her hand. Such posies were a well-established iconographic shorthand for the medicinal value of a botanical garden. In other words, the anonymous engraver suggests that Baret herself possessed botanical knowledge, independent of Commerson. If so, then she was likely a 'herb woman', working in a largely oral, traditionally female preserve, dispensing folkloric remedies while also supplying male physicians and apothecaries with the raw plant materials that were the foundation of their medicine cabinets. If Baret was an herbalist before she met Commerson, then it is easy to imagine the herb gatherer and the passionate botanist meeting in the field, Commerson recognising Baret's knowledge as complementary to his own. So when Commerson was named ship's naturalist on Bougainville's proposed first French circumnavigation of the globe, and was mandated to collect flora and fauna to feed and clothe France's imperial masters and subjects, who better should he appoint as his expedition assistant than the woman who was already his lover, housekeeper and fellow explorer of the plant kingdom? Together, Baret and Commerson hatched a plan whereby she would present herself on the dockside as a young man, eager to sign on as Commerson's assistant. But while the ruse apparently worked in getting Baret on board, the couple had not foreseen what might happen once she was there.

From the various journals kept by members of the expedition, it is clear that rumours that Baret was really a woman started to circulate within a few days of the ship leaving port. The naturalist's assistant was never seen to relieve 'himself' at the heads like other men and, when challenged by hostile crew members below decks, Baret claimed to be a eunuch, taking care always to be armed with pistols after that confrontation. When *L'Etoile* sailed across the Equator on 22 March 1767, Baret was the only crew member to remain clothed for dousings associated with the naval rite of passage of Crossing the Line. Given the limited dimensions of her floating world, it was inconceivable that Baret's true sex was not known. Journals kept by expedition members other than Bougainville hint at a mix of feelings towards this single woman among so many men: animosity and superstition among the crew, tempered with grudging respect for Baret's tireless physical work. With her breasts flattened uncomfortably by strips of linen wound tightly around her upper body, Baret went ashore to botanise under Commerson's direction at every opportunity, hauling the cumbersome equipment of an eighteenth-century field naturalist for her 'master'.

From early December 1767 to late January 1768, the expedition ships inched through the Strait of Magellan, repeatedly sounding the depth so as not to risk ripping open the hulls on submerged moraine. All this time, Baret's exertions ashore were visible from the ships' decks, and an officer characterised her as Commerson's 'beast of burden', labouring up the slopes of the Strait under the burgeoning weight of specimens and their containers.

According to Bougainville, Baret's story finally unravelled in April 1768 on Tahiti. As the officers and men were surrounded by Tahitian women making clear their offer of multiple sexual partners for each man, Baret was apparently surrounded by a group of Tahitian men who saw through her disguise. Bougainville's best-selling journal, *Voyage autour du monde par la frégate du Roi La Boudeuse et la flute L'Etoile 1766–1769* (published in Paris in 1771), would claim that Baret admitted to her disguise as she called for help to extricate herself from an uncomfortable situation. But Bougainville's account of events on Tahiti is only one version of what occurred there.

Four other narratives of the expedition – two journals kept by the surgeon François Vivès, one kept by Charles Othon, Prince of Nassau-Siegen, and a memoir by naval officer Nicolas Pierre Duclos-Guyot – all insist that nothing unusual happened regarding Baret on Tahiti, but that she was forcibly stripped by crew members when the expedition stopped to re-provision on New Ireland in the New Hebrides. Why is the truth of what happened so elusive?

In locating Baret's exposure on Tahiti, Bougainville's narrative sanitises the later actions of his crew and exculpates expedition officers from earlier failures to act on the widespread belief that Baret was indeed a woman. Had Bougainville knowingly allowed a woman to remain on board, in contravention of the royal ordinance prohibiting women on navy ships, he would have rendered himself liable to court martial on his return to France. Had he acknowledged that

Baret was finally forcibly exposed by members of the crew on New Ireland, he would have cast aspersions on the conduct of the French and jeopardised his naval career by having allowed such a breakdown in discipline to occur. The fiction that Baret chose to reveal her identity on Tahiti in order to save her honour was a fiction that protected him.

From New Ireland, the expedition sailed on to New Guinea, Java and Mauritius, where Commerson was released from his expedition contract to stay and work in the French East India Company botanic garden of Pamplemousses at the request of its director, Pierre Poivre (the Peter Piper who picked a pepper of nursery-rhyme fame). Baret stayed with Commerson. Bougainville's problem of a woman aboard was solved. But after Poivre's recall to France and Commerson's death from fever in March 1773, Baret was thrown out of their shared home, separated from over 6,000 leafy, flowering, squawking, scuttling specimens which formed a record of the circumnavigation and represented seven years of Baret's life and work. She would never see the collection she had helped to build again: its final destination would be the Muséum National d'Histoire Naturelle, where it today forms part of the French national herbarium. When Baret was finally able to secure a passage back to France and landed in La Rochelle in late 1775, nine years after first setting sail, she became the first woman to have completed a circumnavigation of the globe.

Baret spent the next year litigating to receive monies she knew Commerson had willed to her, competing for a share of his estate against the claims of his brother-in-law. Quite separately, Bougainville petitioned the Ministry of Marine for an annual pension for 'this extraordinary woman'. When the petition was finally granted, Baret became the first woman known to have received a state pension on account of her service to the advancement of knowledge.

Though Baret charted her own unique path, she never told her own story – that was left to a handful of men, all compromised by the truth of what had happened. When she died in 1807, the single genus that Commerson had named in honour of her, Baretia, had already been reclassified and renamed Quivisia, inadvertently writing Baret out of the history she helped to make. And so it would be until 2012, when a new species, *Solanum baretiae*, was finally named for her.

Dangerous women may sometimes be erased from conventional histories, but they have a habit of returning – embodying the perennially potent idea that the seemingly impossible is sometimes achievable, and that gender is no barrier to achievement.

A coda to the story of Jeanne Baret in the age of #MeToo

This chapter is a birthday present: specifically, my birthday gift to Baret. While there are fewer documents than one might imagine that attest to the life of this remarkable woman, her birth was recorded in French parish records as having occurred on 27 July 1740. Since the publication of my 2010 biography, *The Discovery of Jeanne Baret*, I always try to do something on that day to commemorate Baret in a way that might bring her to the attention of more people. For all those women written out of conventional histories, belated recognition makes a sort of historical amends; in telling their stories, we give a voice to those who were often silenced or sidelined during their lifetimes. Every time her story reaches new groups of people, I see online comments suggesting that Baret's life would make a great movie or TV series. (I've even been asked about my dream cast.)

But shortly after my book's first release in 2010, and well before the hashtag #MeToo raised awareness about the sexual harassment that women in many walks of life report as a depressingly ingrained part of their work culture, I realised that some of my book's reviewers were reluctant to countenance one of the book's conclusions: that Baret was gang-raped by a group of her fellow sailors on New Ireland in the New Hebrides. (I've also been told that my inclusion of this makes Baret's story of less interest to filmmakers than it might otherwise have been – apparently there are limits as to how much should be uncovered when recovering untold histories.) Four members of the Bougainville expedition mention Baret's presence on the first French circumnavigation of the globe: Bougainville himself, ship's surgeon François Vivès, gentleman passenger Charles Othon, Prince of Nassau-Siegen, and junior officer Nicolas Pierre Duclos-Guyot. All but Bougainville insist that something significant occurred when Baret went ashore with other servants on New Ireland. Vivès gives two separate accounts of what he says occurred there, trying the effect of different styles and metaphors in his two tellings: in one of his manuscripts, he refers to an inspection of Baret using the metaphor of a gun's lock-plate being drawn back; in a second manuscript, his metaphor is the men's location of the 'concera veneris' or conch shell they had been seeking. In both accounts, Vivès concludes that – after what happened – he should start referring to Jeanne Baret as 'Jeanneton'. As I detail in my book, this is the title of a traditional French folk song, renditions of which can readily be found online, and its subject is the gang rape of Jeanneton (the diminutive of Jeanne) when she goes into the field to cut the corn. Sadly, the song conjures up a world in which the assault of female agricultural labourers is represented as unexceptional.

It concludes with an exhortation to female listeners that, if they have no idea what the song is about, then they should go into the fields themselves, where they will soon find out.

Those reviewers who wish to insist that there is no evidence for Baret having been raped on New Ireland do not address why three out of the four men who mention her presence on the expedition allude to that very crime, nor does anyone who is critical of my conclusion have any explanation as to why Vivès would end his account of events on New Ireland with the assertion that Jeanne had become 'Jeanneton', given all the connotations of the folk song. Vivès had no reason to fabricate details in his private journals. It was Bougainville who would publish a best-selling account of the voyage, an account which presents hardened French mariners as embarrassed by the sexual freedom they encountered on Tahiti, and in which Bougainville resists introducing anything that might trouble a polite reading public. In her lifetime, Baret was caught in an impossible situation: a woman who had embarked upon a proposed circumnavigation of the globe by sea, disguised as a man, was clearly someone who had set out to deceive all onlookers. How could she challenge the received version of events and expect to be believed? That Baret did not attempt to make herself heard during her lifetime is perhaps not surprising; that two officers and one gentleman passenger on the Bougainville expedition do challenge Bougainville's account of events and yet, historically, have not been regarded as credible is a testament to the power exercised by well-connected men such as Bougainville to shape a public narrative.

One reviewer of my book thought it a pity that I had made Baret 'a victim'. Though the phrase came in a review published well in advance of the #MeToo movement, it was notable that the rise of #MeToo provoked a backlash in which a number of columnists and bloggers, both male and female, complained of what they perceived to be the movement's 'obsession with victimhood'. But to follow historical evidence – or modern testimony – where it leads should not be regarded as embracing victimhood. One of Baret's fellow voyagers, the Prince of Nassau-Siegen, wrote in his journal that Baret 'dared confront the stress, the dangers, and everything that happened that one could realistically expect on such a voyage. Her adventure should, I think, be included in a history of famous women'. Nassau-Siegen is not describing a victim, but nor is he sugar-coating a brutal reality: what might the reader 'realistically expect' would happen to a defenceless woman, alone among over 300 men? To suggest that Baret's many experiences on her circumnavigation included wonder and terror does not diminish her and, if it makes her story less palatable to some, then that surely says more about what some readers want from stories of achievement rather than the messy truths they often contain. To be without a voice – unable to tell one's story – is to be powerless. To have one's story heard is not to claim victimhood, but power.

Yaa Asantewaa: Queen Mother of the Ashanti Confederacy

Chantal Korsah

Chantal Korsah is a British-Ghanaian emerging writer and playwright. She has had several poems and short stories published in literary blogs and anthologies and is currently working on her first novel.

Yaa Asantewaa
Obaabasia oko premo ano
Waye be egyae
krokrohenkro yaa waye be egyae

Yaa Asantewaa
A woman who fights before cannons
You have accomplished great things
You have done well

So goes the refrain sung by the residents of the village of Edweso in the Ashanti Confederacy (now the Ashanti region in Ghana, West Africa), praising their former queen mother, Nana Yaa Asantewaa, who was the leader and commander-in-chief of the fifth and final Anglo-Ashanti War, which lasted from 1900 to 1901.

To most Western scholars, she is known as Africa's Joan of Arc. But what were the circumstances that led to her extraordinary decision to become the most dangerous woman in that region of Africa, to commandeer the entire Ashanti army against the greatest colonial power at the time, the British?

The Ashanti Confederacy was one of the most sophisticated kingdoms in Africa at the time in terms of its influence, wealth and organisation. It was established in 1701 by the first Asantehene (king), Osei Tutu, who led an army and defeated the regional power, uniting the individual village-states into a confederacy. The establishment of the Ashanti State also has some mythology attached; Asantehene Osei Tutu's right-hand man and high priest Okomfo Anokye was said to have called forth the Golden Stool, the symbol of the Ashanti throne, from the sky, and it was reputed to have fallen into Osei Tutu's lap, confirming his ascendancy to the throne.

The confederacy's great defender, Queen Mother Yaa Asantewaa, was born in 1840 in the village of Besease, near Edweso, the village that she eventually grew up to rule, into the Asona matrilineal royal clan of Edweso. She was the oldest of two children; her younger brother Afrane Panin eventually became the Edwesohene (Chief of Edweso). Her childhood passed without major incident, and she was said to have been a major farmer, cultivating many crops in her farms in Boankra village. She married a man from Kumasi, the first wife in a traditional polygamous marriage, and she had one daughter with him. Yaa Asantewaa would have ascended to the throne sometime in the 1880s, inheriting it from her mother or grandmother, as throne inheritance is matrilineal and not patrilineal in Ashanti culture.

During this time, the Ashanti Confederacy had seen major upheaval, with no fewer than four wars having been fought between the British and the Ashanti. The last war, fought in the 1870s, had brought about great destabilisation in the Ashanti. The state capital Kumasi had been set on fire and ransacked; the British had set up a fort opposite the Manhyira (Ashanti Palace) and had implemented forced labour and a compulsory tax of around £160,000. The confederacy was then plunged into a civil war after the last Asantehene was de-stooled and several successors had emerged, fighting until one was crowned.

Against this backdrop, Yaa Asantewaa's brother died and her daughter's son, Kofi Tene, inherited the position and became a strong ally of the Asantehene eventually crowned in 1888, Prempeh I. In 1896 the British demanded the Golden Stool and complete surrender of the Ashanti Confederacy to them. When Prempeh refused, he and other chiefs, including Kofi Tene, were forcibly arrested and deported to Sierra Leone. After four years of constant negotiations and refusals by the British to release the Asantehene and the chiefs, the last straw came when the British governor at the time, Frederick Hodgson, demanded the Golden Stool as a symbol of sovereignty of the British over the Ashantis. That night, Yaa Asantewaa goaded the chiefs to war by refusing to pay Edweso's share of the tax, and when several chiefs protested that the British were too powerful to take on, she gave a rallying speech:

> How can a proud and brave people like the Ashanti sit back and look while white men take away their king and chiefs, and humiliate them with demand for the Golden Stool? The Golden Stool only means money to the white man; they have searched and dug everywhere for it. I shall not pay one *predwan* to the

> governor. If you, the chiefs of Ashanti, are going to behave like cowards and not fight, you should exchange your loincloths for my undergarments.

She then grabbed a gun and fired a shot into the air, and that evening, she and all the chiefs 'drank the gods' (drinks poured out as an offering) and took a solemn oath to rid the Ashanti of British rule.

With this fiery speech and strong will, Yaa Asantewaa was appointed leader and commander-in-chief of the Ashanti forces, a role only held by men previously. The tactics she employed in this war were the most impressive of all Anglo-Ashanti Wars fought previously, so much so that it is primarily known as the Yaa Asantewaa War.

In the beginning, she turned her village-state, Edweso, into the headquarters of the resistance, as the British had established themselves in Kumasi. There was tremendous fear of the British initially and many of the Ashanti men refused to join their state armies. To overcome this, she enlisted the help of their wives by ordering them to withhold sex from their men until they joined. To encourage them further, she also ordered the wives to march every day around their villages and perform victory rituals in a show of support and solidarity.

This war also marked the first time that the Ashantis used stockades, building one outside each village and using them as traps against the British. They had much early success with this tactic. Yaa Asantewaa made it a point to send out generals and troops to monitor strategic points in and around Kumasi. She also ordered a siege of the British fort in Kumasi, preventing food and ammunition supplies from reaching the British who resided in the fort, including the governor, so they could not fight from the inside. In this way, she managed to regain control of Kumasi.

Yaa Asantewaa also subverted the common view of Ashanti women not being allowed on the battlefield; in the early days of the war, she was often seen on the battlefields holding a gun, though she did not fire herself. Another powerful psychological strategy Yaa Asantewaa employed was the use of the Ashanti talking drums to convey to the British several messages during warfare: one beat was reported to mean 'prepare to die', three beats meant 'cut the head off', and four beats meant 'the head is off'. This caused much fear among the British.

The British, however, fought back by destroying many stockades and conquering several villages, forcing Yaa Asantewaa to change her tactics. She merged the single village-state armies into one central army, and when the British were closing in on Edweso, her own village and the headquarters for the resistance, she fed them information that the current general had been changed, thus providing a decoy and leading the British in a different direction, while she was able to escape and set up a new headquarters in Offinso, the village of her friend and fellow warrior queen mother Nana Afrenewaa.

Eventually, though, the British proved victorious. They conquered Ashanti villages one by one, with the help of Hausa and Sikh armies that they recruited and imported into Ghana from their vast colonial empire, and the help of several treacherous Ashanti chiefs and ordinary men who revealed her tactics and hideouts to them in exchange for rewards. Yaa Asantewaa was finally forced into surrender when she received word that her daughter and some of her grandchildren had been captured by the British and were being held in the fort in Kumasi. This brave queen mother was exiled to the Seychelles by the British along with her most prominent generals, and she died there in 1921.

Her legacy, however – as a patriotic defender and a strategic leader of the Ashanti Confederacy army in the fifth Anglo-Ashanti War – lives on and cements her place in history as a dangerous woman.

Further Reading

Boahen, A.A., 2003. *Yaa Asantewaa and the Asante-British War of 1900-01.* Melton: James Currey Publishers.

Mensah, N.P.W., 2010. *The Queen Mother of Ejisu: The Unsung Heroine of Feminism in Ghana.* Dissertation thesis. University of Toronto.

Gabrielle Suchon: A Dangerous Philosopher

Véronique Desnain

Véronique Desnain is a senior lecturer in French at the University of Edinburgh. She specialises in seventeenth-century French literature and philosophy, with a particular interest in gender.

From the late 1200s to the end of the 1600s, there raged in France a debate known as the 'Woman's Quarrel'. The arguments between attackers and defenders of women go back and forth, mostly in texts written by men, with a few exceptions like Christine de Pizan (1364–c.1430, *The Book of the City of Ladies*) or Marie de Gournay (1565–1645, *The Equality of Men and Women*). While it is not surprising that few women took part in the debate, given the level of education they were usually afforded, it seems astonishing that one of the most complete and convincing works by a woman published on the 'woman question' has been all but forgotten. Or perhaps it is entirely unsurprising, given the dangerous nature of Gabrielle Suchon's 1693 text, *A Treatise on Morality and Politics*. Behind this rather neutral title hides a remarkable attempt to address the legal and cultural subjection of women, as revealed by the subtitle: *Freedom, Science and Authority. Where we see that women, despite being deprived of them have a natural aptitude for them [...].*

In this work, Suchon analyses and responds to the arguments that have been used over the centuries to justify women's inferior position, whether in religious texts, law or literature. She puts forward the stories of notable women from antiquity to her own time and enjoins her female contemporaries to educate themselves in order to fight their oppression. Most subversive of all, though, she suggests that to be free, women must live alone (i.e. out of marriage or religious ties). In her second book, *Celibacy Freely Chosen* (1700), she gives practical advice to women on how to achieve this.

Suchon's work is unique in many respects, and it represents an important contribution to the discourse on women which occupied much of the early modern period and to our perception of women's own take on it. As a vast overview of some of the most crucial social and theological issues of its time, this work is an important historical document, as well as a literary and philosophical one. The two treatises she writes between 1693 and 1700 quite simply constitute the most extensive text on *la condition féminine* written by a woman at the time. Suchon's work is important because it is part of the growing body of evidence which proves that, although they may not have been deemed worthy of entering the 'canon', although we may not yet have heard of all of them, women have always taken part in cultural production. It also shows that women have been aware of the mechanisms used to keep their experiences hidden and have attempted to counteract men's efforts to exclude them from history.

Even from a purely anecdotal perspective, it seems astonishing that a figure such as Suchon should have made so little impact: here is a woman who writes philosophical treatises when most women have little or no education. She dares to criticise the institutions of marriage and convents at a time when the Catholic Church was clamping down on 'dissidents' after the threat of the Reformation. As Church and state insist on keeping women under control and strictly subdued to male power, Suchon demands the right for women to be educated, independent and free in all aspects of their lives, before moving on, with her second treatise, to a defence of female celibacy outside the Church. With this, she posits, in essence, a new legal status for women. So the fact that few of us will have heard of her until very recently seems incongruous.

Yet the reason for this lack of recognition is simple: Suchon was dangerous because she was writing in the hope that her work would encourage women to demand equality. One crucial difference between Suchon and her predecessors is that she does not affirm the superiority of either sex. Instead, she relies on a 'different but equal' position and argues that each individual should be dealt with in accordance to their abilities rather than their gender. She argues that female subjection is part of a social and political order, rather than a natural one. This notion was a threat to male hegemony, but was also entirely novel. Perhaps Suchon's work found few echoes in her own time because of its very originality. As Elsa Dorlin points out in *L'Evidence de l'égalité des sexes*:

> Only texts that theorize the natural inequality between men and women are made public and commented. Only those are deemed true and taught. Thus it is not the relative value of arguments or their scientific rigor which determines whether they are discussed, but their position in relation to a specific order of knowledge and power.

Indeed, a number of features clearly distinguish Suchon's work from that which had come before. Unlike the male writers of the 'Quarrel', Suchon is more interested in discussing the topic than she is in demonstrating her rhetorical skills, and she dismisses the essentialist views of both detractors and advocates of women. Unlike Christine de Pizan, she does not address women as wives and mothers, but as autonomous individuals who may dedicate themselves to any vocation they choose. And unlike Marie de Gournay, she does not primarily address an audience of educated male readers, but rather makes it very clear that her intended audience is composed of women. In all those respects, her work can be seen as far more explicitly subversive than that of her predecessors. Her advice on practical issues, meanwhile, can be read as an encouragement to actively resist male supremacy.

Beyond its content, the very existence of Suchon's writing is significant. For too long we have been told that literature, philosophy, sciences and the arts in general were overwhelmingly male domains simply because women had not produced any work of note. The obvious response to this argument is that female access to such practices has been restrained until very recently, not by lack of talent, but by lack of education and by the practical obstacles put in their way. But recent research has demonstrated, quite convincingly, that there is an even more insidious reason for the perceived absence of women from the history of literature, art, philosophy and the sciences: even when they were there, we do not hear about them. They are marginalised from the discourse of history; they are erased from history itself.

Thus, as Gianna Pomata writes in her chapter in the 1993 *Femmes et Histoire*, writing – not just fiction, but any form of writing which illustrates her own experience – becomes, for a woman:

> the power to give shape and impact to one's being through words … It is the power not only to comprehend the past but to validate and justify the present, and to project oneself into the future. It is the power to create a precursor for those who will come after, to establish a pattern, to invent appropriate names and images corresponding to one's knowledge of oneself, and to leave these names and images as beacons for others.

Indeed, Suchon's whole project can be seen as such a 'beacon' which she consciously leaves for her successors. She has little hope to see change in her own time, but seems to have anticipated future social shifts: 'Women *in my time* will never attempt to dispossess men of their might and authority,' she says, perhaps reassuringly for the potential male reader. But the restrictive 'in my time' makes it clear that she thinks, and hopes, that others will in the future.

Perhaps one of the most modern and subversive aspects of Suchon's writing is that it identifies the mechanisms of oppression and the more practical issues behind the theoretical discourse. As such, her method and arguments are relevant to the examination of any form of oppression, and the implications of her writing may be more radical than they first appear. Indeed, despite the need to remain within the orthodox doctrine in order to avoid censorship, especially when her arguments find their source in religious texts, the attentive reader soon discovers, as Pierre Ronzeaud explains in 'Note sur l'article de Paul Hoffmann':

> the existence between the lines of a hidden, far more fascinating side, which is revealed by the aggression of some of her statements and to which Suchon refers through allusions to corrosive and dangerous ideas left unspoken.

While her contemporaries may have preferred to ignore those 'dangerous ideas', her absence from modern philosophy or feminist history is more surprising.

Eileen O'Neill offers a number of reasons for the 'disappearance' of women from the history of philosophy which may well apply to Suchon. In her work on early modern women philosophers, she states:

> One such reason I called 'the purification of philosophy'. The bulk of women's writings either directly addressed such topics as faith and revelation, on the one hand, or woman's nature and her role in society, on the other. But the late eighteenth century attempted to excise philosophy motivated by religious concerns from philosophy proper.

Modern critics are still in many ways influenced by the assumption that, to be valid, philosophy must distinguish itself from religious concerns. Suchon's defence of women is deeply enmeshed with issues of faith and theological discussions regarding the distinction between human and divine, the nature of vocation and the relationship between God and his creatures. Whereas the gender of the author may have been enough reason for many male critics to ignore her work, the religious nature of her writing is sometimes seen as a disappointment by feminists.

Yet Suchon's reliance on Church authorities in her project is both to be expected in the context of her times, and also a useful rhetorical strategy which should not distract from the subversive potential of her texts. Brought up in a society in which the Church was at the heart of all social interaction, having spent many years in the convent (she was made to enter orders as a teenager and did eventually get released from her vows in her forties), it is unavoidable that the author should perceive religion as an integral part of life; yet it is all the more remarkable that she should use, as the cornerstone of her defence of women, the distinction between genuine faith and the repressive institutions which use it for their own benefit.

What's more, her theological position allows Suchon to construct a logical demonstration that operates in the same realm as those of detractors of women. She bases her arguments on her interpretation of authorities which have been acknowledged as valid by those whose arguments she is attacking. Tackling this issue within their own frame of reference enables her to expose the flaws and fallacies of their arguments.

It may also be that, in the wake of the Reformation and the Catholic Church's attempt to reassert its control, there was a greater need for female believers such as Suchon to profess their faith and demand the means to practise it according to their own spiritual needs. While this may be obvious in terms of doctrine, the androcentric nature of religious institutions means that women had long been left out of the equation. Suchon reduces female inferiority to a *custom* and contrasts it with *vocation*. Her defence of women is therefore based on an opposition between the secular and the divine, between historical specificity and the immutability of divine purpose.

In this context, to see Suchon's use of religion merely as rhetorical or as a smoke screen for radical ideas about gender – or indeed as irreconcilable with such ideas – would be tantamount to dismissing historical circumstances and imposing an anachronistic frame of mind on her work. It would also, to a large extent, posit female spirituality as a mere adjunct of male spirituality, denying the very possibility that women could take their own position on dogma and spiritual practices, as opposed to being passive followers of an institution which oppresses them.

All these factors ensured that Suchon's legacy remained hidden for 300 years. Now is the time to rediscover her. We may well find that this woman is still dangerous.

Further Reading

Fragments from Suchon's work have been translated into English:

Suchon, G., 2010. *A Woman Who Defends All the Persons of Her Sex: Selected Philosophical and Moral Writings*. Ed. and trans. by Domna C. Stanton and Rebecca M. Wilkin. Chicago, IL: University of Chicago Press.

'Plucky Little Adela': Australia's Unruly Pankhurst

Geraldine Fela

Geraldine Fela is finishing her PhD at Monash University, Melbourne. Her thesis examines the experiences of HIV and AIDS nurses in Australia prior to the introduction of anti-retroviral therapy. Her research looks at the intersection of oral history, labour history, histories of gender and sexuality and social movement studies.

Adela Pankhurst, what have you done?
Meddled with poison, handled a gun?
Nine months gaol from Notley Moore,
For openly pleading the cause of the poor.

R.H. Long, 1917

We will go up to Parliament to see Billy Hughes in spite of the Police. I believe in action not words!

Adela Pankhurst, September 1917

In August and September of 1917, Adela Pankhurst – revolutionary socialist, feminist and exiled daughter of Emmeline Pankhurst – was perhaps the most dangerous woman in Australia, or at the very least in Melbourne. By November of the same year, she was locked up in Pentridge Prison. Australia's Prime Minister Billy Hughes must have breathed a sigh of relief. Adela had been 'making herself a damned nuisance' for months now, and he hadn't known quite what to do with 'the little devil', Verna Coleman explains in her 1996 book *Adela Pankhurst: The Wayward Suffragette 1885–1961*. For Hughes, prison was an answer, albeit a temporary one.

So what made Adela Pankhurst so dangerous? Why, just weeks after marrying her long-time comrade Thomas Walsh, did she find herself miserable and alone in the cells of Melbourne's most infamous women's prison? To understand this, we need to look not only at her activity in late 1917 but also her years of campaigning against the Hughes government and the First World War.

Adela arrived in Australia in March of 1914, leaving behind her an unhappy political and personal rift with her mother and sister Christabel. Upon her arrival, under Melbourne's steely grey skies, she threw herself into political activity. A staunch pacifist, she opposed the Great War and published a widely distributed pamphlet *Put Up the Sword*, the goal of which was 'setting forth the causes and disastrous social effects of war'. Known in the leftist paper press as 'plucky little Adela', she did speaking tours across the country, delivering her anti-war message and packing out regional town halls and inner-city theatres.

Over the course of 1915, she became increasingly dangerous to the federal Labor government. As the disastrous and gruesome Gallipoli campaign dragged on into the second half of 1915, the number of men enlisting fell. Passionately pro-British, Billy Hughes, who succeeded Andrew Fisher as Labor Prime Minister in October 1915, decided after visiting Britain and the Western Front in the first half of 1916 that Australia needed to introduce conscription. To maintain the nation's contribution to the war effort, Australia's forces, which were suffering deadly losses, would need to be replenished. Hughes would have a fight on his hands. The unions – the power base of his party – and rank-and-file Labor members were opposed to conscription. What followed was a bitter struggle stretched over two referendums. Adela stood proudly at the helm of the 'No' campaign, fighting against the conscription of working-class men into, what she called in *Put Up the Sword*, a senseless war waged 'by small gangs of wealthy men' in the name of 'the bastard Imperialism'.

Adela spoke at countless rallies and meetings of the 'antis' or anti-conscriptionists. These were passionate and often difficult affairs. Adela was, by most accounts, a revelatory speaker. A 28 September 1916 report from Vida Goldstein's left-wing women's paper *The Woman Voter* described one of her addresses in Adelaide in ecstatic terms:

> Adela Pankhurst has been in Adelaide, and Adelaide is different because Adela has been in it ... She did more propaganda work in a few days than all of us in a year, and she is absolutely irrefutable and irrepressible. When it was known that she was going to speak in the King's Theatre on Sunday night, the 17th inst., it was as if the Wind had breathed over the Valley of the Dry Bones, and, behold! The Bones arose and were living, breathing men and women, who made a solid rush at the theatre and packed it from floor to ceiling...

Adela spoke to adoring crowds, but also faced the wrath of soldiers, some of whom loathed the anti-conscription campaign and consistently invaded and interrupted mass meetings.

Worryingly for Hughes and his government, Adela showed a talent for neutralising these situations and pleading her case.

In December 1915, at the Bijou Theatre in Melbourne, a group of angry and drunk soldiers interrupted a mass meeting. According to the Melbourne daily *The Argus*, in a 20 December article, they invaded the stage crying 'down with the pro-German.' Adela took to the stage and made her case, arguing for 'an honourable peace so that the brave men at the front could return and enjoy it.' Adela pointed to the hypocrisy of a government who wanted men to 'fill up cards and go fight' but could not promise jobs upon their return and was doing nothing for their families at home. *The Argus* reports that the men were quiet as Adela spoke and a lull fell over the crowd. When she finished, the soldiers became rowdy again, singing the national anthem loudly to a room of silent 'antis.'

It's impossible to know what impact Adela had on those particular soldiers, but her ability to captivate and hold even the most hostile of audiences was, by all accounts, astounding. It must have been terrifying for Hughes and his government, and surveillance files – First World War Intelligence section case files and investigations into Queensland persons and organisations suspected of disloyalty – suggest that over this time Adela was under an increasingly close watch. Hughes' fears were well founded. On 28 October 1916 a plebiscite was held, and the 'No' vote won. The result split the Labor Party down the middle. As far as Hughes' conscription agenda was concerned, Adela was probably the most dangerous woman alive.

Her threat to the government only increased as Australia entered a painful stretch of wartime poverty and strife. In August and September 1917, the states of New South Wales and Victoria were rocked by a massive strike, a spontaneous revolt against wartime hardships. Wages and standards of living were falling and the senseless carnage of the war was becoming increasingly apparent. Though the strike in the railways and coal mines sharpened the hardships of many families, who relied on coal for heating, there was mass popular support for the workers, as Judith Smart describes in her 1986 article 'Feminists, Food and the Fair Price'.

In Melbourne huge demonstrations were held in solidarity with the strikers and, predictably, Adela led many of these. These so-called bread riots defied the War Precautions Act, which forbade gatherings in certain public spaces, particularly near Parliament House. The demonstrations escalated over the month of August, and on the thirtieth Adela was arrested along with two other women. According to common law files, she addressed a crowd of around 6,000, calling on them to 'defy the police, break into parliament, if necessary, and see Billy Hughes to know what he will do to give food for the starving children'. She led the demonstration in a march on Parliament House before being summarily arrested.

Adela was charged and released, but it seems this only sharpened her determination and willingness to push the boundaries. Following her arrest, she gave a number of speeches encouraging the use of what she referred to as 'other methods'. The demonstrations became increasingly daring, and on 3 September a crowd marched on Parliament, smashing shop windows as they went.

Despite this escalating activity, it wasn't until a mass demonstration on 20 September that Adela was finally deemed too dangerous to stay on the streets. She delivered a rousing speech to a crowd of thousands, calling on them to 'touch the pockets' of the government and big business, Smart explains in the same article. As the crowd marched on Parliament House, troopers wielding batons halted them and a street battle broke out. The crowd dispersed and began smashing shop windows up and down Melbourne's main streets; soon the demonstrators headed towards the wharves, smashing the office windows of a number of unpopular firms, including J. B. Ellerker Pty Ltd, which was famous for its use of scab labour during the strike. In showing herself willing to incite property damage, Adela had become a threat not only to Hughes but to Australian business. It was for this demonstration that she was imprisoned in November 1917.

On 8 November, Prime Minister Hughes, having split from the Labor Party and now leading the Nationalist party in a coalition government, announced another conscription referendum. Perhaps he hoped that with 'plucky little Adela' in a cell, he might have better luck the second time around. But the work of the anti-conscription campaign and, of course, indefatigable Adela had torn irreparable holes in Hughes' pro-war, pro-British agenda. On 20 December 1917, the Australian people rejected conscription once again.

Adela's time in prison was, by all accounts, miserable. However, her imprisonment is not the true tragedy of the Adela Pankhurst story. Far sadder is the story of her political degeneration. Once a staunch communist, the rise of Stalinism in the 1920s saw her reject leftism in its entirety. Her rabid anti-communism led her further and further to the right. Throughout the 1920s she worked with the government in a number of industrial disputes, helping to break strikes. In the early 1940s she helped found the proto-fascist Australia First Movement, though this was an uneasy relationship, as Adela opposed Australia's war with Japan in the Pacific. Never comfortable with the strict atheism of her childhood, in 1960 Adela converted to Catholicism and died a year later, on 23 May 1961.

Adela ultimately betrayed the causes she fought so hard for between 1915 and 1917. She rejected feminism and the politics of class to line up behind conservative governments and even, for a time, behind the Nazi regime in Germany. This, perhaps correctly, has precluded her from fame in Australian feminist or labour history. Nevertheless, Adela was, for a moment, a courageous defender of the oppressed. The Adela of 1915, 1916 and 1917 held a deep regard for human life and fought for a world that matched this regard. It was this conviction that made her so dangerous to Billy Hughes, a prime minister hell-bent on dragging working-class men into the carnage of the First World War.

Adela was also dangerous because she had little regard for the sanctity of property. She felt the hardships of working people deeply and was not afraid to break laws or smash glass to fight for better conditions. As Adela astutely observed in 1917, unlike the starving children of Melbourne, 'glass windows have got no feeling whatsoever'.

Further Reading

Coleman, V., 1996. *Adela Pankhurst: The Wayward Suffragette 1885–1961*. Melbourne: Melbourne University Press.

Smart, J., 1986. 'Feminists, Food and the Fair Price: The Cost of Living Demonstrations in Melbourne, August–September 1917'. *Labour History* 50: pp. 113–31.

Redefining Female Agency

Kayleigh Tervooren

Kayleigh Tervooren is socially involved and combines a strong analytical focus with a creative and hands-on approach. She explored her passion for equality and human rights during her MA in Gender Studies at Utrecht University. Her research focused on how stereotypes of women involved in terrorism as victims relate to women's individual experiences of agency. Motivated to strive towards positive change, she started working for a labour union and is now working as a coach to support workers in their personal and professional development.

Investigating dangerous women and how they are socially perceived is yet another way to illustrate how gendered binaries structure social ideas. Are we not overtly exposed to narratives of men as oppressors and women as their innocent victims, instead of the other way around? Not often are women seen as the subject of violence in social and political debate, because their capacity to subvert traditional femininity is exactly what makes them dangerous.

My master's thesis investigated how stereotypes of women involved in terrorism as victims relate to women's individual experiences of agency and how this relationship can be interpreted. Women engaging in terrorist violence are an example of how women can complicate traditional notions of femininity. Since violence and terrorism are pre-eminently acts that are perceived to be masculine, the dominant narratives about women engaging in terrorism illustrate the pervasiveness of the gendered lens through which political action is viewed. During my analysis of Dutch news media, I found strikingly little coverage on women's involvement in terrorism. Additionally, when women were mentioned, they were predominantly portrayed as brainwashed, manipulated by men, and as submissive 'jihadi brides'. Connecting these findings to existing feminist investigations of women and violence, I found that even in academic writing, there is something missing in the exploration of such women's narratives.

I think it is safe to assume that, for a feminist audience, the misrepresenting of women and the lack of female voices in contemporary media is not something I have to prove once again. In the case of dangerous women, like women engaging in terrorism, representations are problematic as well. Media portrayals obscure female agency by representing women as controlled by men or as monstrous deviants, or by trying to find other explanations to prove their acts are rare exceptions. Accordingly, women's political and ideological motivations to conduct terrorist violence remain under-explored.

Media representations explain away female violence by reinforcing the stereotypical idea that women are naturally peaceful. Laura Sjoberg, for example, argues that violent women's agency is denied 'because women's incapacity to commit acts of terror is essential to maintaining our current idealized notions of women and femininity'. Feminist critiques on the public/private distinction illustrate how violent women challenge traditional gender constructions. Carole Pateman and Sherry B. Ortner, for example, explain how the separation of private and public spheres consequently means a separation between a male and female domain. Pateman argues that, based on the division between political power and paternal power in the family, women are socially assigned to the private, domestic sphere and are subjected to male authority. Thus, representations of violent women that deny their capacity to act as an autonomous subject arguably serve to restore patriarchal constructions of femininity.

The 2012 article 'Gendering Terror' by Jessica Auchter was a main source of inspiration for me to connect problematic media representations to academic writing on women and terrorism. She challenges how the concept of agency in relation to terrorism is used in academia, including in feminist theory:

> Agency remains the attribute which marks entrance into the legitimate political community. Whether or not one is considered an agent has a real-life effect, specifically on women's lives and their ability to participate in significant political action. However, we act as if agency is a matter of common sense rather than questioning how it has come to frame our perception of certain issues.

The problem she identifies is that scholars are often driven by the desire to inscribe women with agency, assuming that 'woman as agent' is their natural state. Scholars, therefore, predominantly study women and their political practices in relation to a strict agent/victim dichotomy; women are either studied in their roles as victims of patriarchy or as agents that oppose a patriarchal system. Relying on this understanding of agency – resistance against male oppression – prohibits scholars from questioning what agency actually means for individual women. Additionally, Saba Mahmood argues that the concept of female agency should also entail acts that may not be seen as pursuing an emancipatory goal. As she focuses on Muslim women specifically, her work is relevant here, since the dominant terrorists in my media analysis are deeply rooted in Islam themselves. Since Islam is often considered by 'the West' as intrinsically opposed to their liberal values, Muslim women are instantly perceived to have an unequal position and lack agency.

However, women's agency is context-specific. Therefore, women who engage in religious practices that from a Western point of view are deemed oppressive should not automatically be defined as non-agents, just as resistance to patriarchy cannot be the only precondition for female agency. Relying on this narrow conception of female agency can actually reinforce patriarchal structures. It reaffirms violence as a male characteristic, while women are naturally peaceful and merely use violence to achieve Western emancipatory goals.

This approach leads scholars to perpetually rely on the existing binary framework that has contributed to the subjugation of women, as they try to transform it into a tool that in the name of feminism can be used to achieve female political emancipation. But, as Auchter argues: 'simply appropriating a framework as your own does not dissolve the problems that are inherent within the existing framework'. Neglecting the multiplicity of experiences that shape individual women leads to generalised representations of female agency. Consequently, the involvement of women in terrorist organisations is continuously underestimated. It is my objective here to investigate alternative stories that might provide a different view of their engagement in terrorist organisations.

As a matter of fact, the London-based Institute for Strategic Dialogue (ISD) published a report by Erin Marie Saltman and Melanie Smith in 2015 that provides insights into the lives of women who joined the terrorist organisation Islamic State. Saltman and Smith try to deconstruct the stereotypical idea that radicalised women simply serve as passive 'jihadi brides'. Even though women's roles within ISIS are first and foremost as wives and mothers, they play crucial roles in state-building processes and spreading propaganda. Saltman and Smith argue that women join Islamic State for multiple different reasons, ranging from a desire for belonging to a community to a strong sense of religious duty. A translation by Charlie Winter of a manifesto by the Al-Khanssaa brigade, a female Islamic State 'police' group, illustrates this as well. The document shows that instead of perceiving their role as oppressive, these women see their domestic duties as a valuable contribution to the caliphate. In this manifesto, women illustrate how they experience their position as being the orchestrators of the organisation:

> It is always preferable for a woman to remain hidden and veiled, to maintain society from behind this veil. This, which is always the most difficult role, is akin to that of a director, the most important person in a media production, who is behind the scenes organizing.

Thus, the idea that women's traditional domestic roles are merely a private matter and are fundamentally restrictive might not always correspond to reality.

As part of my thesis research, I held an interview in March 2016 with an analyst from the Dutch organisation for counterterrorism, Nationaal Coördinator Terrorismebestrijding en Veiligheid (NCTV). Making national threat assessments, this analyst focuses on interior jihadism. She reaffirmed that in their role as mothers and wives, women's state-building contributions are perceived as very significant. According to her, women connected to Islamic State are often strongly committed to the radical ideology, and it in fact serves as a way to enlarge their autonomous domain instead of restricting it. Additionally, it is striking that while the 'caliphate' in Syria is not the utopia that many of these women expected, they still continue to spread propaganda:

> They feel like the hardships in the caliphate are trials they have to go through; they are being tested, but they hold on to the faith that the paradise will come as long as they build it together.

The interviewee emphasises that these women will never openly criticise the Islamic State they so firmly believe in. The 2015 ISD report also provides evidence of women's religious conviction. The report offers an example of a female Islamic State recruiter who claims to encourage women who want to migrate to IS-controlled territory to critically consider their personal motivations. The recruiter urges women to only migrate when they feel it is their religious obligation, instead of becoming a 'jihadi bride'. She explains that women will face many difficulties living in the caliphate, which requires patience and persistence and will not meet the expectations of women who merely migrate for marriage. Nonetheless, it is important to remember that these are just a few examples of the complex factors that play a role in women's motivations to engage in terrorism. Although their contributions are seemingly valued, the restrictions these women live under and the violence that affects them cannot be forgotten. These reports merely serve to illustrate that women's experiences might differ from dominant stereotypes, and that they might engage in violence out of conviction rather than coercion. In no way am I suggesting that these women do not face hardships such as (sexual) violence. My objective is merely to point out that the lived realities of these women are more nuanced than is often portrayed in media and academic work.

As an illustration, another interview I held in March 2016 with a Dutch-Turkish journalist offers a valuable confirmation of the importance of awareness about gendered structures. As a documentary maker, he travelled around several countries to investigate the aftermath of the Arab uprisings and the emergence of Islamic State. He had emotional encounters with different families and, having seen the hardships people face, he understood the young men who saw terrorism as their way out. In contrast, regarding women and terrorism, he expressed a very one-sided view. He reinforced the stereotype that women conducting violence do so under pressure from men and did not address other motivations for their actions. Also, seeing women participate in public life was, for him, an indicator of female emancipation, especially when they were not wearing a veil. Thereby, he reaffirmed the traditional idea that the public is a male-identified space, while a woman's place is in the private sphere. By simply taking up space in the public sphere, this journalist perceived women as emancipated. Again, I want to emphasise that there is no universal female experience, and therefore not wearing a veil and participating in public life cannot uncritically be understood as an emancipatory practice. It has to be investigated whether these women actually experience their position as such. As the journalist spoke from his own experiences, my objective here is not to claim that his observations are false. Instead, his comments illustrate the importance of understanding women's unique social and political context.

Finally, what I valued most about this interview is that the more I questioned him about women involved in terrorism, the more he began to question his initial ideas. He became more aware of how obscured the roles of women actually are and started to question the idea that women merely take up an inferior position:

> Women might just be the ones that determine the structure of the whole organization. Who secures the cities when men are out to fight? And who manages the infrastructure and the distribution of food? And how about the stories you hear about female doctors?

This interview emphasises the importance of looking beyond preconceived gender divisions. As long as female agency is defined by a strict agent/victim binary, it will preclude a full understanding of women's individual motivations and will continue to generalise women's experiences.

In conclusion, through studying the representations of women and terrorism, it is possible to raise awareness of how conceptions of masculinity and femininity continue to structure dominant ideas about violence and security. A too-narrow conception of female agency leads both the media and academics to obscure the fact that there are politics in domestic duties. In their supportive roles, women might actually feel empowered and play a pivotal role in societies that do not reflect Western ideas of emancipation.

Further Reading

Auchter, J., 2012. 'Gendering Terror'. *International Feminist Journal of Politics.* 14.1: pp. 121–39.

Mahmood, S., 2001. 'Feminist Theory, Embodiment, and the Docile Agent: Some Reflections on the Egyptian Islamic Revival'. *Cultural Anthropology* 16.2: pp. 202–36.

Ortner, S.B., 1998. 'Is Female to Male as Nature is to Culture?' *Feminism, the Public and the Private.* Ed. Joan B. Landes. Oxford: Oxford University Press: pp. 21–44.

Pateman, C., 1989. *The Disorder of Women: Democracy, Feminism and Political Theory.* Cambridge: Polity Press.

Saltman, E.M. and Smith, M., 2015. *'Till Martyrdom Do Us Part': Gender and the ISIS Phenomenon.* Institute for Strategic Dialogue.

Sjoberg, L., 2009. 'Feminist Interrogations of Terrorism/ Terrorism Studies'. *International Relations* 23.1: pp. 69–74.

Winter, C., 2015. 'Women of the Islamic State: a manifesto on women by the Al-Khanssaa Brigade'. *Quilliam Foundation*, 18.

Narratives of Female Fighters: Self-Defence Classes for Women in Revolutionary Cairo

Perrine Lachenal

Perrine Lachenal obtained her PhD in social anthropology in 2015 from Aix-Marseille University in France. Her thesis is an ethnographic study conducted between 2011 and 2012 in Cairo on certain defence practices that have emerged in recent years in Egypt. Her dissertation conceives self-defence training for women as not only revealing but also producing 'revolutionary' physical and technical repertoires in which the emotional, gendered, social and moral dimensions of the period's political upheavals are embodied.

Self-defence courses for women initially emerged in the Cairene urban landscape in the wider context of the mobilisation of civil society to fight sexual harassment. Harassment in turn had become a worrying trend and a public cause. The first women's self-defence training was probably organised around 2002 at a cultural centre close to downtown Cairo. In the years that followed, similar courses multiplied in social centres and NGOs, and the popularity of self-defence classes for women continued to grow. The revolutionary period can be seen as a turning point since it gave birth to a huge 'security market' that included self-defence classes as well as private security services and self-defence accessories like pepper sprays. The marketing was mainly aimed at appealing to women in the socially affluent districts of Cairo. The deep feeling of vulnerability that spread across Cairo after the Egyptian revolution of January 2011 contributed to legitimising the choice, for many women, to learn how to fight back and to acquire combat skills such as throwing kicks and punches.

By making visible the socially and sexually situated modalities by which categories such as 'legitimacy' and 'illegitimacy' are produced with respect to violence, self-defence classes for women constitute a valuable vantage point from which to contribute to a wider discussion about 'dangerous women'. In self-defence classes, how do attendees and teachers describe and label violence? In which ways do they frame and justify the possibility for a woman to react physically? By focusing on the ways female violence is articulated in self-defence classes – the words and categories used to describe it – it is possible to identify different kinds of narratives which are used to describe women fighters.

The narrative to which people most commonly appeal relies on the association between female violence and 'popular' or working-class areas, reflecting some mechanisms of social distinction at work within Egyptian urban society. It is important to specify here that most of the self-defence classes organised in Cairo take place in the wealthiest neighbourhoods. The attendees I met explained that they chose to learn how to fight 'just in case' and that they want to acquire techniques they plan never to use. According to them, there is a huge difference between being able to use violence and actually using it. They clearly oppose the possibility of violence (what might happen) to its actual performance (what does happen). The second option is relegated to the side of social otherness – and to 'other' women to whom they cannot be compared. These female figures' capacity for being violent is articulated with specific representations of their bodies, depicted as oversized – sometimes monstrous – and scary. Mona, one forty-year-old attendee, explained to me: 'Women from popular areas are huge. Their husbands are so tiny compared to them! There, husbands are afraid of their wives ... I saw on Facebook that there are a large number of men beaten by their wives in Egypt.'

The second narrative regarding women fighters relies on the impossible alliance – so the compulsory negotiation – between women's capacity to fight back and conjugality. Doing self-defence can be judged problematic by the attendees themselves since most of them have reached the strategic age when it becomes crucial to find husbands and to conform to classic expectations of femininity. Their words depict models of conjugality in which gender roles are clearly defined, implying that the man is supposed to give protection to the woman. Because they do not want to scare away potential husbands, female attendees remain discreet about their unconventional defence abilities. Sarah explained to me: 'Girls are afraid to appear too strong and not to be able to find any husband for this reason. Men want to protect women. What would happen if women were strong? Men might feel useless! Girls feel concerned about that because marriage is a fundamental issue for us.'

In order to preserve the classic gender divide, the transgression linked to the fact of being a girl and being able to fight back has to remain partial. Women can legitimately use violence only under certain conditions, which include there being no man present whose role is to protect them. Fady, a self-defence teacher, explained, for example, that 'women learn defence techniques only in case there is no man around because it would shame a man to fight back on your own instead of calling him!' Female violence has to be subordinate to male violence.

Another narrative, which is the continuation of the previous one, links women's ability to fight to the risk of becoming men. The self-defence attendees I met express the fear that acquiring fighting techniques, commonly associated with men, could masculinise them. The bodily transformations resulting from physical training are perceived as particularly problematic, as Mona explained to me: 'People tell me they can't understand my choice [of practising martial arts]. They say that it is not feminine and that I will become a man, with muscles and so on, and that no man around me will accept to marry me.' For a single young woman, ceasing to be 'fragile' – or at least giving the appearance of fragility – is perilous, and physical power has to remain dissimulated. To cancel the masculinising effects of attending self-defence classes, the female attendees consequently engage in compensation attitudes, aimed at maintaining the appearance of femininity. Their aversion to muscles and their preoccupation with remaining thin, and therefore constantly dieting, offer good illustrations of their fear of being physically transformed – and perceived as less attractive by potential future husbands – as a result of self-defence classes. Nevertheless, it is worth mentioning that the female ability to fight can sometimes be considered positively, even as a characteristic that could please men. Yasser, a self-defence teacher, posted a video on his Facebook wall, showing a woman successfully decking ten male opponents, and wrote underneath the following comment:

'What a girl! I would love to marry her!' Here, the reference to conjugality seems to undermine the feminine transgression by integrating it in a more conventional experience. Teachers also sometimes address female fighters in aesthetic and even sexualised ways: the feminine use of violence is admitted under the condition of remaining connected to heteronormative matrimonial and seduction projects and of not threatening the sexual order.

The final narrative I identified while doing my fieldwork at self-defence training classes for women in Cairo is related to the Egyptian revolution. The revolutionary period has indeed given birth to a new frame in which the use of violence by women is admitted, and even positively represented. The transgression – the fact that women are not supposed to employ fighting techniques in their daily lives – is justified by the historical importance of the events. In times of emergency or exception, violence can be seen as a possible feminine resource. Radwa explained to me that she was fully part of the revolt since its first days, standing at the front lines and throwing stones at policemen: 'Women always fought hand in hand with men. Even the Prophet was helped by women fighters during some crucial battles.' Quoting famous female figures, especially from the Qur'an, the attendees justify their choice to practise self-defence by referring to the intensity of the crisis and to the political cause. Not to mention that the deep feeling of insecurity that arose with the revolution gave obvious intelligibility to self-defence initiatives. This revolutionary narrative reveals a spectacular and heroic form of feminine violence, which nevertheless has to remain temporary. Women can exceptionally exceed their conventional attributions, but only until the end of the crisis and the restoration of the classical gender roles.

Popular, monstrous, subordinate, masculinising, sexy, spectacular or even revolutionary: the words of Cairene self-defence attendees and teachers reveal different representations regarding the use of violence by women in times of political transformations. All these narratives give visibility to female fighters, while undermining the subversive potential of their experiences. The transgression of being a woman and simultaneously capable of physical violence – of being a 'dangerous woman' – destabilises social and sexual hierarchies and must be carefully restrained and framed.

Childless by Choice

Jasmine Tonie

BBC Radio 4 Xtra regular contributor and Britain's Got Satire *sketch show finalist Jasmine Tonie is a comedy writer from the Midlands. Professional credits include: 'What A Time To Be Alive' for* London Podcast Adventures, *'Britain's Got Sentiment' for* Sketch! Please! *and her TV debut 'The Family Trump' for* That's TV Manchester. *Jasmine is a writer for Britain's leading female comedy platform* Funny Women. *Her situation comedy and her debut black comedy book series* Existential Animals In Crisis *are both currently in development.*

> When I see children, I feel nothing. I have no maternal instinct… I ovulate sand.
>
> *Margaret Cho,* Revolution, *2003*

I am a dangerous woman. In my opinion, the most dangerous kind. I'm dangerous because I simply do not want a family; in fact, I couldn't think of anything worse. I lack the broody, motherly, maternal sensibility which inevitably leads to vulnerability, and I possess all the discipline, drive and dedication to continually work at my career as a scriptwriter without ever having to think of anyone or anything else. Selfish? Probably. But why not?

I have a life, and it's up to me how I want to live it and what I want to do with it. I am as committed to my decision as I am wholly uncritical of others who choose to procreate and 'settle down'. I'm a firm believer in everyone doing what's right for them; we enter the world alone and we leave that way. For me, there are countries I want to explore that I haven't travelled to yet, experiences to have that I haven't experienced yet and goals I have yet to pursue. Frankly, I make no apologies for pursuing them.

I work hard for my money and I want to spend it on me. I'm not prepared to squander my body, my bank balance and my future to look after another human being; why would I create one myself? The frankly frustrating notion of getting all the things you want to do out of the way before you settle down and have children sounds ludicrous – as if you can no longer do what you actually want to do once you give birth, that effectively your life ends. Well, personally, I couldn't do it.

Feminist movements have come a long way to broaden women's horizons in this country, and I thank my lucky stars I was born at a time where we finally have the freedom to choose. True, there is perhaps residual judgement and discrimination, but on the whole, women like me – and more importantly, these types of decisions – are treated with much more respect than in years gone by.

So why are more and more women choosing not to have children? I know women who feel the world is just too horror-filled and unpredictable to even contemplate bringing another human being into it. Others feel they are unable to balance a successful career with motherhood, at least not without compromising on one or the other. Some women make the informed decision, in my case relatively young, that they simply do not want a child; no maternal instinct lurks, no internal drive to procreate is present, without even a glimmer of that oft-quoted but impossible-to-define feeling: broody.

> It's unconscionable to breed, with the number of children who are starving to death in impoverished countries.
>
> *Ashley Judd,* Sunday Mail, *2006*

This mystical 'emotional need to create' supposedly exists in every woman; I've been told on countless occasions that I will obviously change my mind, that my life 'will be empty without children'. I've been challenged with the apparently horrifying concept of 'who's going to visit you when you're old?' Interestingly, and perhaps inevitably, more often than not it is men who offer these kinds of responses, whereas women usually tend to be more sympathetic to, if not entirely understanding of, my 'radical' views.

I'm a dangerous woman because I made this decision when I was young. I'm confident and self-assured enough to know that I won't ever change my mind, and all this makes me infallible to falling prey to the usual social trappings of womanhood. I'm not on the prowl for a man to sweep me off my feet. I'm fine without one, thank you; actually, I prefer it.

I can hear no loud, intimidating tick-tock of an internal body clock, only the ever-present tick-tock of time clicking by – and I intend to make the most of every second. If I'm lucky enough to reach old age, I'm fine that no children will come to visit me in my nursing home. I won't be there anyway; I'll be lounging on a beach in Thailand, wrinkled and leathery, my sunburnt skin flapping away in the wind. Knackered, battered, but crucially, fulfilled.

'What? No children? Well, you'd better get on with it, old girl.'

'No!' I'd say. 'F*** off!'

Dame Helen Mirren, British Vogue, *2013*

A Serious Kind of Love

Yewande Omotoso

Yewande Omotoso's debut novel Bomboy *(Modjaji Books, 2011) was shortlisted for the Sunday Times Fiction Prize, MNet Film Award and Etisalat Prize for Literature. It won the South African Literary Award First Time Author Prize. Her short stories include 'How About the Children' in* Kalahari Review, *'Things Are Hard' in the 2012 Caine Prize Anthology, 'Fish' published in* The Moth *literary journal and 'The Leftovers' in* One World Two: A Second Global Anthology of Short Stories. *Yewande was a 2013 Norman Mailer Fellow, a 2014 Etisalat Fellow and a 2015 Miles Morland Scholar. Yewande's second novel* The Woman Next Door *(Chatto & Windus, 2016) was longlisted for the Bailey's Women's Fiction Prize and the International Dublin Literary Award, and was shortlisted for the Aidoo-Snyder Prize, the Barry Ronge Fiction Prize and the UJ Literary Prize.* La Signora della Porta Accanto *(66thand2nd), the Italian translation of* The Woman Next Door, *has been shortlisted for the 2019 Premio Lattes Grinzane Literary Prize. Born in Barbados, Yewande grew up in Nigeria and currently lives in Johannesburg.*

When I think of dangerous women, I don't think of women in whose presence I am in danger. When I think of dangerous women, I think of women in whose presence the dangers of life finally meet their match. The kind of dangers I'm talking about are the hypocrisies, the patriarchy, the rules that are not rules at all, but simply ways to cheat freedom and oppress those who dare sing out.

I have known such women; they occur throughout my life. It's not what it sounds like; some do present as fierce but many are soft spoken, calm and of few words.

In my childhood I knew a lot of mothers. My own, Marguerita, was gentle. Her danger may have been in whom she chose to love. It would have been more popular, in the late 1960s at Edinburgh University, to suspect a Nigerian suitor of having a stash of wives back home in 'dark' Africa. Instead my mother, hailing from the island of Barbados, wasn't bothered, and decades later I was given life.

Only as an adult, a woman, do I consider how bold my mother must have been to carry such conviction and to voyage.

I remember being at a party as a little girl and watching the adults. And a family friend whose name I have lost walked up to another woman and said words that didn't belong at a party, very clear words, not disrespectful but not polite either. I've named the person she was addressing Stella in my memory. *Stella,* she said, *don't you know you are already beautiful.*

Dangerous women show up sometimes, they disturb something. Stella was beautiful. She also bore tell-tale signs of the chemicals she was using on her dark skin to lighten it. I must have been eight or nine, and I was startled that someone could speak to another someone that way.

Many of the women on the island of my birth are like this. Their bow tongues launch arrows into the world and never miss their mark.

My grandmother was one such woman. For a very long time she convinced me only of her sweetness, until one day when I commented on how lovely she was; she, holding a pot of boiling water, said, *Muh dear, there was time when I throw this water on you soon as look at yuh.* It would appear, I learnt, that my sweet grandmother once had a temper. Most dangerous women do, an important ability to access their rage whose existence alone runs counter to nursery rhymes we were fed about sugar and spice.

My mother's cousins. Dangerous in the sense that they take up magnificent space; they know what it is to laugh even though they have cried too.

My grandfather's sister, their mother, sits mostly in a wheelchair now, but the other day she said, *Boy if I were young,* and I believed her. I believed that the woman in front of me, frail and sitting, had eaten life, swallowed it completely whole. I imagine she danced, fell in love, made love, made children, made lives, and set people straight with her arrow-words. And you know, danger, in the way it manifests in these women, has never been more allowing or more generous.

This is a new kind of meaning, this danger. A serious kind of love. For oneself, one's kin; and what life is meant for. Dangerous. I didn't say it then; I was too young and answered Doctor or Mother, but ask me now what I wish to be when I grow up.

A Deep Shade of Red

Sujana Crawford

A multilingual poet, playwright and researcher, Sujana Crawford's work mainly explores human relationships, traditional practices and our interconnectedness with nature. Her work often draws inspiration from her childhood in Nepal, interest in folklore and work in gender relations.

In loving memory of Minu Aunty

The day she got married she acquired an official right to the colour Red. Red would mark her new status as a married woman and represent her vitality, fertility and sexuality. Red gave her power and a place at the centre of social life within her community. Her family hoped, as they bade her farewell, that she would never be without Red in the forms of *sindoor* on her hair parting, *tika* on her forehead, *pote* around her neck, *chura* around her wrists and *sari* around her body.

The day she lost her husband, three decades and three children later, she lost her right to Red also. Like everything else in her life – her name, her nationality, her home – it was never truly hers to begin with. Within hours of her husband dying, her neighbours and relatives gathered to ritualistically wash every trace of Red off her. With this, it was expected that she let go of every earthly pleasure she might have learnt to take comfort in, and launch her journey as a widow. In the absence of a husband to give meaning to her existence, society dictated that her life no longer served any real purpose and therefore held no value. From now on, she was meant to be in a state of mourning that was to last the rest of her life. To represent this state, she was to limit herself to wearing the plainest of colours and avoid any make-up or jewellery. She also no longer had the right to actively participate in any of the social and religious events. She was to live on the fringes and blend into thin air as much as possible. By stripping Red off her, she was reduced to a living corpse, both in the eyes of the society and her own.

Fading away isn't simple, though. Just as Red speaks volumes through its vibrancy, in its absence too it screams for attention. Where it comes with prestige and power, when evicted, it leaves behind stigma and unwanted attention. During festivals, in a sea of bright colours, unsmiling, unadorned faces often stick out, their sadness, and perhaps resentment, obvious. It is always these faces that stick in one's mind and she was now expected to be one of them.

Growing up, there were other women like her around us. Women who had lost their husbands and had quietly accepted life on the fringes. It was simply accepted as a way of life, a part of our culture. Nobody ever seemed to give it much thought or attention. When I realised we only ever bought plain saris for my two aunts, both widowed, I simply assumed that was what they liked. I thought they were antisocial when they didn't actively seek to bless new brides or asked my mother to take their offerings to the temple during religious ceremonies instead of doing it themselves. So natural and trivial it all seemed that my young mind never made the connection between their behaviour and them having lost their husbands. It was never mentioned, never discussed, never questioned. It was simply accepted. I wouldn't be surprised if my aunts had long forgotten the connection themselves.

Once, after noticing how unkind my cousin's husband was to her, in my naivety (and rage), I commented to my mother that my cousin would be a lot happier if he (her husband) were to die. At the time, I thought the severe scolding that followed was melodramatic but warranted given the meanness of my remark. The possible repercussions for my beloved cousin, were my curse to come true, were not explained to me, then or later. They are the kind of things you are meant to pick up and understand along the way. Besides, where would one start, so many are the rituals girls and women are meant to observe! Many years later, I would come across this line in a book – 'one of the few things widows are not forbidden to do is laugh, but given the many restrictions and biases they face, not many would want to'. And that little exchange with my mother would come rushing back. I would finally understand: life with an abusive husband was a million times better than life under the shadow of a dead one.

For two years, buried under the cloud of grief, she quietly accepted the life that was offered, discarding everything she was expected to. She was now to live for her children, people often said. There was to be no more living for herself. This life was what God had planned for her and she had to accept it, she was told. A subtle reference to the belief that she must have harboured some bad karma to have been unable to ward off her husband's death before her own. In other words, a better woman would have died before her husband. Once she began to see past the grief, however, she started becoming aware of the resentment that was beginning to replace the joy and love she held in her heart. Living on the fringes as an outcast was not how she wanted to spend the rest of her life. For the first time, she found herself paying attention to the unfairness behind the customs she felt obliged to observe. She was expected to give up so much in return for so little. While this had been true most of her life, this was the first time she felt she was expected to feel grateful just for being allowed to remain alive. Not long ago, women in her position would have been reduced to ashes in their dead husbands' pyres. Reclaiming Red was not a decision she took lightly, nor could she afford to. In reclaiming Red, on the one hand she would be breaking every social decorum expected of her, while on another, she would be reclaiming herself. And the latter was the only way she could be true to her children and her work, but most important of all, true to herself. But it wouldn't be easy.

When she started dressing as she pleased, in colourful saris and red lipstick, she was one step closer to being her true self. But at every step, she pretended not to notice the shaking heads and gossiping tongues. In breaking the rules, she was challenging the practices held dear for hundreds of years. The balance was delicate, and by being obstinate, people thought (and it's always about what other people think!) she was risking toppling the entire society. Despite the subtle and not-so-subtle social shunning, she persevered. She continued to wear the colours she had loved since she was a little girl but that had been snatched away since her husband's death. She began to actively participate in social and religious functions. She missed her husband, but she knew that she was never just an extension of him. Nor was she now a mere shadow of someone long gone.

It was never just about reclaiming Red, for one colour alone could have never fully represented her at any stage. It was about having the right to choose from and own a colourful palette, instead of being symbolised by the presence or absence of just one colour. It was about refusing to be defined or reduced for the convenience of society. It was reclaiming herself, and living as a whole – a feeling, thinking, seeing human being. She understood that now, and it was time the wider society did as well. Over time, her choices forced more and more people to rethink current norms and enabled them to embrace change.

It's been over a decade since she reclaimed herself. She no longer quickens her steps when she notices a disapproving glare thrown her way, nor does she look away. It's still not easy, but she is no longer embarrassed or ashamed. She full-heartedly blesses new brides and dances when her favourite song comes on. Newly retired, she travels between continents to visit her children whom she loves fiercely but isn't a burden to. To me she personifies strength; to others she is an inspiration. And for being all of these things, and for various other reasons, she is also a dangerous woman.

Headscarves

Nada Awar Jarrar

Nada Awar Jarrar was born in Lebanon to an Australian mother and a Lebanese father. She has lived in London, Paris, Sydney and Washington, DC and is currently based in Beirut. Her journalism has appeared in the Guardian, The Times, *the* Sydney Morning Herald *and Lebanon's English-language newspaper the* Daily Star. *Her first novel,* Somewhere, Home *(Heinemann, 2003) won the Commonwealth Best First Book award for Southeast Asia and the South Pacific. Her latest novel,* An Unsafe Haven, *was published by the Borough Press and was launched at the Edinburgh International Book Festival in August 2016.*

I saw her hair for the first time – thick ringlets of dark brown that formed a circle around her delicate face – midway through the semester, when she appeared in my creative writing class minus the veil that usually covered her head. Her clothes were different too, casual and more appropriate for her age, I thought. Before I could stop myself, I blurted out in front of the whole class: 'Wow, Rabab. I love your hair.' Her reaction – a watery smile that did not reach her eyes – warned me not to comment further.

It was several months later when, to my surprise, Rabab decided to take another writing class with me. I was surprised because I thought I had offended her by pointing out the change in her appearance.

The course, entitled 'Writing Identity', explores the ways that we as writers fashion changing identities for ourselves through our work. Rabab submitted a childhood memoir in which she described the first day she had to go to school wearing a headscarf as the moment she was admitted into 'the sisterhood of Greys & Whites', the moment she became just one of many nameless little girls wearing white veils and grey uniforms, the moment she could no longer reveal her true self to the outside world. 'I was a rainbow coated with grey and white,' she wrote, 'but still they failed to decolourise me on the inside.'

When I recently sat down to talk to Rabab, she told me she had not been coerced into wearing the hijab. It was 'the norm', she said, at her Islamic school for girls who had reached a certain age, a tradition she also accepted because the women in her family had always been veiled.

But from the moment – aged eight years and ten months – she was made to wrap a scarf around her head that also covered her ears and neck, Rabab no longer felt like herself, hated what she saw every time she stood in front of the mirror before she went out. In time, she also developed an eating disorder that she attributed to her anxiety over wearing the veil. Then at nineteen, having endured a relentless inner struggle, she felt she finally possessed the wherewithal to approach her parents and try to convince them that removing her headscarf was the only option if she was to remain true to herself.

It took months of extensive research on Islam for Rabab to conclude – and to point out to her mother and father – that while wearing the veil was recommended in Islamic tradition, it was not considered a religious duty in the same way, for example, that prayer and fasting are. Her parents, prominent members of their community who worried about how the extended family might react, were open-minded enough – and ultimately loving enough – to go along with their daughter's wishes despite the possible repercussions to themselves and to their place in the community.

'I remember the day I was preparing to go to university with my head bare, my mother helped me brush my hair while at the same time scolding me about going out without a scarf,' Rabab told me with a smile. 'She was feeling guilty, I think, about having brought up a girl who could think for herself.'

Growing up in Beirut in the 1960s and until the outbreak of Lebanon's civil war in 1975, the only veiled women I came across regularly were the Druze religious initiates in my father's mountain village. The women wore floor-length black dresses and long white scarves that not only covered their hair but often their mouths and noses as well, so that the only features visible to the outside world were their eyes. But these were initiates, I knew, who had vowed to devote their lives entirely to God and were, at least when it came to spiritual matters, separate from the rest of the community.

In our mixed Beirut neighbourhood, where Muslims and Christians lived amicably alongside one another and where there was a thriving, international expat community, we did occasionally come across veiled women. But I was brought up in a secular, liberal household that encouraged me to believe that these women were the exception rather than the norm, so seeing them did not make much of an impression on me as a child.

After the end of the civil war, when I returned to Lebanon from nearly twenty years of studying, living and working abroad, I began to notice an increasing number of veiled women in my old Beirut neighbourhood, as well as everywhere else it seemed. The demographics of the city had changed, I knew. The fifteen-year conflict had forced people living in the capital to move away from dangerous areas and to settle permanently elsewhere. At the same time, the twenty-year Israeli occupation of Southern Lebanon drove tens of thousands of families out of their villages and to the outskirts of Beirut. Still – and despite the circumstances – the sight of so many women whom I believed had been made to cover their heads against their will disturbed me.

Then we began to hear of how a number of European countries had passed laws banning full-face Islamic veils in public places. There were disturbing images on television of girls not being allowed into school and news of growing anti-Muslim sentiment inspired by these laws. I was appalled by what was going on, but also found myself wondering if banning the hijab might not be a way of freeing these girls and women of a deeply sexist custom forced on them by their communities. It was some time, however, before my prejudices made way for a deeper and ultimately more compassionate understanding of my fellow Arab women.

Working first as a journalist covering Lebanon and the region, and eventually publishing four novels that attempt to explore the effects on the everyday lives and relationships of ordinary men and women of the many conflicts that continue to plague the Arab world, I have come across women for whom the idea of removing the veil would be akin to going out in public in one's birthday suit. During my conversations with these women in Beirut and around the country – and more recently, with women from rural areas in Syria who have taken refuge in Lebanon – I learned that while wearing a headscarf may not always be a personal choice, it is one that is deemed, by some communities, as necessary for women and their families to live piously and therefore enjoy a secure existence.

I was also astonished to discover that some women make the decision to cover their heads willingly. During the two years of my mother's illness, and before her death in 2016, she was treated at home by a family physician who appeared one day with a scarf wrapped around her usually bare head. When I asked her why she had decided to put on a veil in middle age, she said she had been so moved by her recent pilgrimage to Mecca that she resolved to remind herself every day of that intense spiritual experience through wearing the hijab. A short time after her return from the haj, her teenage daughter said she wanted to take the same step, but the doctor forbade it, saying that this decision had to be an informed one, not taken merely because of a desire to conform. Perhaps, I deduced, for well-educated, middle-class women, the decision becomes a personal one.

All these close (as well as distant) encounters with fellow Arab women have given me significant food for thought, so that when it came to considering the question of what it meant to be a 'dangerous woman' and I contemplated writing about my mixed feelings about the veil, I was able to come to a conclusion of sorts (although I acknowledge that even that might change in the future).

A dangerous woman is one who, despite the constraints put on her by society – whether religious and conservative or secular and free-thinking – insists on remaining true to herself, whatever the sacrifices she has to make to achieve this. If this is indeed the case, then I, as a committed feminist, cannot presume to speak for all Arab women on the issue. As sad as it often makes me feel to see young girls wearing headscarves in school playgrounds, and as disappointed as I sometimes am to meet women I have known well who suddenly decide to start wearing the hijab, my opinion hardly matters.

I console myself with the thought that even for a young woman as brave and intelligent as Rabab, who struggled long and hard both with her own conscience as well as with her family to find convincing reasons to remove the veil, the decision to do so was indeed important, but it did not change her in fundamental ways.

'My beliefs, perceptions and personality in general did not change as a result of removing the veil,' she explained. 'It's just that by taking off the hijab, my outer appearance became congruent with who I actually am.'

Outside the Camp

Janet Lees

Janet Lees has worked with people of all ages and abilities, using creative ways of retelling the Bible, bringing to the foreground characters and episodes that have previously been in the background of the text. She is a writer and a member of the Lay Community of St Benedict. Janet has frequently been accused of 'making the Bible up.' Here is an example of one such episode in which she pairs two texts: the story of Miriam being sent outside the camp and the story of creation. Outside, Miriam's encounters with nature help her recover her sense of self so that she returns to the camp stronger. You can read about Miriam's punishment in Numbers chapter 12: it's much shorter. It is one of the texts of the Hebrew Bible that confirms women as dangerous; so dangerous they have to be sent 'outside the camp.'

Miriam was outside the camp. Alone. She was afraid and cold. It was getting dark. Her skin was flaking off and she didn't understand what was happening to her. She understood how she'd got here: men had dragged her outside the camp and her brothers had allowed it to happen. They'd been in the worship tent and it had been decided. She had to spend seven days outside the camp – for what? For her part in the criticism of her brother Moses and his wife. The finger had been pointed at her: she was to blame. Everyone else kept quiet and kept their eyes down. The women said nothing as she was dragged away.

It was beginning to get dark. The pink sky was beginning to go velvety blue. She would be outside the camp in the dark. There would be no comforting firelight, no sheltering tent, no cosy covers. It would be cold. She would be alone.

As the velvety night began to deepen, a star came out. A bright pinprick of light far away in the universe, it lent Miriam a tiny bit of light. Once she noticed it, she focused on it; putting out her hand, she pointed at the star, using her index finger to cover it up. She pointed and then the light was covered up. She took her finger away and it appeared again, pointing and un-pointing several times. Each time the star disappeared and reappeared again. 'So this is light,' she thought. 'It's good.' She curled up in a ball under a small busy tree and tried to sleep.

When she woke up, it was still dark. Even darker than the first dark. But also lighter. There were more stars. She crawled out from under the small busy tree and looked up. There were millions of stars stretching right across the sky; so many she could not cover them with her fingers, although she could put her hands in front of her face and hide from them. She uncovered her face and turned it upwards to the stars. They snaked across the sky like a shawl, and others lay scattered either side. It was as if the sky was a huge dome and the stars were scattered all over the inside of it. She traced the path of the shawl of stars. 'So this is sky,' she thought. 'It's good.' She walked over to a nearby rock and sat down with her back to it, looking at the stars, and she fell asleep again.

When she woke the second time, she was cold. There was some dew on her hair and clothes. The deep velvety sky was receding and some pinkness was coming back into it. Away on the horizon to the east, the pinkness was increasing as if a fire was raging over the horizon. She sat and waited, pulling her slightly dewy shawl around her. Gradually, gently, without much fuss, but with thousands of birds heralding the moment, the sun rose. The giant ball of light and heat emerged from out of the earth at the place where the sky dome ended. As it did so, the air began to glow, and that glow warmed her. 'So this is sunrise,' she thought. 'It's good.'

How long it took for the sun to free itself from the line of the horizon she couldn't say. It was probably about the same amount of time it took every day, except that she didn't always notice. Not when she was inside the camp, in the sheltering tent and the cosy covers. Now she was sorry she'd missed it so often. To be outside the camp meant bathing in the sunrise. It was beautiful.

She found herself thinking about bathing. Bathing in sunlight was fine, but washing would be good. She knew that whilst she was outside, she was expected to stay clear of the river and the wells the women from the camp used. So where was she to find water? She stood up and looked around her. Where would water be? Maybe if she got up on the rocks, she would get a better view. Slowly and carefully she climbed through the rocks, picking her way from one boulder to the next. She tied up her skirt and let her bare legs and feet do the work they had been made for. It made her breathe heavily, but it felt good. After some time, she came to a place near the top of the rocks. She stopped on one rock, as she heard the sound of running water. There was a stream, a tiny one, flowing down from the rocks, over the boulders and back into the earth. Reaching the stream, she put out her hand and touched the stream of water with her finger, just like she'd pointed at the star on the previous night. The stream of water lopped over her finger and continued on, over the rocks with all the other water. She turned her hand round and cupped it, brought it up to her lips and lapped it. Then she licked her fingers. 'So this is water,' she thought. 'It's good.'

Of course, she'd had water before. Every day since she was a small child, she fetched water with all of the other women, but that water was not like this water. That water was for the camp. She'd found this water herself. She took off her shawl and splashed the water onto her arms, her face and her head. It gave her a lovely tingling feeling. She looked around to remind herself where the water was. She'd need it again, after all. Then, taking back her shawl, she carried on up the small gully the water had made to the top of the rocks.

At the top there was a small tree bending over the stream. Its branches were heavy and weighed down with something. There were small birds in the tree and as she approached, they flew up and away. The branches of the tree sprang back up when the birds had gone and she saw that each branch had many small black fruits growing on it. The birds had been eating them, so maybe she could too. She took a small fruit between her thumb and finger and bit into it. It was sharp but not unpleasant. The dark juice stained her finger. She licked it off and took another fruit. 'So this is fruit,' she thought. 'It's good.' And she ate some more.

After a while, she sat down under the tree. It was warm now and she was tired. As she sat there, still and alone, the small birds came back. They landed on the branches of the tree and began to chatter and sing as they ate the fruits. Each one called something to its neighbour and the others would join in. The sound was light and bubbly. She listened to it more carefully than she ever had before. 'So these are birds,' she thought. 'It's good.'

As she sat there, she became aware that a lizard had crawled out onto a nearby rock. The lizard was also interested in the heat of the sun, and the warm rock was the ideal place to benefit from it and to catch flies. She watched the lizard, sometimes basking, sometimes catching flies, and she smiled at its simple life there on the rock. 'So this is life,' she thought. 'It's good.'

After the day had passed its hottest point and the sun began to slip down again in the sky, she got up. She followed the small stream back onto the plateau and as she followed it, she saw plants growing alongside or in the water. She marked them in her mind, knowing she might need to come back for them. Eventually the stream ended in a small pool. It was in the shade of the rocks and seemed to bubble up out of the ground. Around the spring the clear water lapped on pebbles and sand. She sat down again and tasted the water. As she dipped her head down to catch the drops, she caught sight of herself. Her reflection was perfectly formed there in the pool of water, as if she was in the water and reaching out from it to touch her own face. She marvelled at it, how clear it was, how lovely. 'So this is me,' she thought. 'It's good.'

For the next six days, Miriam stayed by the pool. There was shelter, water and food. Each day she found something new to enjoy or wonder at. As she wandered along the stream or sat under the trees, she'd think about the camp and what had happened there. She thought about her life, her family and friends. But she also remembered the disputes, the rules, the jealousies. It was difficult to disentangle her part in it all, just as it was difficult to take a strand out of the water. Each time she put her hand in, the water just flowed round and over it again. As she bathed in the pool and dried herself in the sun, the flakiness of her skin seemed to lessen. Her skin was returning to its familiar firmness and brightness. The reflection in the pool affirmed she was her true self.

She thought about her brothers and the men who had dragged her out of the camp. They had been cruel and hurt her both physically and more deeply. She didn't trust them. They seemed to think they could make up the rules. She thought about the women, her neighbours, and how they had said nothing and kept their eyes down. Yes, she understood, it could have been them. Better to say nothing and stay within the protection of the camp, with its sheltering tents and cosy covers.

Only it wasn't like that. If she'd stayed in the camp, she wouldn't have found all these good things. She whirled round and took them all in, and then again and again as the whole world started to swirl and whirl around her. She stopped suddenly, staggered and laughed. Her laugh was like the water bubbling up in the pool. 'So this is happiness,' she thought. 'It's good.' She bent down and picked up a dried seed pod; it rattled when she shook it. She shook it gently at first and then faster and in more varied ways, and as she shook, she danced. And she danced and danced and danced.

On the morning of the seventh day, she made her way down the gully and back across the plain to the edge of the camp. She took some of the seed pods wrapped in her shawl, which she tied around her waist so that they rattled as she walked. When she got to the camp, she saw her brothers waiting outside with some other men. The women were inside the camp. She could just see some of their faces in the tent doorways and around the cooking fires. She walked slowly and steadily. As she approached them, she did not slow her pace or stop and turn to them. She walked right on into the camp, the rattling sound of the seed pods accompanying every step. Aaron, her older brother, tried to interrupt her with one of his pompous pronouncements. But Moses put out his arm and stopped him. They let her go into the camp. As she walked past the women, she took seed pods from her shawl and gave them away. The last person she met to whom she gave a seed pod was her sister-in-law. And then she went into the tent.

The Teacher

Meltem Naz Kaşo Corral Sánchez

Meltem Naz Kaşo Corral Sánchez is an Istanbulite living in Barcelona and working as a UX researcher in a consulting company. Previously, she was an investigative journalist for a Turkish daily newspaper. In addition, she contributed to various publications around the world, including the newsletter of the University of Chicago, Armenian newspaper Hetq, *Spanish newspaper* El Periódico, *Spanish feminist magazine* Pikara, *Turkish travel magazine* Fly Pegasus, *and* Barcelona Metropolitan, *and was involved with the Dutch NGO for international education, Nuffic. Meltem is also the author of a short story titled 'Candied Chestnuts' which was published in Fabula Press's anthology* Nivalis 2015. *Follow her on Twitter @MeltemBarcelona and check her podcast anchor.fm/meltem-naz-kaso-corral-snchez*

When an adventure-seeking agnostic woman like me volunteers to help women from different faiths communicate, an American storyteller goes outside her comfort zone in search of knowing her Muslim other, and a missionary Turkish woman dares to tell her story, social patterns that usually set us apart begin to dissolve. We become dangerous to the persistence of prejudices with regards to xenophobia and Islamophobia. Here is what I am talking about: I was lucky enough to listen to the story of a Muslim woman who has taken a path very different to mine, along with an American woman whose background did not match mine. I am inspired to share our story, to make a home for it, and give you an opportunity to meet a Muslim woman behind her veil, behind her closed doors.

On a hot summer day, I travel to the Çarşamba neighbourhood of Istanbul to help a young American photojournalist meet ultra-conservatives. Çarşamba resembles Saudi Arabia, if that is possible in Turkey. The women cover their faces, leaving only holes for seeing. Bearded, robed men emerge from the time of the Prophet Muhammed. Çarşamba people don't trust commercially produced perfumes and make their own according to strict Islamic standards. Residents of Çarşamba practise a strict version of Shari'a, the holy laws of Islam.

I meet the photographer, and we search for the building that fits the description of a Quranic school for young girls. Ahmet, a Çarşamba resident I met in Yavuz Sultan Selim Mosque, suggested that we go there.

We are somewhere between the Fatih Mosque and Yavuz Sultan Selim Mosque when I realise that we are lost. It is one of the warmest days of the summer, and we are dressed in layers so as not to offend anyone. It is Friday, a holy day. My sweat pours from my forehead into my eyes.

I see a woman in a black chador. It is hard to tell whether she is fat or thin, old or young, smiling or frowning. She comes so close to me that no one else can hear her voice. 'Follow me,' she says.

She unlocks the door of one of the silent buildings. We close it behind us and we enter into a world of colours. 'Merhaba, I'm Sabaahat,' she says. Surrounding us are a dozen young women dressed in grass green, red, yellow, light pink and leopard designs. They have on matching headscarves and loose dresses.

'Girls, bring me my navy-blue headscarf, please,' Sabaahat says. She has a tiny nose, a wide smile and no make-up. Wrinkles around her eyes tell me that she is in her fifties. 'And bring our guests a pair of slippers.'

Wearing slippers, we climb the stairs to the teachers' room. There, Sabaahat tells me that she has approximately eighty students and fifteen volunteer teachers. 'The teachers are not paid. They do it for the love of God,' she explains.

Sabaahat's students have chosen her school over the state-run high schools. Each of them completes one to four years of education. Ultimately, they receive a certificate from Sabaahat that has no official value. Still, they are lucky. 'Back in my day, my Quranic school was covered in black curtains. Police raids and break-ins by counter-terrorism teams were a daily occurrence. Our teachers were taken to court,' Sabaahat says. 'Some of them were even arrested.'

Ten years ago, Sabaahat and her sister founded the Quranic school. They teach the Quran, conversational Arabic, the history of Islam, the rules of prayer and fasting, and theology. The teacher on duty wakes the students up at dawn for the Fajr prayer, while recitations of the Quran resound from both mosques. After completing their prayers, the students go back to bed until eight o'clock. Meanwhile, the teachers prepare breakfast. At nine, everyone finishes eating and starts their first lecture. They study until ten o'clock at night and have a lunch and dinner break, and four more prayers throughout the day. After dinner, the students have dessert. In winter, there are cookies, and in summer, there is ice cream.

Students pay a tuition fee of approximately one hundred Turkish liras per month. 'In fact, costs are much higher,' Sabaahat explains. Her family owns a five-star hotel in Taksim, the business and tourist centre of Istanbul. She doesn't need the money to run the school. 'Money is important for parents. Even if they give ten liras, they care more about their daughters' performance.' That's the only reason, Sabaahat says, that she charges her students.

'My daughter, Meltem,' Sabaahat smiles, 'you two came to us during lunch time. Let's eat and then I will answer your questions.'

A bowl of shepherd's salad arrives at our table, along with a pot of cooked beans, and four jugs filled with a traditional yogurt drink, *ayran*.

'Sabaahat, are you originally from Çarşamba?' I ask. She says no. Her headscarf is not secured with a pin; it keeps falling off.

'I was born in a *yalı* in Beylerbeyi. I spent my high school years in Nişantaşı. For college, I went to Bosphorus University to study chemical engineering.'

This comes as a surprise. An average *yalı*, a mansion on the immediate waterside of the Bosphorus strait in Istanbul, costs millions of dollars. Nişantaşı is one of the most modern and European neighbourhoods of Turkey, and Bosphorus University is the most prestigious educational institution in Turkey, originally founded by Americans.

'And your sister too?'

'No, actually, she studied finance in London. My dad was not religious and didn't discriminate by gender. He enrolled us in the most expensive schools. We went to prestigious universities. What he had in mind for us was to become world citizens,' Sabaahat says as she reaches for her salad. 'My father wanted us to experience life abroad and then come back to Turkey to climb the professional ladder.'

One day, after attending her university lecture, a miniskirt and high-heel-wearing Sabaahat was talking with a friend. He said that there was a talk later in the evening given by a soft-spoken and well-read spiritual leader known as a *sheikh*. This friend asked Sabaahat to join him. She liked the young man. He had green eyes and a wide smile. She said yes. Now, they are married with two sons.

Islamic mysticism says that a *sheikh* is the one who holds the seeker's hand in their journey towards God. According to Sabaahat, a *sheikh* is the one who chooses his students the moment they are conceived inside the womb. 'In the spiritual realm, when Allah asked, "Am I not your God?" I said, "Yes." God Almighty sent my *sheikh* to save me.'

Around the time that Sabaahat was a college student at Bosphorus University, what she calls 'anarchists' tried to break into her family's mansion. It took a long time before the police came to Sabaahat and her family's rescue. It was in the late seventies, the peak of fighting between leftist and rightist groups in Turkey. Some 5,000 people died in the violence between right-wing ultra-nationalists and left-wing groups. Sabaahat felt insecure, targeted and confused.

'But I was curious about Islam long before that,' she added. 'My parents were Muslims, but they didn't truly know Islam. "Pray, fast, and that's it," they used to say. The soul of our faith was lacking. I was searching for something to fill that gap in my heart.'

The teachers take away the empty plates and bring chocolate-marzipan cake along with Turkish tea. The tea is poured into a glass with a thin waist. Most Turks I know say that they cannot taste their tea if their fingers aren't touching this particular small teacup. Sabaahat is no exception.

She takes a sip from her hot tea and says, 'I don't understand why the world is fearful of Muslims. We know non-Muslims, and to a certain extent, we have even internalised their thoughts, feelings and lifestyle. They propagate it in the media, on the streets, everywhere. But they don't make the slightest effort to get to know the real us.'

Sabaahat is disappointed that women with headscarves, even more than those who are 'Westernised', show hatred towards women like her and their chadors. 'They are embarrassed by us. They think that the secular segment of Turkish society doesn't accept them because of "extreme examples" like us.'

'Listen, my Meltem-daughter,' Sabaahat says. 'Of course, Muslims want God's rules to reign in the world. But the important thing for a true Muslim is to be able to live Shari'a peacefully even in a secular state. Can I fulfil all the Islamic rules? The answer is yes. This is my Shari'a. This is my Islam. Nobody forces anyone to do anything. All we wish to do is to introduce Islam in a loving environment to the younger generations.'

The rest is small talk. My photojournalist friend says she has taken enough notes. We thank Sabaahat for her kindness and generosity. She tells us it is her duty.

As we pass by the Golden Horn, a narrow and isolated peninsula that separates the historic centre of Istanbul from the rest of the city, the women wearing chadors disappear as if into the past.

Eve: The Enduring Legacy of the Original Dangerous Woman

Katie Scott-Marshall

Katie Scott-Marshall is a writer and communications professional living and working in London. She holds an MA with Distinction in Modern and Contemporary Literature from Newcastle University. Her writing features in the print anthology The Bi-ble: New Testimonials *from independent publisher Monstrous Regiment (2019), and her essays have appeared online with* Moxy Magazine, Entropy, Bright Lights Film Journal *and others.*

When we think of Eve, the notorious 'first' woman in the Book of Genesis in the Old Testament of both the Hebrew and Christian Bibles, we conjure up images of snakes, of forbidden fruit and of the Garden of Eden. The story of Eve is undoubtedly one of the best-known didactic narratives in the world: Adam and Eve, the first man and woman on Earth according to the creation story, happily resided in the Garden of Eden. God's only request of them was that they were not to eat fruit from one of the trees, but Eve was tempted into doing so by a treacherous serpent, and she shared the forbidden fruit with Adam. God punished them by expelling them from the Garden of Eden and condemning Eve to a lifetime of painful childbirth and subservience to her husband:

> I will greatly increase your pangs in childbearing;
> in pain you shall bring forth children
> yet your desire shall be for your husband,
> and he shall rule over you.
>
> Genesis, 3:16

Eve became known as the source of original sin, responsible for the fall of mankind, and she became a blueprint figure for all subsequent women: the reason for their menstrual suffering, their pains during labour, and a cautionary tale as to why they should submit to their husbands. The prevalence of Judeo-Christian discourse in Western culture has meant that the story of Adam and Eve has endured, and over 2,000 years of cultural contributions to the figure of Eve across a range of traditions and disciplines means that a comprehensive biography would be impossible. My intention here, however, is not to recount the story of Eve, but to draw attention to her ongoing reputation as a dangerous and overtly sexualised woman, even in the present day, and to raise the question of what Eve's legacy means for modern women. Ultimately, Eve is just as relevant a figure as ever in womankind's long historical struggle against patriarchal violence.

The story of Adam and Eve still permeates modern culture, and in particular, the association of women with serpents persists in art, literature and popular culture. Indeed, from Debra Paget's erotic snake-charming dance in Fritz Lang's 1959 film *The Indian Tomb* to Britney Spears's iconic performance with a live python on stage at the MTV Music Video Awards in 2001, the serpentine has been inextricably linked with the feminine, and more specifically, with overt displays of female sexuality. A quick Google image search of 'snakes and women' reveals thousands of sexualised images of women and snakes. There is an entire sub-genre of man-eating 'snake lady' movies, positioning the expression of such female sexuality as both intoxicating and threatening, with titles such as *Night of the Cobra Woman* (1972), *The Snake Queen* (1982) and *Snake Club: Revenge of the Snake Woman* (2013). The image is so ingrained – and commercialised – that it is even possible to buy a sticker of Eve and the serpent to be placed on a MacBook, Eve's hand encircling the Apple logo (an apple being most commonly chosen to represent the forbidden fruit). As recently as 2014, an advert for Airwaves chewing gum featured a man going back to a woman's apartment, expecting to spend the night but instead finding her bedroom to be full of snakes and fleeing in horror. The figure of Eve has a highly erotic and sexualised history in various art traditions, having been repeatedly depicted as a nude, particularly during the Renaissance. Perhaps most famous of these is the detail from *Adam and Eve* by Lucas Cranach the Elder (1528), which depicts Eve as naked and with a coy expression on her face while the serpent looks on. She holds an apple in her hand and conceals her sex with a fig leaf.

Throughout history, the serpentine and the feminine have not only been associated, but even conflated, resulting in a number of artistic depictions of the serpent as actually being gendered as a woman, sometimes by having a woman's face or breasts. One such example is *Temptation of Adam and Eve* by Masolino da Panicale (*c.*1425), in which the serpent is depicted with a woman's head and hair the same colour as that of Eve. In Michelangelo's *The Expulsion from Paradise* (1510), too, the serpent has a female anatomy down to the buttocks, whereupon the legs morph into a snake's tail, wrapped around a tree. This conflation is quite transparent in its revelations about society's perceptions of women: the creation story makes it abundantly clear that the snake is a seducer, a liar, a manipulator and a hateful creature sent by the Devil. Take, for example, this passage from Ford Madox Ford's *No More Parades* (1925), the second novel in his quartet *Parade's End*, a classic twentieth-century modernist text including an archetypal 'dangerous woman', the beautiful, selfish and sexually promiscuous temptress Sylvia Tietjens. Her husband imagines her:

> coiled up on a convent bed... Hating... Her certainly glorious hair all around her... Hating... Slowly and coldly... Like the head of a snake when you examined it... Eyes motionless, mouth closed tight... Looking away into the distance and hating...

This cold, negative portrayal of Sylvia as snake-like, 'coiled up' on a bed with 'motionless' eyes, is telling in its association with monstrous femininity. The reader is aware of Sylvia's feminine traits, such as her 'glorious hair', and Christian themes and sexual boundaries are hinted at in the inclusion of the 'convent bed'. The image of the serpent is once again bound with the threat of female sexuality, in view of Sylvia's sexual transgressions, but also with female deception.

The fall of Eve was frequently alluded to in Victorian literature, which often relied on biblical motifs to depict 'fallen women' and mirror society's then-preoccupation with the virgin/whore dichotomy. Thomas Hardy's *Tess of the d'Urbervilles* (1891), a novel which famously chronicles the downfall of its working-class protagonist, Tess, is ripe with imagery and symbolism relating to Eve and the Garden of Eden. Her character is seduced (or more accurately, raped, although critical opinion differs and there is more than one version of the text) by Alec, a devilish sexual libertine, under a tree, echoing Eve's fall from paradise. The name of the forest where this encounter takes place is 'the Chase', in a deliberate nod to the way in which Adam and Eve were chased from the Garden of Eden. The imagery of fruit is used to further consolidate Tess's role as a kind of Eve, with Alec offering her strawberries at one point in the novel, which she accepts. The fallen woman appears as both a weak sinner, vulnerable to seduction, but also as an inadvertent temptress and a sinner of her own making, foreshadowing later media depictions of female sexuality as something threatening and out of control. Franz von Stuck's Victorian-era painting of Eve, *The Sin* (1893), capitalises on the seductress theme and depicts Eve as a dark and sensual woman who is fully complicit with the serpent, her face half-submerged in shadow and the serpent entwined around her, its head at her bare breast.

The Bible declares that Eve was made from the rib of Adam, to be his 'helper', and so she is often cited by traditionalists as evidence of God's intentions for gender essentialism and complementarianism, rather than the idea that gender might be fluid or that full gender equality should exist in terms of shared tasks and responsibilities. Complementarianism, the idea that men and women were created 'equal but different', has been hotly disputed by feminists, theologians and scholars alike. In *The Alphabet of Ben-Sira*, an anonymous medieval Jewish text, Eve is Adam's second wife, and his first is a woman named Lilith. Lilith refuses to have sex with or to submit to Adam, and when he attempts to coerce her into an inferior position, she voluntarily leaves Eden and engages in sexual relations with demons. God sends angels to her, who threaten to kill her new demonic offspring unless she returns to Adam. She refuses, and so God makes a second wife for Adam, Eve. Lilith's character and her fate vary across different sources and texts, but like Eve, she is often depicted in a sexualised manner alongside a snake, which is presumably the same one as that in Genesis. For example, John Collier's 1887 Pre-Raphaelite painting *Lilith* shows a naked Lilith lovingly basking in the attention of two snakes that entwine her legs and torso.

Although the story of Lilith is not commonly known, it is fascinating to consider an alternative figure to Eve from the original paradise narrative, who not only defies patriarchal order but also manages to evade the same punishment. Lilith's rejection of complementarianism and Eve's sentencing to a life of being 'ruled over' by her husband are struggles that carry enormous relevance for modern-day women, who still take up the majority of caring roles and are often assumed to be primarily responsible for child-rearing. A huge number of contemporary feminist issues, including the objectification and sexualisation of women, equality for women in relationships and in the workplace, rape culture, violence against women, and the reproductive value assigned to women – all of which have been at the fore of media conversations about gender and sexuality in the wake of the #MeToo movement – find their origins in biblical scripture, and in Genesis and the creation story in particular. Contemporary feminists have repeatedly argued for Eve's 'punishment' as entirely unjust. In her book *Eve Was Framed: Women and British Justice* (1992) the British lawyer Helena Kennedy has even put forward the case that Eve was set up:

> Transportation from Paradise is one thing, but a sentence of eternal damnation when the conviction had to be based on the uncorroborated testimony of a co-accused must surely constitute a breach of international standards on human rights. Poor old Eve.

Subjecting the creation story to rigorous analysis in fertile and previously unconsidered arenas such as law provides new opportunities to foreground and affect real change. Upon publication, Kennedy's polemic caused a storm in the British courts for its exposure of how the justice system was consistently undermining and disadvantaging women.

It might seem somewhat strange to be appreciative or even in admiration of Eve, given that patriarchal religious traditions so often cite her as the sole cause of all women's woes and encourage us to blame her for them. Of course, for the majority of atheists, she was invented entirely as an example of deviant womanhood in order to provide justification for the oppression of women. Yet the figure of Eve and, perhaps even more so, the lesser-known figure of Lilith are hugely significant in the patriarchy's configuration of women as a threat in the first place. These are not women who submitted to their husband, or even to God. The enduring legacy of Eve is not that of original sin, as we would be led to believe, but of the original dangerous woman. In view of society's longstanding ill treatment of, abuse of and discrimination against women, it is almost comforting for contemporary feminists to remember that the beginnings of Western patriarchal discourse on gender and sexuality started with a rebellious and transgressive woman.

Thecla: Dangerous 'Chick Lit'

Catherine Kennedy

Catherine Kennedy is a PhD candidate at the University of Sheffield investigating Bible materials for children and the communities which use them.

What did a dangerous woman look like in the ancient world? A temptress like Cleopatra was a one-off and so arguably not dangerous for long. There was no Cleopatra ideology to inspire a movement. In contrast, perhaps the most socially disruptive women of the Greco-Roman world were as far from the glamour of Cleopatra as could be, and they are brilliantly represented by the fictional heroines they created. My favourite of these is Thecla. Thecla is quite a gal: part nude Xena warrior princess, part St Clare dispensing alms to the poor and the good word to anyone who'll listen. To be fair, she only ever sets out to play the second role, but like any dangerous woman she attracts some unwanted attention and in fighting it off she lands herself in the Roman arena fighting for her life. Just as well God is on her side!

Thecla appears in the *Apocryphal Acts of Paul and Thecla*, an entertaining little book which was penned around the time of the biblical pastoral epistles – the ones addressed to Timothy, and from 'Peter' and 'John'. In this apocryphal book, a character called Paul is travelling around the Empire preaching a new religion which venerates a certain Jesus. His message is slightly different from the biblical one, involving swearing off sex as a basic condition for salvation. Young people flock from far and wide and decide to stay single. Wives leave their husbands or refuse them their conjugal rights... this probably won't end well.

In other books of *Apocryphal Acts* women drive a husband to suicide (Agrippina), cause another woman to be murdered (Agrippina again), desert their live-in lover together (the four concubines of prefect Agrippa), flee naked by night from an amorous husband (Mygdonia) and get imprisoned in a tomb and miraculously rescued (Drusiana). The original 'Princess Bride' is another of these colourful stories. The ethics are often questionable, but the plot lines are as dramatic as secular novels from the time, where star-crossed lovers are abducted by pirates, threatened by cannibals and generally have a hard time. The crucial difference is that in the secular stories, true love of the heterosexual married kind conquers all, whereas in the apocryphal plot lines marriage and sex are precisely what the women are all desperate to escape. With implacable resolve. As fanciful as these stories may be, they reflect the deadly serious threats any woman could face if she dared to question the inevitability of marriage; threats which remain a pressing reality for many women and girls across the world today.

At the start of her tale, Thecla is a privileged teenager engaged to a rich young man chosen by her mother. The absence of a father suggests that the mother, Theoclia, has remained single after being widowed in order to retain control of her fortune and her daughter. Many wealthy women in antiquity did this rather than surrender their freedom again, although it was hardly a working-class option. In a perfect world, this independent-minded mother would empathise with a headstrong daughter, but the world is not perfect and Theoclia proves to be the sort of mother who takes disobedience personally.

Thecla overhears Paul preaching his celibate Christianity in the house next door and she is fascinated. For days she hangs on his every word through her bedroom window and refuses to come down for meals. Her fiancé is sent to talk some sense into her, to no avail. He takes it badly and has the preacher arrested for disturbing the peace by persuading women not to marry and to become bad wives. So that night Thecla creeps out of the house and bribes her way into the cells. Falling at his feet, she begs Paul to preach to her in person.

Meanwhile, the whole town is out looking for her and when she is found there is uproar. Teenaged rebellion is not recommended for girls in antiquity. Thecla is not just a class traitor; she has betrayed her sex by refusing to marry and betrayed her mother by publicly refusing to back down. Theoclia demands her daughter be burned at the stake as a warning to other youngsters who might get uppity after hearing this newfangled religion. The governor passes sentence on the spot and Thecla is only saved by divine intervention.

At this point, we can be sure we are dealing with fiction. However, while Roman courts may not have actually been in the habit of executing disobedient daughters of the aristocracy, girls were not at liberty to refuse their parents' choice of suitor. Marriage and childbearing were legal obligations, and fathers made and unmade their offspring's marriages as suited their business interests. The paterfamilias had theoretical power of life and death over his children as long as he lived for much of Roman history and what went on behind closed doors was entirely the householder's business where discipline was concerned. The 'honour' killing attempted against Thecla is fiction, but it was fiction with a point to make. No woman was free in such a system, and for some, the best option was to opt out altogether.

On with Thecla's adventure. Paul has been flogged and thrown out of town, so Thecla sets out after him and they travel to a different city. Here, a local chap takes a fancy to her and tries to 'embrace' her in the street. Thecla is having none of it. She beats off her attacker, yelling that she's not faced death by refusing one man to end up being mistreated by another. Predictably, he takes offence and drags her into court, where it turns out that he is a big noise and pals with the governor. She is condemned to die by wild animals as a public spectacle. There is an outcry, with the ladies of the town taking her side, but they don't make the rules. Thecla is paraded into the theatre naked and battles valiantly for two days with various creatures (including man-eating seals), being saved each time by some miracle. Ultimately the authorities give up and she is freed to rejoin Paul, who gives her his blessing to go on her way as a fully fledged believer and teacher of their version of Christianity. The richest of her supporters, now her adoptive mother, signs a vast fortune over to her and Thecla sets out on a life of poor relief and preaching. She is everything the writers of the Pastoral Epistles feared: not under male control, not shut in the house, taking a role in public instruction and attracting hostile pagan attention. Quite the 'nasty' woman.

So why was sex a problem when antiquity was so open about it? Victorian prudery was a long way off, but the idea that sex was entirely unspiritual was quite widespread across the Greco-Roman world, and committed philosophers often formed celibate communities. Philo of Alexandria describes one of these, the Therapeutae, in glowing terms, with women as full members. Whether these were all widows deemed to have 'done their bit' for keeping up the birth rate Philo doesn't say, but we can be fairly sure that they were not just walking in off the street. Membership would have required independent means and the right connections. The ancients were terrible snobs and a life of contemplation was quite beyond ordinary folk. People of breeding clung to the idea that only the well-bred could attempt life on a higher plane.

And being a woman was very much second-best. The female body was deemed less human, less perfect, than the male. Women couldn't help it. Their reproductive functions just got in the way of them ever growing up and becoming rational, spiritual grown-ups. (Yes, the two went together back then.) The best they could hope for was to become an honorary man by avoiding using their plumbing for making babies. These biological ideas went back a very long way, even at the time, and although early Christianity went out of its way to stress that ladies were just as 'saved' as gentlemen, the combination of powerlessness that went with marriage and the stigma attached to female biology, inspired many Christian women to go celibate and enjoy a life of independence where they could get out and about, working and doing their own thing in all-female communities. They genuinely felt this was a net gain, and theirs was one of the first belief systems to support that sort of choice. Unlike the philosophers, these were ordinary women making an unorthodox choice which attracted condemnation from mainstream society. It was their ordinariness, their refusal to bow to male supervision and their firm belief that everyone and anyone could lay claim to their intellectual independence which made them dangerous. As Thecla illustrates, any woman or girl who gets wind of the fact that she is a person in her own right may just walk out on everyone's expectations and discover that she has it in her to take on the world.

Celibate female communities were extremely controversial in an age where a stigmatised group might fall foul of a lynch-mob or judicial discrimination. Not on the scale of Thecla's adventures, to be sure, but the pressures and dangers symbolised in the narrative were real. As the Church became ever more institutionalised, female independence was often seen as problematic there as well. But the all-female groups continued to reinvent themselves and flourish as environments where women could realise their potential. They are currently very much on the wane. Since modern developments in medicine and in relationships have broadened women's options, it is easy to forget that for these very early foremothers of feminism, religion and celibacy were revolutionary and empowering. Far from being hamstrung by a quest for male approval or seeking after their ultimate 'soulmate', these dangerous women were proving that they needed no one but themselves and their beliefs to live to the fullest.

Further Reading

'The Acts of Paul and Thecla'. In Elliott, J.K., trans., 1993. *The Apocryphal New Testament.* Oxford: Oxford University Press. Available at: www.tonyburke.ca/wp-content/uploads/Acts-Paul-Thecla.pdf

Davies, S., 1980. *The Revolt of the Widows.* London: Feffer & Simons, Inc.

MacDonald, M.Y., 1996. *Early Christian Women and Pagan Opinion.* Cambridge: Cambridge University Press.

Torjesen, K.J., 1995. *When Women Were Priests.* New York, NY: HarperCollins.

A Dangerous Woman Speaks of Her Bewilderment...

Jo Clifford

Jo Clifford is a playwright, performer, proud father and grandmother who lives in Edinburgh. She is the author of over 100 plays, many of which have been performed all over the world. These include Losing Venice, Every One, Faust *and* The Tree of Knowledge. *Her* Great Expectations *makes her the first openly transgendered woman playwright to have had a play in London's West End. Recent work includes* Eve, *which she wrote and performed for a National Theatre of Scotland production. Other recent successes include* Five Days Which Changed Everything *on BBC Radio 4 and* The Taming of the Shrew *at the Sherman, Cardiff, and the Tron in Glasgow. She revived her* Gospel According to Jesus, Queen of Heaven, *also at the Tron Theatre, Glasgow, for its tenth anniversary in 2019, before taking it to Birmingham and São Paulo. During lockdown she has been creating online work for the National Theatre of Scotland, Pitlochry, Paines Plough, the Royal Lyceum in Edinburgh, and filming a weekly online blessing from Queen Jesus. You can find more information and her blog on www.teatrodomundo.com and www.queenjesusproductions.com*

Somebody has made a film about me on YouTube. The man is filming himself sitting in his car outside the church in which I am performing.

He tells the camera that what I am doing is against the canon law of the Church of England and he holds up a much-thumbed book to prove it.

The book is the canon law of the Church of England, apparently, and it looks like it's the poor man's only line of defence against a disturbing and dangerous world.

A world that is disturbing and dangerous because I am in it.

He says he's been invited in to talk about it, but he can't go in. He has to go and preach the word of the Lord.

And besides it's perishing cold.

And he starts his engine and he drives away.

And as I watch him, I think: is this really about me? Am I obviously so dangerous?

Apparently, I'm worse.

There's another film just next to his which talks of me with the greatest scorn and derision.

But which at the same time warns its listeners that I am one of the ungodly men spoken about in the book of Jude (1:4).

That I'm bringing the grace of God into lasciviousness and immorality.

Worse even than that: what I am saying is blasphemous, damnable heresy.

It is a sign, apparently, a sign of the Last Days and the imminent coming of the end of the world.

And my picture comes up on the screen and the voice says:

'Here is the demon playing Jesus.'

And that's me.

Why am I a demon? Demons are dangerous, aren't they?

I thought I was a human being.

A human being with a woman's passport and a birth certificate to tell the world I am female.

So why am I a danger? What have I done?

After years of trying to hide the truth from myself and from the world, I have begun to live as a woman. And I find, for the first time in my life, that I feel comfortable in my own skin.

Is that so very dangerous?

And I have written, and performed, a play which imagines Jesus coming back to earth in the present day as a trans woman.

A play in which she reminds her audience that the most important thing in the Gospel is that we learn to love each other and that we do not pass judgement.

Is that so dangerous?

It seemed like such an obvious thing to me, and I still can't really understand why it enraged so many people so much that they demonstrated in the street outside the theatre where I first performed it.

Or why an archbishop should take the trouble to denounce me. As a dangerous affront to the Christian faith.

Am I so strong? Or the Christian faith so weak?

And why did hundreds and thousands of people feel it necessary to express their online anger and rage against me?

Is their sense of identity so fragile?

Or the whole structure of gender in our world so weak?

Is it because women are dangerous?

Or because when in my play Jesus tells us to love our neighbour, it is the truth?

Is the truth so dangerous?

I don't really understand. I don't want to be dangerous. I

want to be able to love my family, write my plays, enjoy beautiful music, cook delicious meals and enjoy the sensation of being true to my own dear self.

But perhaps these, too, are dangerous.

Perhaps to try to live a decent life in indecent times is dangerous:

A clear and present danger in so dangerous a world.

When Lesbians Became Dangerous: The New Woman Discourses of the Fin de Siècle

Laurie Garrison

Laurie Garrison has a PhD in Victorian literature from the University of London and an MSc in Human Computer Interaction from the University of York. She is the author of Science, Sexuality and Sensation Novels: Pleasures of the Senses *(Palgrave, 2010) and general editor of* The Panorama: Texts and Contexts *(Pickering and Chatto, 2012). She is currently balancing the writing of a novel about William Morris in Iceland with volunteer work for the Women Writers Network and a series of day jobs in User Experience Research.*

We can identify a specific moment in history when lesbians became dangerous, nearly down to the exact year. We might argue that it was in 1893, when Sarah Grand coined the term 'new woman' in a media debate with the novelist Ouida. Or that it was in 1892, when Richard von Krafft-Ebing used the term 'lesbian' to describe women who were sexually attracted to women in *Psychopathia Sexualis*. In any case, this was the moment when a popular (rather than medical) discourse of the

New Woman became synonymous with rebellious, masculine women who preferred the company of other women. Regardless of where the precise starting point was, the *fin de siècle* saw a growing discourse of the New Woman that represented a threat to man's position as the only gender that could be professionally employed, earn a living and support dependent family members.

So widespread was the discourse of the New Woman that we can find examples in every level of writing – from high literary texts to the very popular and now obscure. Vivie Warren from George Bernard Shaw's *Mrs Warren's Profession* is perhaps the most famous example. Vivie takes honours in the mathematics exam at Cambridge and refuses any sort of ordinary life in favour of doing actuarial calculations in her friend Honoria Fraser's chambers in Chancery Lane. Other examples include Olive Chancellor in Henry James's *The Bostonians* or Rhoda Nunn in George Gissing's *The Odd Women*. Rhoda Nunn, like Vivie Warren, eschews male companionship and marriage for the independence of running a business, one that works to prepare women to financially support themselves. Along with Sarah Grand, women who wrote about the New Woman included novelists Olive Schreiner and Mona Caird. The New Woman was a regular figure in the popular press, and she was satirised by *Punch*. The New Woman was also a type in reality: a feminist campaigner who had newly become a threat to patriarchy, as the work of first-wave feminism started to come to fruition in the *fin de siècle*.

Prior to the *fin de siècle*, discourses of female same-sex desire could be found in both medical and popular texts. However, in order to locate them in medical texts, we must look to the many treatises on sexual health that were circulating during this time. These were usually written with the purpose of curing masturbation, which was considered a harmful addiction. The more famous and widespread examples include Henry Smith's *The Private Medical Friend,* Tissot's *A New Guide to Health and Long Life,* or the book that has been considered a Victorian birth control manual, *Elements of Social Science* by George Drysdale.

These sexual health manuals focused primarily on men and male sexuality. The reason for this was that masturbation was seen to be more of a problem for men. Male masturbation had both physical and social consequences. It was believed that masturbators were plagued with a loss of energy, a wasted look and increasingly antisocial habits. For female masturbators, which were always assumed to be much fewer in number, the consequences were almost entirely social and only a threat in the most extreme circumstances. Most female masturbators would become timid and antisocial, and a smaller number might become prostitutes or be driven to adultery. Women who masturbated were thought to be suffering from a pathologically intense form of sexual desire. Masturbators often learned 'the habit' – as it was usually referred to in these popular medical works – from other women in all-female settings, such as boarding schools. Most could be cured. Some women supposedly became uninterested in sex with their husbands, preferring masturbation instead. However, there is little anxiety that women may honestly prefer women to men in these texts. The worry is more that female masturbators will have sex with large numbers of partners, male and female alike.

These medical discourses can be seen in the literature of the early to mid-nineteenth century, in the sense that female same-sex relationships were transgressive but not deeply threatening. In Samuel Taylor Coleridge's long poem *Christabel,* a strange woman called Geraldine comes to visit and entices Christabel into bed with her. In Joseph Sheridan Le Fanu's *Carmilla,* the heroine is seduced by Carmilla until the relationship is discovered and the vampire slain. In both narratives, women transgress with other women, but there is no real threat to the practical, everyday heterosexual order. There is no possibility that Christabel and Geraldine or Carmilla and Laura will forge a life together separate from men. Another example of female same-sex desire can be found in Wilkie Collins's *The Woman in White,* where the characters Marian and Laura frequently express their intimacy with kisses, touches and sleeping in the same bed. At the end of the novel, Laura marries the hero Walter and they live with Marian in an oddly triangular relationship. Nonetheless, Laura and Walter have a child together. With the women needing to rely on Walter financially, their intimate relationship is no real threat to patriarchy.

By the *fin de siècle,* medical discourses of female same-sex desire changed considerably and were no longer confined to discussions of masturbation. In Krafft-Ebing's *Psychopathia Sexualis,* four types of lesbianism are documented, ranging from mild and curable to intense and incurable. Interestingly, the trajectory of mild to intense is determined by the extent to which the woman looks and behaves like a man. The woman who falls into the most extreme category 'possesses of the feminine qualities only the genital organs'. Lesbianism is directly linked with the adoption of traditionally male behaviours and 'may nearly always be suspected in females wearing their hair short, or who dress in the fashion of men, or pursue the sports and pastimes of their male acquaintances'. Havelock Ellis argued in *Sexual Inversion* in 1897 that the women's movement 'must be regarded on the whole as a wholesome and inevitable movement' but that 'It has involved an increase in feminine criminality and feminine insanity ... In connection with these we are scarcely surprised to find an increase in homosexuality'. Overall, these medical texts about sexuality focus more on social behaviour than sexual practice in order to establish their markers of deviancy.

Throughout New Woman novels as a genre, the struggle between those who want to preserve the social order and those who want to transform it can be seen over and over. In Henry James's *The Bostonians*, for example, this very struggle is at the heart of the plot. Olive Chancellor, the New Woman figure of the novel, is hard and deliberate. She believes in things so strongly that she intimidates nearly everyone she interacts with. Basil Ransom, her cousin and nemesis, detests the idea of any sort of reform, especially that of the women's movement. He refers to Olive as 'morbid'. Their ideological struggle is played out through their rivalry for the love of Verena Tarrant, the daughter of an itinerant performer who discovers and exploits his daughter's unique talent for public speaking, especially about the wrongs of women, while she is in a sort of trance. Early in the novel, Olive is not a sympathetic character. She is financially independent and comes to support Verena, who lives with her for a time. However, once the tables turn and Basil becomes engaged to Verena, our sympathies are guided to Olive. Patriarchy wins over the woman who wants to support her lover, but it is at a very great cost, having left both Olive and Verena bereft of their relationship. James has long been assumed to have experienced same-sex desire himself, which might explain this awareness and apparent sympathy for Olive.

New Woman novels written by women were much less likely to include manly women and their love interests. This does not mean that female same-sex desire did not exist in these novels.

Rather, female New Woman writers were more likely to look to the past when writing romantic relationships between women. Such relationships can be seen in Mona Caird's *The Daughters of Danaus* or Isabella Ford's *On the Threshold.* Like Wilkie Collins's depiction of a romantic friendship between women, New Woman novelists wanted to highlight the sense of sisterhood, collaboration and mutual support that could be achieved between women, whether this was a sexual relationship or not. In fact, it is arguably easier to identify New Women in reality who had intense, quite possibly sexual relationships with other women. Regardless of Olive Schreiner's support of heterosexual relationships in *Woman and Labour*, she was known to have had very close, arguably romantic friendships with her fellow New Woman writers Eleanor Marx and Amy Levy. Perhaps most famously, Katharine Harris Bradley and Edith Emma Cooper lived and wrote poetry together under the pseudonym Michael Field.

Writers and activists of the late nineteenth-century women's movement did indeed have to be careful how they made their arguments. Increasing power of decision for women when it came to marriage, divorce or sexual partners could easily be dismissed by detractors as a slippery slope that would lead to moral depravity rather than a more equitable social order. The increasing recognition and representation of the newly termed 'lesbians' associated with the women's movement came primarily from a reaction against it. Because the new discourse of female same-sex desire was largely negative, New Woman writers did not often take it up. It was too difficult to twist it into something closer to the positive representations of women's romantic friendship that they wanted to promote. Thus, the dominant discourse of female same-sex desire in the *fin de siècle* was that of the dangerous lesbian. I would argue that it would not be until the publication of Virginia Woolf's *Orlando* in 1928 that a representation of a lesbian in literature offered a clearly positive alternative to the manly New Woman.

Shaming the Shameless: What Is Dangerous About Anaïs Nin?

Ruth Charnock

Dr Ruth Charnock is a writer, artist and independent researcher. Her work, which is often at the intersections of the creative and the critical, is interested in contemporary culture, feminism, gender and affect. Her latest edited collection Joni Mitchell: New Critical Readings *was published by Bloomsbury in 2019. She is currently writing a book about Anaïs Nin, bad sex and shame.*

Anaïs Nin went from being a marginal writer from the 1930s, known only for being Henry Miller's mistress, if at all, to a feminist icon in the early 1970s and a doyenne of erotic fiction in the late 1970s, to a figure for critical derision in the 1990s when a journal detailing Nin's incestuous relationship with her father was published. Since then, her cultural star has been on the wane, although her name surfaces occasionally in unexpected places: on the name of a perfume bottle, or as an exemplar for communication in the digital age.

As a whole, though, nobody has paid much attention to Anaïs Nin since the 1990s, when her attitudes, writing style and cultural persona were widely trashed by the voices of 'high' culture. Certainly, you would be hard pushed to find anyone in quarters such as the *New York Times* literary pages who would think of Nin as dangerous. 'Shameless self-promoter', 'nymphomaniac' and 'fabulist' would be fairer guesses.

What is it about Anaïs Nin, then, that could possibly be deemed 'dangerous'?

I didn't start out by being ashamed of Anaïs Nin. No doubt, reading *Delta of Venus* for the first time around nine was something I kept hidden, but it was titillation, intrigue and mystification that ruled – feelings allowed to flourish in secret but without fear of being caught, blushing and reading, in a childhood home, and without a concept of unsuitable reading material. Yet through the course of my PhD, which looked at the way Nin disrupts narratives of intimacy in psychoanalytic, feminist and modernist cultures, I started to feel uncomfortable about working on a writer who seemed to command so little critical respect in academic fora.

Giving papers at conferences became an exercise in negotiating other people's titillation and/or disapproval, particularly when I was discussing Nin's relationship with her father – a relationship that turned sexual when she was in her thirties and he was in his fifties. Responses ranged from the disgusted (a disgust that always, incidentally, accreted around Nin and not her father) to the prurient. 'Oh, yes,' sighed one male academic, who barely held back from rubbing his knees, 'I remember reading her erotica in the seventies. But she never wrote anything *serious*, did she?'

Responses such as the latter, which came from female academics as much as male, made me feel uneasy in ways that I couldn't, initially, pinpoint. I had anticipated that academic audiences might balk not just at the fact of Nin's affair with her father, but the way in which she renders it: as a swooning piece of romantic fiction. Unarguably, too, there is much that might produce the wrong kind of rise in Nin's erotica – in particular, she presents scenes of pederasty not only without moral judgement, but with a sympathetic, kindly attitude towards her paedophiles. However, whilst Nin's refusal to occupy a position of judgement, shame or condemnation when it came to either her own sex life or the lives of her fictional characters struck me as complex, politically radical and provocative, for many of my interlocutors the facts (and fictions) of Nin's sex life engendered a desire to shut her down. She was a liar, a nymphomaniac, mad. At best, she was the author of moderately successful (and one wonders quite how this success was being measured) erotic fiction – a curio of the modernist Left Bank who floated to the surface, briefly, in the 1970s. There was little else to be said – bearing in mind that she never wrote anything really 'serious'.

Faced with these reactions, wanting to be a serious academic myself, I began to dislike Anaïs Nin and dislike having to talk about her in public. Whereas I had long believed Nin was a dangerous woman for all the right reasons – she was fearless; she went into the stuffiest, most patriarchal-seeming spaces, such as the psychoanalyst's office, and shook them up; she believed, to the last, in her own artistry despite constant disbelief from others – it began to seem as if Nin was going to be dangerous for my career, dangerous for me in all the wrong ways.

Somewhere around the time of taking up my first full-time job, I must have made the decision (although I can't remember when or how) to stop writing, thinking and talking about her. She became my dirty little secret. At the time, I didn't think of my turn away from Nin as playing it safe – it felt, rather, as if I had done all I could with her. But, looking back, I wonder if the constant fielding of prurient or censorious comments had inculcated in me the sense that to work on Nin was to place my own legitimacy as an academic under suspicion.

Coming back to Nin, almost five years after I submitted my PhD, I have realised that what is most dangerous about her is not just the type of sex she had, or who she had it with, or how she wrote about it, but the fact that all three combined have the power to make us feel so uncomfortable. It was this discomfort that I wanted to back away from as a PhD researcher and it is the same discomfort that I wanted to theorise in my forthcoming book on Nin: *Anaïs Nin: bad sex, shame and contemporary culture.* In it, I argue that it is the points at which Nin has most irritated critics – which are the moments at which she has appeared to be the most shameless in her attitude towards sex – that have the most to offer us in handling contemporary depictions of sex and shame. The reason Nin feels so uncomfortable, so dangerous to read, is because she refuses to be ashamed of the kinds of sex conventionally deemed as shameful. Nin's shamelessness is frightening because it reveals the potential for different kinds of sexual and romantic relationships, as well as also staring the titillated, passive consumer of transgressive/taboo sex writing in the eye.

During my PhD, I became preoccupied with parsing the often venomously hostile reviews that have greeted Nin's work, both fictional and autobiographical, from its earliest publication onwards. All of the most negative reviews (and there are plenty), but particularly those that greeted the publication of Nin's unexpurgated diary *Incest* in 1990, hum with indignation, irritation and, often, disgust at Nin's sex life. Time and again, critics cast her as brazen, a nymphomaniac, a fabulist, blind to her own bad writing, narcissistic, a monstrous seductress. They wonder at her gall or her neuroses, depending on persuasion –

how could she sleep with her father and write about it in great, lurid detail and yet these accounts display no embarrassment, humiliation or disgust? Where is her shame? When critics are disgusted with Nin, when they find her shameful in some way, it is more often than not when she is shameless and so at her most dangerous.

Put simply: Nin is dangerous where she is most shameless, and she is most shameless when it comes to our culturally held sexual taboos – those to do with incest, non-monogamy and S&M, to mention just three of the terrains Nin's work explores. As taboos, these are dangerous terrains. And, particularly in her treatment of incest, Nin refuses to tread the prescribed path.

Nin slept with her father in her early thirties and described it as 'a great adventure'. She lived for around thirty years as a bigamist, reasoning that this was the only way she could embody all of her potential: as a lover and wife. In order to keep her two lives on separate tracks, she developed a complex index card system of lies, half-lies and pseudonyms. Prior to her bigamy, she revelled in numerous, often simultaneous affairs – undoing the contracts of monogamy and marriage again and again. Often residing at the borders of her own sanity, she sought out those who felt dangerous too: artists such as June Miller, Henry Miller, Antonin Artaud.

Then she invited these fellow hedonists and nihilists to take one more step with her towards the edge: of their capacity to feel, of their creative practice, and of their sexual identities. She seduced her psychoanalysts. She set up her own printing press and painstakingly hand-cranked every individual letter of her novels. She was a Surrealist amongst the Beats in Greenwich Village, an audacious fabulist in the confessional consciousness-raising groups of the 1970s. She rewrote whole swathes of her diary for public consumption and then denied any rewriting had taken place. She lied about her age, she denied she was married. She spoke in front of feminist audiences but refused to define herself as a feminist. Instead, she wrote a book entitled *In Favor of the Sensitive Man*. In short, Nin is an exemplar of what it means to live without limits. This certainly makes her dangerous as far as cultural conventions, and those who would seek to espouse and uphold them, are concerned.

Nin is dangerous because she makes us feel things that we don't want to feel. She embarrasses, shocks and arouses us in equal measure. In her life, she slept with whoever she wanted to, flouted cultural convention at every opportunity, and refused to stay comfortable in what, ostensibly, was a comfortable existence: as the wife of a wealthy, adoring banker. In her writing, she refuses to moralise. Instead, she shows us the dingiest, most labyrinthine corners of human sexuality and relationships: the petty deceits, the self-aggrandisements, the fetishes, power games and transgressions. Reading Nin can be frightening because of how she revels in excess. Where one adjective would do, she uses three. Her characters 'ensorcell' (a Nin favourite), enchant, seduce and rant. She refused all editing of her writing, and thus reading it feels like following the gradually unfurling thread of someone's madness. Nin was a self-confessed graphomaniac: writing page after page of a diary that, initially at least, she hoped no one would read, so filled was it with secret affairs, desires and others' confidences.

It is not that Nin invented a new kind of sex – and she certainly wasn't the first to have transgressive sex and to write about it. But the vociferous critical opprobrium that she has attracted over the years suggests that there is something very particular about her way of having, and writing about, sex that feels culturally dangerous. I think this is why Nin's work has either been discounted or denigrated for so long, and why it is so crucial to theorising our own attitudes towards sex and shame in the contemporary world.

Anaïs Nin's writing sometimes forces, sometimes cajoles us into asking:

Why are there such different standards for sexual conduct when it comes to men and women?

Why slut-shaming, but no male equivalent? Why slut-shaming at all?

And what is it that feels dangerous when we read a woman writing, fearlessly, about sex?

Confronting the Black Jezebel Stereotype: The Contentious Legacy of Brenda Fassie, South Africa's Pop Princess

Chisomo Kalinga

Dr Chisomo Kalinga is a Wellcome Trust Medical Humanities Fellow in the Department of Social Anthropology at the University of Edinburgh. Her Wellcome project is titled 'Ulimbaso "You will be strong again": How literary aesthetics and storytelling inform concepts of health and wellbeing in Malawi.' It examines how indigenous literary practices (performance, form and aesthetics) are used to address community health. Her research interests are disease (specifically sexually transmitted infections), illness and wellbeing, biomedicine, traditional healing and witchcraft and their narrative representation in African oral and print literatures. She is working with colleagues at College of Medicine and Malawi University of Science and Technology in Malawi to support the Malawi Medical Humanities Network (www.malawimedhumsnetwork.com). She is also an Africa section editor of the forthcoming Palgrave Medical Humanities Reference book on Race and Ethnicity.

The South African pop singer Brenda Fassie (3 November 1964–9 May 2004) was affectionately titled 'MaBrrr' by her fans and proclaimed by *Time* magazine as the 'Madonna of the Townships'. Her outspoken, brazen and rebellious personality garnered unparalleled notoriety across Africa. She has long reigned supreme in my memory as the embodiment of the ultimate African diva (and you need only do a quick image search to see the variety of personas she inhabited).

On stage, she played the muse; her voice was melodic and her dancing, particularly when she wore traditional beaded Zulu-inspired miniskirts, was playful and vivacious. In her personal life, her indulgence and bacchanalian exploits were well documented in the media. Her drug and alcohol abuse also drew comparisons to other fallen idols, as *Vice* magazine branded her the 'African Edith Piaf'. But these Eurocentric monikers never afforded full justice to the complex and unique figure she was in Africa. She neither hid her addictions from the public nor did she retreat from inquisitions into her tumultuous relationships with both men and women lovers, which played out in the tabloids for most of her two-decade career.

By traditional and conservative African standards, she was by all means not a 'good girl'.

The full force of her provocativeness only made her superstardom across the continent even more enigmatic. This is taking into account the double standard that embraces the same level of self-destructiveness from male artists as a nuance that complements their creative genius. And yet, despite her over-the-top and out-of-control diva personality, she was respected by her contemporaries throughout Africa and transcended the standard of success for black women set by her dignified elders such as singers Dixie Kwankwa, Dorothy Masuka and Miriam Makeba.

On the one hand, her popularity was justly gained through her presentation of powerful ballads about injustice such as 'Black President' (1990), a call to arms for the release of the then incarcerated Nelson Mandela, which became an international hit and a rallying cry against apartheid. In 'Sum' Bulala' ('Please Don't Kill Her/Him') (1997), she pleaded with South African taxi drivers to end escalating violence amongst rival operators in townships.

On the other hand, it was her carefree stage persona as evidenced in a 2001 performance of her best-selling, upbeat wedding song 'Vul'Indlela'('Open the Gates') (1997) that embodied everything that the public loved about Brenda.

She pranced barefoot in a short dress and jumped in the air, landing in the splits position with her pants exposed in the presence of Nobel Peace Prize Laureate and then President of the Republic of South Africa, Nelson Mandela. Every audacious move was met with cheers of support. Moments later, she leaped offstage and danced her way towards his table, first into the arms of his wife, Graça Machel, and then his. She pulled him away from his table and coquettishly pleaded with him to sing with her: 'Madiba… please, sing! Please, please!' He offered one abrupt syllable into her microphone before giving up. Her message was clear. At that moment, she, and only she, was in charge. And she had won him and the entire audience over.

Perhaps few outside the African continent are familiar with her legacy as a singer, a cultural icon and an outrageous success story to rise from the segregated townships of Cape Town. When IASH introduced the Dangerous Women Project and called for essays reflecting upon the question 'What does it mean to be a dangerous woman?', I felt compelled to share Brenda's story within the context of the black Jezebel narrative and stereotypes of black female sexuality that should have hindered her rise to fame.

Brenda was known as the 'bad girl' whose music even *gogos* (grandmothers) liked to dance to. Her success was in part defined by an unapologetic command of her sexuality both on and off stage. She was a libertine and *enfant terrible*, yet she strategically confronted the Jezebel stereotype by challenging racial binaries and heterosexist patriarchies that sustained this narrative within the South African apartheid social construct. Her celebration of South African traditions in her image and sound created an important space for deconstructing black female autonomy.

Despite the turbulence that affected her personal relationships, her fame and popularity were buoyed by her fans' acceptance of her narrative of empowerment against detrimental interpretations of black identity promoted by the apartheid regime. From the late 1990s onwards, her songs were less focused on English language, in favour of Sotho, Xhosa and Zulu. On stage and in her videos, she adorned herself in personalised traditional costumes reflecting the versatility of South Africa's indigenous textile cultures. Her music, which was first infused with Western pop sounds, soon adopted the local kwaito beats, a late twentieth-century African aesthetic that emanated from South African townships. For a brief overview of her career, have a look at Liz McGregor's 2004 obituary in the *Guardian*.

Watching Brenda Fassie in recordings of her performances, interviews and music videos, I often feel that she did not contrive to brand herself into an African feminist icon. Rather, there was an innate and raw disdain for injustice and oppression that informed her style, performance, imagination and sound. If her rebellion was ingrained, it perhaps was tested by a combination of her nature and a reaction against the apartheid state that she grew up in.

The black Jezebel narrative, within the context of feminist thought, is a trope that establishes a distorted and dehumanising framework to hypersexualise and objectify black women's sexuality; it historically demeans and overshadows the complexity and diversity of romantic experiences faced by women of colour. In its historical roots, particularly in the context of the European colonisation of Africa and the transatlantic slave trade to the Americas, it attributes shame and culpability for sexual interactions between white men and black women as a result of entrapment due to the manipulative and lascivious nature of African women, as Evie Shockley explains in her article 'Buried Alive'.

The stereotype traces its origins to hermeneutical interpretations of the New Testament in the Book of Kings; Jezebel was a Phoenician princess and idol worshipper who persuaded her husband, King Ahab, to abandon worship of Yahweh (God) in favour of pagan deities. In artistic representations, she is portrayed as a lascivious, dangerous woman who uses her sexuality to lure men into sin and other misdeeds. Hence, applications of the black Jezebel stereotype during colonialism, postcolonialism, slavery and the Jim Crow era justified rape, sexual exploitation and degradation of black women by emphasising their feral sexual nature. Augustine Asaah, in 'Images of Rape in African Fiction', affirms that dominance over the African female body in creative representation continues to be framed by histories of postcolonial patriarchy, particularly in depictions of women's sexuality.

In African culture, the question 'Is she a good girl?' at face value is a polite inquiry; however, this question can also be a thinly veiled code to ascertain the level of promiscuous behaviour that a woman engages in. It reflects the conventional way that women are viewed within the troubling binary of either a 'respectable', 'honourable' African lady or a 'prostitute'. The anglophone African application of the word 'prostitute' classifies a spectrum of women who engage in sexual activities that involve premarital sex, particularly with multiple partners. This is contrasted with common applications of the word in a Western construct where it either identifies sex industry workers or is meant to insult a woman's sexual agency by associating her with sex workers.

The woman who has been labelled a prostitute in African discourse is devoid of humanity and is usually depicted as the source of demise, particularly through disease; she exists only to entrap the morally conflicted male to teach a lesson about promiscuity.

She is a Jezebel.

Paula Treichler examined the dialogue about female sexuality during the AIDS epidemic and revealed that although scientific discourse had a tendency to present women in general as 'incompetent transmitters of HIV, passive receptacles', this consideration did not apply to African women and sex workers. She argues in her 1999 article 'AIDS, Homophobia and Biomedical Discourse' that these two specific types of women in the public imagination were:

> seen as so contaminated that their bodies are virtual laboratory cultures for viral replication. ... [Their] exotic bodies, sexual practices, are seen to be so radically different from those of women in the [West] that anything can happen in them.

It demonstrates the severity to which the black Jezebel narrative had become entrenched in anthropological, communal and scientific understandings of black female sexuality.

Brenda Fassie used her music as a platform to confront *both* the African 'good girl' and 'Jezebel' narratives. In her song 'Good Black Woman' (1989), she woefully pleaded against her brother's imprisonment to apartheid police officers. Her frustration powered the melody, as she chastised the officers for having a bad attitude towards her and appealed to them to respect her value as a 'good black woman': one who fights against injustice.

While her music provided one avenue to discuss injustices against women, particularly during apartheid, she also used it as a platform to challenge perceptions that a measure of a woman's 'goodness' is conditional on her sexual demureness. In her aptly titled dance track 'I Am Not A Bad Girl' (1990), she responded to media criticism about her behaviour by declaring that she's not a bad girl seeking publicity, but just 'an ordinary girl' seeking acceptance to be 'the way I am.' In interviews, she matched these sentiments very candidly, particularly about her same-sex partnerships, and offered that her unrepentant stance of self-acceptance had a slight negative impact on her fame. In a 2003 interview with *Mamba Magazine*, she said:

> I am a lover. I've always been with women. When I was still married, I was also with women. ... People knew. ... Before people thought it was a bad thing in God's eyes. ... They don't bother me. It's nice to be the way I am.

In her last years, she came out as a lesbian. She was particularly adamant that who she loved should not prohibit her from also self-identifying as a good African woman.

The impact of the Jezebel narrative is most troubling in its tendency to both overtly and subconsciously undermine the sexual expression, identities and desires of black women. Many black women across varying cultures feel compelled to counter this stereotype by projecting an overemphasised demeanour of wholesomeness, piety and chastity. Asaah argues that this is reflected within African self-representations of female sexuality in particular: 'in spite of their thematic interest in the subject of sex, [African narratives], at the stylistic and technical levels, are muted and euphemistic portrayals of the sexual'.

Brenda Fassie, whose life and music were defined by racism, sexism and a counter-narrative of empowerment, set forth an important dialogue that resonated across the continent through an interrogation of oppressive ideologies against Africans and women. Privately, she was a complicated and self-destructive character; but as an artist, she was a self-assured revolutionary. She offered herself and the South African music scene to the entire continent as a platform to converge and rebel against the legacy of ownership of black identity and sexuality. She seemed unfazed by the public exposure of her private life and allowed it to inform her activism and legacy.

Mireille Miller-Young argues in her 2008 article 'Hip-Hop Honeys and Da Hustlaz' that contemporary hip hop culture and its emphasis on pornographic, explicit and crude displays of black sexuality tend to cause anxiety within black communities and incite controversy around exactly what constitutes 'appropriate' representation of black sexuality. Though she acknowledges that misogyny and homophobia are rampant in hip hop culture, she advocates against withdrawing or toning down images of black sexuality as a protection and preservation mechanism against the historically rooted exploitation of the black Jezebel stereotype. Additionally, bell hooks, the prominent black feminist scholar, has advocated in the past for an 'oppositional gaze' or a new way of looking at and challenging the ways society has accepted certain stereotypes about black women.

I found the life story of Brenda Fassie intriguing because she used her celebrity to publicly denounce the principle that sustains the sexual expression of an African woman as an acceptable measure of her character. Instead, her articulation and embracing of her own sexuality encouraged us to theorise it as a practice of resistance against the black Jezebel narrative.

Black African female sexuality receives considerable analysis under heteronormative frameworks of postcolonial resistance and patriarchal subjectivity and fetishism. This engagement is vital to contextualise gender and feminist studies in Africa, but we need to engage more with the full range of experiences that the modern African woman faces. As a humanities scholar, I aspire to integrate more diverse narratives within the framework of African studies, particularly gender and LGBTQI+ experiences.

Brenda Fassie had an extraordinary ability to convert the discomfort that her sexuality elicited into an invitation to adore her. One of my favourite stories is how she handled a wardrobe malfunction at Zanzibar nightclub, a now closed venue in Washington, DC once popular with the African diaspora. Several of my relatives were in attendance that evening, and during a vibrant dance set, Fassie's breasts burst out of her corset in front of a stunned audience. Interpreting their silence as discomfort, Brenda paused her performance and cupped her hands under her bare breasts. She faced the audience and unapologetically declared, 'This... is Africa!' Once again, she was met with rapturous applause.

Brenda Fassie, at her best, epitomised black female empowerment and sexual liberation.

So what makes a woman dangerous?

The dangerous woman is an African woman who embraces her sexuality, who refuses to conceal it as an act of self-preservation against an antiquated narrative that vilifies her as a dark, voluptuous and indecent being. The dangerous woman is an African woman who is not afraid to challenge traditional perceptions of what it means to be a 'good girl'.

Brenda Fassie was a dangerous woman because she was a free spirit who wanted the world to love her unconditionally as a sexual black woman.

And we did.

Further Reading

Asaah, A.H., 2006. 'To Speak or Not to Speak with the Whole Mouth: Textualization of Taboo Subjects in Europhone African Literature'. *Journal of Black Studies* 36: pp. 497–514.

Asaah, A.H., 2007. 'Images of Rape in African Fiction: Between the Assumed Fatality of Violence and the Cry for Justice'. *Annales Aequatoria* 28: pp. 333–55.

'Brenda Fassie: A Very Human Hero'. BBC News, 10 May 2004. Available at: news.bbc.co.uk/1/hi/world/africa/3700309.stm

hooks, b., 1992. *Black Looks: Race and Representation*. Boston, MA: South End Press.

McGregor, L., 2004. 'Obituary: Brenda Fassie'. *Guardian*, 11 May.

What Does It Mean to Be a Truly Dangerous Woman, in This Dangerous World?

Bidisha

Bidisha is a broadcaster, journalist, film maker and stills maker. Her latest publication is an essay called The Future of Serious Art *and her latest film series is called* Aurora. *As a journalist and broadcaster, Bidisha specialises in international human rights, social justice and the arts and culture, and offers political analysis, arts critique and cultural diplomacy tying these interests together. She writes for the main UK broadsheets (currently as an arts critic for the* Observer *and the* Guardian*) and presents and commentates for BBC TV and radio, ITN, CNN, ViacomCBS and Sky News. Her fifth book,* Asylum and Exile: Hidden Voices *(2015), is based on her outreach work in UK prisons, refugee charities and detention centres. Her first short film,* An Impossible Poison, *premiered in London in March 2018. It has been highly critically acclaimed and selected for numerous international film festivals.*

We live in a dangerous world, and that danger comes from male violence. It is hardly radical to point this out, as it's a fact: governments know it, the police know it, crime reporters know it, judges know it and victim support workers know it. Statistically, this violence is perpetrated by men and boys against women, girls, other men and other boys. Statistically, it is males who rape, traffic, terrorise, buy and sell and rent, harass, exploit, use and abuse females and sometimes other males. Statistically, it is men who physically beat and brutalise women and other men.

This abuse is supported by an inescapable network of macho social and cultural misogyny in which male authority figures with money and power head up every area, be it politics or the arts, finance or the charity sector, medicine or academia, law or engineering. Meanwhile, but for some few exceptions, women are kept in the lower echelons of each organisation and are often paid less for the same work as men, discriminated against, sexually harassed, dismissed through ageism, punished for becoming mothers and overlooked for promotions.

In a patriarchal society like this, women are punished through comparison with negative stereotypes, impossible ideals and hypocritical double standards which sexist men invent and reinforce among themselves to ensure their own dominance (although many women have absorbed and internalised the same values): an assertive woman is shrill, while her male counterpart is assertive; a friendly woman is a tease who deserves what is done to her by any man who abuses her, while a friendly man has easy charm; a child-free woman is a selfish careerist, while a new mother is a matronly sap who can't be trusted to concentrate at work, whereas a man with kids is a 'family man' even if he does no actual parenting and leaves the childcare labour to the mother or a female nanny.

And so on.

In culture and in the mass media, women are ignored, sidelined or under-represented as writers, directors, artists, experts, architects, designers, photographers, composers, conductors, panel speakers, whatever it is. If it involves money, influence, self-expression, the power to influence images and narratives, to create great spectacles and show the world our creative vision, we are kept out – whether that's making films or getting on best-of lists or prize shortlists or receiving big commissions and exciting work trips as DJs, as scientists, as academics, as poets, or whatever it might be. Those who are not 'lucky' to be treated like this in full-time, middle-class professional employment are struggling as exploited workers in 'flexible' jobs which offer no pension, no stability, no progression and no safeguards.

At the same time, in the home, many men still use women's labour as cleaners, cooks, child-raisers, sexual service providers, family admin organisers and parent-carers. And yet providing all of these free services for a man who does far less than 50 per cent of all the work does not mean that a woman will not be beaten, raped, bullied, controlled, deceived or betrayed by him; two women a week are killed by their male partner or ex-partner. And when a woman is abused, and she speaks out about it, she will be told she is lying.

Women are cornered and trapped in their lives by severe funding cuts which have affected domestic violence, rape, legal aid, housing, early years education and elderly care charities. Women are bearing the brunt of a macho government's sadistic 'austerity', where those at the bottom of society – always women, and in particular women of colour – are punished again and again and sometimes kept in abusive situations through lack of a way out, all because the Chancellor doesn't want to tax rich, privileged chaps like himself.

Yet it is not we who are the liars. Narratives and images about women in mass culture, from films to music videos to adverts, do not derive from reality but are chock full of malicious lies and patronising, belittling insults. So often, the stories we ingest as part of our daily entertainment are full of slanders against women, and they give us a pantheon of females who represent everything that sexist men really think about us. At the very best, we can hope to be sexually objectified as a 'hot' body to be used and then discarded, or a crying and desperate kidnap victim to be saved. We can be turned into pornography and masturbated over, or rented and used by the hour to give a man sexual gratification and a feeling of power and control. We can be patronised as an infantile and endlessly supportive love interest or pityingly leered over as a murdered prostitute on a mortuary slab. There is the useless frump, the nagging wife, the interfering mother-in-law, the hard-faced police detective, the petty fusspot, the pathetic yet predatory 'cougar'. We are either stupid bimbos to be used then ignored, or scheming, dried-up witches to be mocked then ignored.

When our very youthful beauty fades, the true hatred and derision felt for us is revealed.

And at the very worst, we are represented as dangerous women who will destroy the world out of our irrational malice if we are not stopped. The succubus, the ugly hag, the sinister crone, the cold bitch who can't take a joke, the demonic castrator, the shrill feminist who overreacts to every tiny thing, the shrivelled spinster aunt, the baby-hungry woman, the demanding high-maintenance girlfriend, the shallow high-maintenance wife, the 'psycho' ex-wife, the scheming harridan, the un-maternal career woman 'ballbreaker', the embittered former beauty queen, the vengeful stalker who's mad, sad and bad and lives to emasculate men.

These images bleed out of the arts and culture and are used to judge and attack all women in public life, especially in politics and business leadership. Women who aim for power of any kind, in any area, are represented as ravenously ambitious, selfish, inhuman witches who want to take something away from men. Actually, forget about trying to get power; when a woman wants justice, basic justice in law, against a man who has harmed her, and she is strong enough to go to the police and even through a court to get it, it is she who is put on trial, said to be lying, psychologically exposed, cross-examined and destroyed in front of strangers.

There are many dangers for a woman who dares to claim more than what is offered to her. More than a life of drudgery and abuse, of being objectified or belittled or ignored or exploited or undermined or treated as stupid. More than a world in which women are only tolerated when we can be used, and where we encounter verbal violence, structural violence or physical violence when we test the limits set down for us.

But what does it mean to be a truly dangerous woman, in this dangerous world? Forget about film and TV myths for a moment. In a woman-hating, woman-exploiting, woman-abusing, perpetrator-excusing world, a dangerous woman is one who points out the obvious. A dangerous woman is a woman who is made, like all of us, to go through the gauntlet of misogyny all day every day, who sees perpetrators lionised as pillars of society and victims tortured and punished, and like the little boy in *The Emperor's New Clothes*, shouts out that something isn't quite right and wonders why everyone is colluding with the illusion. The sheer amount of slander directed at women who do this is simply a way of deflecting attention from the obvious truth about the perpetrators of virtually all the violence and abuse in the world.

The slander and resistance are themselves a form of abuse.

You wouldn't think that words alone could make you a dangerous woman.

In a militarised, violent, capitalistic world, individuals are considered dangerous if they have ammunition of a literal or metaphorical kind: if they are carrying a gun, or have a lot of economic or political power, or if they have a record of hurting others. Yet if I were to put this article up on my own website, I would immediately receive emails and Tweets from abusive men enraged by my claims about abusive men. I am only pointing out what is obvious and ubiquitous and endemic – what is, indeed, on the front pages of news sites every single day – and yet simply to say it causes them such blistering panic that they immediately lose their minds and confirm exactly what I am saying. I have become, in their eyes, a dangerous woman who must be shut up and hounded out, just for using language to express the truth.

At the very best, they would call me stupid or physically hideous. At medium, they would say I am mad, which is sexist men's most malicious and longest-standing insult against women. And at worst, I would receive threats of rape and death; these are clever threats, given that men's raping of women is endemic and perpetrated with impunity in societies all over the world, from war zones to university campuses.

That is all it takes to become a dangerous woman. When women tell the truth about what they have experienced and witnessed, from casual workplace misogyny to gang rape, men (not all men; just enough for every single woman commentator on the planet to have experienced it countless times) say that we are mad. I am certainly mad, as in very angry. And that anger gives me energy and immense, anarchic power.

You become a dangerous woman when you decide that you've had it, when your anger pushes you out of your silence, out of your head, out of your room and into the world to express your fury and woe and to begin changing things. A woman becomes dangerous when she threatens the status quo.

A woman makes herself dangerous, and gains power, when she throws off the shackles of propriety, feminine decorum and modest silence – all of which protect perpetrators – and instead opens her mouth and speaks frankly about what she has gone through, what she's seen, what she thinks and what she feels. A woman becomes dangerous when she talks about her mother's life, her sister's life, her daughter's life. A woman is dangerous when she points out what is hiding in plain sight. She is dangerous when she speaks the simple truth about what she has survived. And she is dangerous when she stands with other women, in her words and in her deeds, against abusive men and against the macho misogyny which oppresses us and makes us feel afraid, with just cause, even when we are making the ten-minute walk home from the station.

To continue with that image, despite the dangers a woman senses on that walk home, sometimes a woman is herself considered dangerous simply for going from A to B. To be out in the world is to claim space, and a woman is dangerous when she claims space. A woman is considered dangerous when she dares to occupy the workplace, public transport and the street. In all three of these places, sexual harassment by men, insulting casual misogyny by men and intimidation by men (such as following, hissing, sexual noises, baiting and outright assault) are endemic. The perpetrators harass us not because they admire our beauty and long to be friends with us, but because they gain a sadistic enjoyment from our confusion, fear or fury; because, ultimately, they want to drive us out of these places and back into the home where we supposedly belong, cleaning up men's dirt and bringing up men's babies for free.

A woman is dangerous when she challenges what patriarchal culture says about her and about other women. A few years back, I wrote an essay called *Emotional Violence and Social Power*. It described in horrific psychological detail how an industry peer, a feminist, socialist man, well known and well liked by many, groomed and sexually exploited me. Ten thousand people have read that article and many other victims and witnesses got in touch with me. I learned that he was a compulsive abuser with a long history.

Writing the piece, which was the absolute truth, felt like slashing a line straight through the female silence and male cronyism that protected the perpetrator. The piece – just a piece of writing – had power *in itself*, because it was true. It was dangerous, the truth was dangerous, to a terrifyingly two-faced perpetrator. It was *so* dangerous that he teamed up with a male lawyer and together, nightmarishly, they threatened me.

There is nothing more horrific than receiving a scathingly aggressive and sexually detailed letter from a male stranger in the law profession, in which he stands shoulder to shoulder with the man who abused you, in full fraternal support and belief and power and money and misogyny, as if they are long-time friends. They threatened me because they said I had damaged the perpetrator – because I had told the truth about him, and the truth about him was terrible and damning and caused decades-long scars. For his victims. It is a mark of the cowardice and self-pity of narcissistic, abusive men that what they fear most is one of their own victims showing them a mirror; the most dangerous thing they can envisage is simply the truth about themselves becoming known.

A woman is dangerous when her desire to express her rage and pain begins to outweigh all other reservations. It is men, not women, who get hysterical when women tell the truth. Yet there are so many of us, writing chapters like this, that the same old arguments which used to be deployed to shut us up no longer work: the claims that we are mad, or malicious, or mistaken, or exaggerating.

A dangerous woman holds something in her hands which does not cost anything but is priceless. When she reveals it openly, the world shakes subtly on its axis, even though she may not think it has, and even if she is destroyed in the process.

A dangerous woman is truth incarnate.

Speak Out! Dangerous White Woman

Pegi Eyers

Pegi Eyers is the author of the award-winning book Ancient Spirit Rising: Reclaiming Your Roots & Restoring Earth Community *(Stone Circle Press, 2016), a survey on social justice, decolonization, nature spirituality, earth-emergent healing and the holistic principles of sustainable living. Pegi self-identifies as a Celtic Animist, and is an advocate for the recovery of authentic ancestral wisdom and traditions for all people. She lives in the countryside on the outskirts of Nogojiwanong in Michi Saagiig Nishnaabeg territory (Peterborough, Ontario, Canada), on a hilltop with views reaching for miles in all directions. Find her at www.stonecirclepress.com and on Twitter @PegiEyers*

For me, the everyday question has become 'Do I share what I know, or remain silent like everyone else?' Making the rounds in my own community and calling out the implicit bias I hear from friends and neighbours, or the imbedded colonialism in our gracious cultural institutions, or the cause-and-effect of endless consumer choices made possible by white privilege (and how our lifestyle is killing the planet), can get me in a world of trouble.

And heaven forbid I point out that we live in a white supremacist society – that one really paints a bullseye on my back! And yet I can't help it – rejecting Empire and participating in 'whiteness speaking back to whiteness' is who I am, and I am a Dangerous White Woman. There is no turning back.

I feel for the white folks who freak out, or turn away, or ignore me, or block me on social media and in the real world, I really do. It wasn't too long ago that I was blithely unaware of the harsh realities of the white supremacist, capitalist, abled supremacist, cisheteronormative patriarchy, but instead of fulfilling my destiny as an artsy zoomer, I had to go and get decolonized. Over the years, my bohemian need to relinquish the corporate dream for a simpler life had already put me on the margins, so to speak, and coming to terms with critical race theory, white privilege and allyship for the first time was not such a big deal. And contrary to my outward upscale jovial appearance (I do dress neat!), poverty and a lack of opportunity also kept pace with me on the outskirts of middle-class life. From my own experiences, I was able to identify with marginalized folk, and the other contributing factor to my career as a Dangerous White Woman and my blossoming as a radical dissident author-activist was my pain-in-the-butt habit since childhood to question everything (including authority).

I am incredibly grateful for the explosion of social justice training and individual or collective actions in recent times that have dramatically enlarged my understanding of the intersectional oppressions. My personal journey through these movements has led to a more neoteric alignment of my heart and mind, and like activists everywhere, I am dreaming the collective dream of a world free of patriarchy, white supremacy, racism and the insatiability of capitalism. Part of my work is to encourage other white folks to have the same epiphanies and learning opportunities that I have had. On the periphery of First Nations community here in Canada, I have seen the effects of the colonial apparatus up close, and I have witnessed the disgraceful legacy of historical and ongoing attacks on Indigenous people by genocide, segregation, residential schooling and assimilation. Outrage is our best response, and discussion and study are the first steps, but our learning will grow exponentially when we actively work for social justice by attending rallies, demonstrations, meetings and cultural events; practice allyship; and join committees and organizations. There is no shortage of tools for the highly relevant learning curve that renowned author, academic and speaker Allen Johnson calls 'racial reconciliation and cultural competency'. And whether we are approaching anti-racist activism as a new direction or have been working as a change agent for years, it is extremely useful to look at the model of 'The 8 White Identities' created by Barnor Hesse.

> Barnor Hesse has argued that 'there is a regime of whiteness that governs society through racial rule and there are socially visible, action-oriented white identities in everyday dialogue with that regime. People (not only white people) may identify with whiteness in one of the following ways.'

The 8 White Identities

1. White Supremacist: maintains and advocates a white society, preserving, naming, and valuing white superiority.

2. White Voyeurism: desires non-whiteness as interesting and pleasurable; seeks to control consumption and appropriation

of non-whiteness; expresses a fascination with culture, e.g. consuming Black culture without the burden of Blackness.

3. White Privilege: may critique white supremacy while maintaining an investment in questions that normalise whiteness; may state a goal of 'diversity'.

4. White Benefit: privately sympathetic to aspects of anti-racism; will not publicly speak or act in solidarity, due to benefitting through whiteness.

5. White Confessional: speaks about whiteness but only for accountability to People of Colour after the fact; seeks validation.

6. White Critical: accepts critiques of whiteness and invests in exposing the regime of whiteness; refuses to be complicit – might be seen as whiteness speaking back to whiteness.

7. White Traitor: refuses complicity in the regime of whiteness; names and speaks about what is happening; intends to subvert white authority and tell the truth at any cost.

8. White Abolitionist: changes institutions historically based on white rule; dismantles the regime of whiteness; does not allow the regime to reassert itself.

For me, initially learning about 'The 8 White Identities' was a great blessing, and I refer to them often, as a way to stay focused when confusion, doubt or weariness creep in. In my own case, hovering between 6 and 8 often makes me feel like the crazy Doomsday Sayer up on a soapbox, and when 'call-out culture' becomes the only option left, the appellation of 'white traitor' definitely applies. Educating others on the history of colonialism, patriarchal white supremacy, the origins of racism, white privilege and how one goes about performing social justice work is key, and with writing, one-on-one discourse, workshops and the free-for-all that is social media, the challenges are immediately apparent. The majority of the whitestream have no interest in breaking their bubble of complacency or getting their hands dirty with real issues in the real world. Yet there is a minority who are open to the altruistic impulse, 'making things right' and contributing to the paradigm shift in themselves and others. Learning about the colonial systems of white privilege and the deplorable machinations of institutionalised racism for the first time can be very unsettling, as we are forced to think about what it means to be white in our time and place. Taking in the truth of our colonial history is difficult, but before anyone can sink into an abyss of guilt, I like to say: 'The shock only lasts for a day or two, believe me; you will soon come to terms with this new information. These are systemic inequalities created by psychopathic white men, and you are not supposed to take it personally!'

Some of us are willing to sit with the truth, but unfortunately many folks indulge in inventive sidesteps and clever justifications to deny these painful realities, and white fragility is by far the most common response. Centring on hurt feelings and personal issues is also typical, but this kind of reaction will never lead to change. Becoming an anti-racism spokesperson automatically makes one a target for hostility, anger, denial and online opprobrium from other members of the dominant society. As I have learned, you will find that there are literally thousands of creative and angry rebuttals those in the overculture will come up with to evade responsibility for their hegemony and privilege. Many white folks feel that their 'whiteness' is above reproach, but this is just not true. In my condemnation of 'whiteness' as the historical colonizer, the dominant culture and the ruling elite, I have been accused of racism against white people, but I refuse to fall into this trap. It is not more racism to see clearly that the source of racism and racist behaviour, both historically and in modern times, is coming from white people; and it is those of us who are white that need to change. After centuries of unquestioned superiority, white folks need to challenge our deep sense of entitlement and learn new skills for honest discussion and actions on 'race'.

Examining and owning my own white privilege has allowed me to truly look at the oppression of the 'other'. The bottom line is realizing that empire in the Americas was founded on a land grab and the genocide of the First Nations people who occupied the land, and built with the labour of black slavery. Clearly, it is wrong that the patriarchal founders and robber barons of empire – the rich, rapacious, entitled, racist, privileged, greedy, misogynist, bloodthirsty, warlord, bible-thumping, immoral, power-mad, dysfunctional white men – and their policies have imposed their will on our bodies, minds and souls, and have dictated the destruction of our world. And Dangerous Women everywhere need to object! Suppressed for so long, the fierce rage of women is the most threatening force on the planet today, and coming into our full power means embracing this transformative energy. Many of us are angry, and we can embrace it as an appropriate response to the elite who shape our reality by controlling resources and power. Instead of hiding our anger, Dangerous White Women can be motivated to speak out on the intersectional oppressions that surround us, and the privileged white people who refuse to take the first steps in understanding these dynamics.

So I will remain on the alert, challenge racist acts directly, and call things out. I will not just think about injustice when I see it online or in the media, I will act! I am obligated to use my knowledge and proficiency in social media, internet activism and community building to make things right. When raising awareness, I will tone down my provocative position with concrete actions that everyday citizens can take. There are exciting new movements happening that promote the enlargement of our empathy by stepping outside of ourselves, discovering the lives of others, and expanding our moral universe. For example, empathy was a major driver for the principles to abolish slavery in 1834, and nurturing this connective power across colourlines, time and space can lead to monumental social change. Forming empathic bonds with oppressed and marginalized people has made me more compassionate, as I feel empowered to speak out, and I believe that at some point in the future a determined collective force will undo racism. According to the original Quaker definition, 'speaking truth to power' means communicating first to those in power, then to the citizenry, and finally to the notion of power itself. In collaboration with all the Dangerous White Women who have resisted injustice in the past, present and future, I invite you to join the struggle!

Is My Sexuality Dangerous? The Questions Asked in the Aftermath of Sexual Violence

Eleanor Cope

Eleanor Cope has worked in the arts for over ten years as an actor, producer and writer. She now works as an events executive, but she continues to write both fiction and non-fiction. She has written several short plays, as well as adapting classic literature for theatre, and is now working on a novel.

I sometimes wonder if I was born with something dark and malignant inside me, like a tiny monster at the back of my mind that truly deserved pain, or at least a good talking-to and a sharp kick up the bum. Perhaps an odd thing to wonder, and I'm not sure now whether the thought developed after I was raped or whether it was always something I feared. After my trauma, I thought for a long time that the rape had happened precisely because my attacker had sensed this monster in me.

Maybe he thought I was a dangerous woman and needed to be taken down a peg or two.

I backed up my own argument about being a secret monster – I'd already experienced some strange sexual encounters in my early childhood and been snogged by a forty-something man when I was fifteen. So, I ask myself, is my sexuality dangerous? Was I somehow a sexual fiend from birth? Did people sense something in me that begged to be exploited?

Actually, I think all women at some point or another have to face this question: is my sex dangerous?

Are we women accountable for instances of harassment and sexual assault by men because the very fact of our womanhood is a temptation, a bait? Are we destined to relive Eve's ill-advised apple moment over and over again, always assuming the blame while Adam chomps away and points the finger?

It may be that a dangerous woman is a woman who wears a sexy dress or a sexy pair of jeans or a sexy massive jumper. Maybe she's a woman who takes a taxi home alone or walks through a park at night. Maybe she is a woman who doesn't wear magic nail varnish that detects rape drugs.

I'm guilty of all of the above.

And I still want to know when the men who shout or whistle at women in the street, who call us darlin', who pat our arses and stare at our chests, who force themselves upon us in some large way or small, will be the ones held accountable. In this instance, they are the ones who pose a threat, and they are a very real and potent danger that needs to be stopped.

Before I was violated and humiliated, battered and broken, I was a weaker person. Even if I did have a treacherous little beast inside me, my friends certainly wouldn't have described me as a dangerous woman. I tried to please, I felt uncomfortable being direct or leading a group or making decisions. I cried easily and often. I had an outer layer of soft downiness.

So perhaps my ferocity arose out of the aftermath of the rape, and my status as a dangerous woman was only won by first being ripped apart.

The guilt and the fear and the shame that I feel has made me push myself both physically and mentally. At first, I ate and ate and ate as if I wanted to make my body into a shape that wasn't associated with me, or any woman at all: I wanted to be a ball, and I did my best to bounce through life in denial. Then I decided I was softer than I'd ever been and I hated that: I threw myself into exercise, desperately trying to be strong and hard. That didn't work either, so I opened a bottle of wine and kept opening more bottles until two years had passed, and I realised it was time to get a home and a job and a life again. During this time, I had been a danger to myself.

Now, I push myself to work.

I work and work until I'm almost a machine and don't know what my personality is any more. Sometimes I'm emotional. Sometimes I'm overwhelmed. Almost always I'm shattered. I have swathes of rage physically coursing through my body. They keep me going. On occasion, I wonder if I'm insane because I think I could scream so deeply and lastingly that the whole world would actually turn inside out, and the monster inside me would burst out and become everything. If this were real, and if I chose to do it, I'd certainly be a dangerous woman.

But as it is, I've chosen to harness this power into helping, into looking after people and making exciting things happen in my community, into fighting for equality between women and men, into seeing the world, learning new things, challenging everyday injustices, even having fun.

So who exactly am I a danger to?

As far as I can see, only to those who deserve to be in danger. If being a dangerous woman means learning to like the inner monster that pushes me forward, expressing anger at sexism, demanding accountability from people who are sexually abusive, running my own business, taking control, making decisions, recognising my own talents and abilities, then I am happy to be that woman.

On my long and often faltering route to recovery, I can take some comfort in the idea that I am dangerous, and that I can be defined as delicate, daring, dynamite.

The First Blast to Awaken Women Degenerate

Rachel McCrum and Jonathan Lamy

Rachel McCrum is a poet, performer and workshop facilitator. Originally from Northern Ireland, she lived in Edinburgh between 2010 and 2016. She was the first BBC Scotland Poet-in-Residence, and Broad of cult spoken word cabaret Rally & Broad. She has taught and performed in Greece, South Africa, Haiti and Canada, and toured her first book of poems, The First Blast to Awaken Women Degenerate *(Freight Books, 2017) across Ireland, Scotland and England in 2017. She was the co-founder of Stewed Rhubarb Press (Callum MacDonald Award 2012). She is now delighted to call Montreal home, where she is curator of the Atwater Poetry Project, co-director (with Ian Ferrier) of Mile End Poets' Festival, and the occasional bilingual series Les Cabarets Bâtards.*

Jonathan Lamy is a multidisciplinary poet and performer from Montreal. He is also a poetry and performance art critic, currently postdoctoral fellow at Université Laval. He has published two collections of poetry at Editions du Noroit, as well as many articles about Quebecois and First Nations poetry. His practice as a performer combines participative reading, sound poetry, poetry-action and intervention in public spaces.

A note about where this poem came from

The coverage of the New Year attacks against women in Cologne and Stockholm in 2015; further reading about other incidents of mass sexual violence against women, for example, Tahrir Square in 2013; the 'corrective rapes' of lesbians, particularly in South Africa; that these are not a phenomenon that happens only outside the UK and Northern Ireland (Dapper Laughs exists, for example); reading *Women Who Run with the Wolves* by Clarissa Pinkola Estés and exploring feminine archetypes around the world; my own feelings as a muscular woman who often feels more akin to a bear than a bird, regardless of what a lot of poetry tells me; the need to free my own voice, to yell and howl and scream against an upbringing that tells me this is uncouth, ugly, excessive; learning about Inuit throat singing, that it is traditionally a female practice, a game, and delighting in how 'unfeminine' and 'ugly' it sounds, and the power that comes from that; my own absolute terror of groups of men, particularly in the streets, of mob think and the violence, the mindlessness, the egging-on that can come from that, my own physical helplessness against those situations, however much I like to think of myself as strong, my need to scream, stomp and rage against that, and my desire to see women able to scream, stomp and rage along with me.

With thanks to Jonathan Lamy, whose vocal support, trust and love enabled this piece to be written.

Listen to the live version, performed by Rachel with throat singing support from Jonathan: soundcloud.com/rachelmccrum/the-first-blast-to-awaken-women-degenerate

The First Blast to Awaken Women Degenerate

I am assured that God has revealed to some in this our age, that it is more than a monster in nature that a woman shall reign and have empire above man.

And therefore, I say, that of necessity it is that this monstiferous empire of women (which amongst all enormities that this day do abound upon the face of the whole earth, is most detestable and damnable) be openly revealed and plainly declared to the world, to the end that some may repent and be saved.

John Knox, The First Blast of the Trumpet Against the Monstruous Regiment of Women, *1558*

The trumpet sounds.
All the monkeys are grooming themselves bald
in the zoos

Women slither out from gutters and under streetlamps
down from bedsits, and from behind garden fences

Foil sail unfolding irresistible as empty crisp packets
from pub table women
Women who sink a bottle of red and rage
with wine lips women

Fury unleashed women
in stamping, stomping, sweating
hordes of women

ranks amassing women.

Give me
gorilla women
and bear women
penguin women
and wolf hound women
blue whale women
and badger women
yeti, yak
and bison women

Give me
caribou women
and bone women
bite back
beefy
women

not quite bird women
not least the sparrow
crow
or wren
women
but
flamingo women
peacock women
eagle women
and pelican women

Give me unnatural women
deranged women
moving

drumming
howling women

Give me mobs of women
chow down on misery women
seismic cunt women
bloody pushy women
like a 2am army's march
through the veins women

Give me ruling women
and yelling women

Give me unsilent unwatchful women
Give me monstrous women
on the pavements of

Cologne women
London women
Tahrir Square women
Belfast women
Stockholm women
Cape Town women

Before the second trumpet sounds.
Before the monkeys can groom themselves bare and repent
Before the streets can fall dark and silent and damned
Please
Give me my monstruous regiment
of women.

You Are a Danger to Our Society: One Woman's Struggle to Become Legally Divorced in India

Papia Sengupta

Papia Sengupta completed her doctoral studies at New Delhi's Jawaharlal Nehru University in 2013, where she works as an assistant professor. Her research interests include minority studies, public policy, Indian and Scottish medicine women, women's rights, language in federal polity, minority accommodation, multicultural policies and governance in democratic politics. Her mentorship was recognised and she was awarded the Distinguished Teacher of the University of Delhi in 2009 by the former President of India A.P.J. Abdul Kalam. She has held fellowships from Cornell University, Brown University, University of Freiburg and was awarded a Visiting Research Fellowship from IASH and the School of Social and Political Science at the University of Edinburgh in 2015–16. Papia has also been working on women and memories of violence, trauma, conflict as well as love, privacy and intimacy. Her first book Language as Identity in Colonial India *was published in 2018 by Palgrave Macmillan. She is presently working on her next book on higher education and inclusion.*

Sitting in a small claustrophobic room, there I was in front of the magistrate who was trying to reconcile me and my husband, against whom I had filed a divorce case based on violence.

The magistrate was a middle-aged man and looked aghast when I calmly told him that I didn't want reconciliation, as I didn't want to live with my husband.

Trying to make me understand, the magistrate started narrating a story from the Hindu epic *Mahabharata*, the great battle fought between cousins Pandavas and Kauravas, where Pandavas killed all Kauravas in order to protect righteousness (*dharma*). After narrating, the magistrate looked at me and stated, 'You know, Draupadi, the wife of the Pandavas, was responsible for the war and decline of the mighty Kuru empire. Women with pride and self-respect always bring trouble with them.'

He went on and on, trying to reform me about values of household, family and holy wedlock. Reasoning with me about how men – due to their impatience – are at times violent, but violence was a form of their love. Women, he said, must be forgiving and not like Draupadi (who could not forgive her tormentors).

While he was immersed in his storytelling, the last sixteen years of my life were flashing in front of my eyes. I had known my husband for all those years, six years of courtship and ten years of marriage. I had known him since I was sixteen years old. That day, there I was, a woman of thirty-two.

I was sitting blankly in silence, but there was a conflicting conversation going on inside me.

I have loved this man, laughed with him, comforted him, and today here I am seeking divorce from him.

Why?

I found myself answering my own question – because I loved him blindly, forgiving all his faults; stood by him through thick and thin. Until then, I had completely forgotten that cruelty is bad but suffering cruelty is worse. And my daughter of two years taught me that. My small, cuddly bundle of joy who – with her screaming as if she had a phobia of her father – showed me how wrong I had been.

I got up without realising why.

The magistrate looked puzzled and looked at me as if saying: 'I am not done yet.'

I smiled at him and said: 'Thank you, I am done.'

By then, I knew the magistrate would never understand me. Why should he? He was himself a victim of patriarchy, just like me. But he didn't stop. Just went on cursing 'education' and 'modernity' and my 'economic independence' for having spoilt me, and for making me bold enough to shake the very foundation of family.

I didn't look back, just kept walking.

Education has made me what I am today. I am so glad my parents educated me to the best of their ability and gave me values of perseverance, confidence, care, love and respect. I had forgotten that we must respect others, but first and foremost we must respect ourselves; I did not remember till that day.

There was no regret in me. I had been working nonstop to provide comfort and happiness to my husband for the past five years, whereas he didn't have a job. I had reasoned out that as a believer in equality between men and women, even if my husband was jobless, it didn't matter to me whether he was working or not. If both the wife and husband are in love, that's what matters, nothing else. What's the big deal if I work all days without any off, even on Sundays? It is fine. I do it for my family.

My ordeal with the judiciary did not end there. I kept on going to the court for ten more years, hoping that one day I would get a divorce.

My case kept getting deferred, with judges being transferred and changes in jurisdictions. At home, with my husband gone, my daughter had grown up from four years to nine, from a timid, scared child always hiding behind the bed, frightened by the man who happened to be her father, to a lovable, fearless, carefree music lover. She calls me 'mapa' at times, meaning 'ma-papa'.

I am growing up with my daughter.

In 2010 my husband signed the first motion of divorce, but he never came to sign the final divorce papers, which is mandatory according to the Hindu Marriage Act of India, under which I was married. The law allows divorce on mutual consent when both partners sign the final papers within eighteen months. The judge told me very matter-of-factly that I had to file a fresh case of divorce.

He said: 'Your husband has not appeared in the court to sign divorce papers, and so you cannot get a divorce. Think about it – life has given you another chance. Look, you have a girl child – who will marry her? Go back to your husband.'

This time I did not smile, just pitied the magistrate and told him: 'Yes, I am a proud mother of a daughter, and even if I had ten daughters, I would still not go back to my husband.'

He retorted: 'You educated women, look at your pride... You never asked for alimony or maintenance for your child. You think you can do everything on your own? You have got so much courage to shake the very foundation of family. You teach your students to question the status quo, to stand for their rights. You are proud to have given birth to a girl child. You are a danger to our society.'

This time when I walked out of the court, I was not only smiling but was as happy as a child. And I was repeating aloud: *I am dangerous. Yes, I am a dangerous woman – and proud to be one.*

The courts in my country are too patriarchal, and I did not have money to waste on court cases and lawyers year after year. I realised it was best to spend my limited resources from my salary on my daughter and her education, rather than wasting it on the court case.

I asked myself: What would the court give me?

Divorce.

But I am free. Nobody can put me in chains except me. I decide for myself.

Yes, I am a dangerous woman. I live on my own terms, fight patriarchy and injustice, stand with my students and numerous women whom I don't even know.

Yes, I am dangerous, because I live with my head held high.

Eventually I got my divorce in 2017, that too because my ex-husband wanted to get married. The patriarchal stereotyping of educated women as independent and dangerous is seemingly a universal narrative in many societies and the legal system in India seems no different. In order to change it, we need numerous dangerous women.

Load Comments

Maria Stoian

Maria Stoian is a Romanian-Canadian illustrator based in Scotland. Her first graphic novel, Take it as a Compliment *(Singing Dragon, 2015), is a collection of real-life stories of sexual violence. Her comics have previously been published by* The New Yorker, The Nib *and in anthologies including* Drawing Power: Women's Stories of Sexual Violence, Harassment, and Survival *(Abrams, 2019) and* We Shall Fight Until We Win: A Century of Pioneering Political Women, The Graphic Novel Anthology *(BHP Comics, 2018). She likes to make zines and is probably checking the news right now. www.mariastoian.com*

10:22am
Load Comments
girlwhothinks
23↓ 2↑
MARIA STOIAN

I think this and this other thing. I have an opinion.
POST

I should put you in ur place
Stop talking before you hurt yourself hun
go get raped

I will find you
I bet u give good head
send pics people would care more lol
dumb whore

I see you
I will shoot u in ur sleep
THIS IS REVERSE SEXISM!!!
Jump off a bridge!
YOU CUNT

Kill Yourself
I should hunt u down
FUCK OFF!
get off the internet before I make you
You'd be cuter if you shut up

SHoo!
STAND BACK
SHE'S ON HER
PERIOD, LOL

Opinion, continued: I also think...

Three Poems: I'm a woman, The Weed, Poem for the Puya

Mab Jones

*Mab Jones is a 'unique talent' (*The Times*). Her subjects are nature, dreams, death, the body, being a woman, being a human, silence, speech, childhood, sexual abuse and mental health. Mab is currently Resident Writer in Cardiff Wetlands, and hosts a podcast about wetlands funded by the Royal Society of Literature. Her latest books are* 111 Haiku for Lockdown *(Infinity Books UK) and* The Land That Grew Me *(Selcouth Station). www.mabjones.com*

I'm a woman

I'm a woman. Measure me. Take the tape
of expectation and wrap it round my form.
Like any thing you own I am a shape,
designed to have a certain use; was born
to be placed on view. My circumference
may determine which shelf you put me on.
Am I ornamental? New? Then it makes sense
to have me on display. Older, I belong
in back. A lip may proclaim me pitcher,
bearer of wine, water, children. Pleasure
brims in me. Drink. Eat. I am a platter,

content to carry what you need. Measure
me, and tell me where I should be placed;
whether I may hold riches, food, or waste.

The Weed

I was never as pure as the lily, never as sweet as the rose;
I was a thing that strangles up, an ugly, dirty bit o' scrub,
That suffocated buttercups and muscled in on marigolds.

Unlike the lily I toiled, and unlike the rose I did not bud;
I was a thing that sprouted, climbed, an ugly tube that grew from slime,
On daisy heads and daffs I dined, and through my roots I ate up mud.

The lily wears an elegant gown, the rose wears elaborate garb;
I was a thin and dirty child, but now I'm fat and strong and wild,
Whole families of flowers have been defiled by my poisoned barbs.

The lily cries sweetly for mercy, the rose bends her soft head and begs;
But I am a thing without feeling or fears, they fall on deaf ears
As I squeeze dry their tears and drink their sweet sap to the dregs.

Poem for the Puya

Written for the wild flower Puya chilensis, *which was in bloom for the first time in ten years at the National Botanic Garden of Wales in 2012. The plant possesses spiked leaves which hook in small creatures and then feed from their blood; however, when it is in bloom, its flowers are full of a sweet nectar which animals and even humans can drink.*

Puya, they call you. The word sticky
in their mouths. You prickle the roof
of the glass house, unsettle the groups
of visiting classes. Like a nettle, your
leaves are stingsharp, laced with thorns.
'Cruel', they remark. Your taste is for
animal flesh, which they hook, pull in, and
starve to death. Their blood is your food.

Your bed more wet with this than dew.
From the Andes to Llanarthney you
came. A monster baby in a way: eight
feet tall and closer to a mutant than
a flower. Towering above the others,
a giant in the nursery. Cursed to slowness,
reliant on your new owners, still you
grew, your brontosaurus neck too thick
for them to prune; a Chilean imposter
that loomed above its human masters.

But now, a decade later, you're in bud,
about to blossom. Your body as round
and fulsome as a woman's. Crowds

come to marvel, wondering at your
beauty. Eyes hunger for your form.
Cameras snap and looks are thrown,
but sweeter than before. You ignore
them; take no note. Your name now
sweet as nectar in every thirsting throat.

Nature and Danger: Women's Environmentalism

Kate Lewis Hood

Kate Lewis Hood is a PhD candidate at Queen Mary University of London, researching contemporary poetry and anti-colonial approaches to the Anthropocene. Her critical work can be found in Green Letters: Studies in Ecocriticism *and* MAI: Feminism & Visual Culture. *She co-edits the online eco-poetry magazine* amberflora.

In her acceptance speech for the 2015 Goldman Environmental Prize, Lenca activist Berta Cáceres stated powerfully: 'Our Mother Earth – militarised, fenced in, poisoned, a place where basic rights are systematically violated – demands that we take action.' Such action is urgently needed: 'We're out of time,' she said. After founding the Council of Popular and Indigenous Organisations of Honduras (COPINH) and protesting actively against the Agua Zarca hydroelectric dam project on the Gualcarque river (which is ancestral Lenca territory), Cáceres herself was out of time. On 3 March 2016, she was murdered in her home by armed assassins. She was one of 201 environmental defenders to be killed that year. Cáceres was considered a dangerous woman by state officials and international corporations with interests in the dam-building project. Her death – and more importantly, her life

– highlight the dangerous nature of the work indigenous women activists are doing around the world.

Cáceres' reference to Mother Earth (*Madre Tierra*) suggests a feminised nature, and similar ideas recur across a wide range of cultures and traditions, each differing according to the specific contexts from which they emerge. However, in ongoing struggles against settlers and neo-colonialism, many indigenous peoples identify a crucial relationship between being and land that differs from Euro-Western notions of land as property and non-human nature as resources. For example, after the Idle No More movement (founded by four women) erupted in the place currently known as Canada in 2012, Michi Saagiig Nishnaabeg scholar and writer Leanne Betasamosake Simpson wrote an article titled 'I am Not a Nation-State':

> Our nationhood is based on the idea that the earth is our first mother, that 'natural resources' are not 'natural resources' at all, but gifts from our mother. Our nationhood is based on the foundational concept that we should give up what we can to support the integrity of our homelands for the coming generations. We should give more than we take.

In Euro-Western frameworks, ideas of nature have evolved differently from this sense of earth as relative. In Western philosophy, myth and literature, a female Nature is often represented as mediating between divine powers and the material world. Responsible for both maintaining order and overturning it, this Nature is at once nurturing and dangerous. In *The Death of Nature* (1981), American ecofeminist philosopher Carolyn Merchant claimed that such an understanding of nature was lost during the 'Scientific

Revolution' in the sixteenth and seventeenth centuries. In Euro-Western thought, nature shifted from a living being to an inert machine and a set of resources, which she argues led to the intensification of ecological exploitation as part of a masculine, capitalist narrative of progress. Challenging this narrative, Merchant links the feminist and environmentalist movements that grew rapidly in the second half of the twentieth century. She advocates for new social structures and practices able to resist and overcome 'the domination of women and nature as resources'. Faced with a patriarchal system of misogyny, sexual violence and ecological damage, it seems tempting to try to reclaim nature as a dangerous woman capable of fighting back.

However, as the Australian ecofeminist philosopher Val Plumwood has shown in *Feminism and the Mastery of Nature* (1993), to do so is to risk perpetuating the potentially damaging implications of the gendering of nature in the Western 'rationalist' accounts discussed above. These ideas essentialise both women and the environment, allowing misogynistic stereotypes and gendered inequalities to be upheld as 'natural'. Challenging this approach, Plumwood argues:

> Not all women are empathic, nurturant and co-operative ... Women do not necessarily treat other women as sisters or the earth as a mother; women are capable of conflict, of domination and even, in the right circumstances, of violence. Western women may not have been in the forefront of the attack on nature, driving the bulldozers and operating the chainsaws, but many of them have been support troops, or have been participants, often unwitting but still enthusiastic, in a modern consumer culture of which they are the main symbols, and which assaults nature in myriad direct and indirect ways daily.

Plumwood's approach is intersectional, considering not just gender and the environment, but also race, class and colonialism. In order to counter the 'rational' enlightenment thinking that subordinates nature to culture, woman to man, blackness to whiteness and indigenous to settler, Plumwood resists simply reversing the terms, instead questioning the hierarchical binary structure that allows them to make sense. She also emphasises ways of living and acting rather than essential characteristics, reminding us that 'women have also played a major role, largely unacknowledged, in a male-led and male-dominated environmental movement, in resisting and organising against the assault on nature'.

In fact, women's environmental activism has long been diverse and influential. A whole host of women have worked globally and locally both to fight against ecological degradation and to contest the terms in which it has been framed. One of the best-known examples is marine biologist Rachel Carson, whose hugely influential work *Silent Spring* (1962) charted the effects of pesticide use on human and nonhuman beings. Written in an engaging style for a non-specialist audience, the book sold hundreds of thousands of copies in the US and further afield, and contributed to a growing environmental consciousness. Nevertheless, when the book was first published, Carson was repeatedly vilified as 'hysterical', 'inaccurate' and a 'communist', a highly dangerous accusation in Cold War America. In 1977, on the other side of the globe, the activist Wangari Maathai founded the Green Belt Movement. This was a response to the increasing problems that rural Kenyan women were having in sourcing food, water and firewood, as a result of intense deforestation and soil erosion. Through climate change and environmental exploitation, good soil was being washed away, leaving only arid land behind. In order to combat this, the Green Belt Movement advocated planting trees, which would work to bind and sustain the soil so that it could support vegetation. In this context, planting trees was not only ecologically beneficial and economically necessary, but it was also a political act; as Rob Nixon argues in *Slow Violence and the Environmentalism of the Poor* (2011), planting became an 'iconic act of civil disobedience' that has grown far beyond its humble beginnings. The Green Belt Movement highlights the ways that practical responses to environmental change developed by ordinary women have subversive potential.

These feminist approaches to nature offer important challenges in what is now being called the Anthropocene, a proposed geological epoch in which humans have profoundly altered the climate and other Earth systems, perhaps irreversibly. The *anthropo* part of the word Anthropocene means 'human', and yet, as critics of the term have pointed out, the Anthropocene neither was caused by nor affects all humans equally. As the United Nations Framework Convention on Climate Change notes, women often face higher risks and burdens from the impacts of climate change where they rely on natural resources for their livelihoods. In addition, a range of studies around the world examine the relationship between climate breakdown and violence against women. For example, collaborative work by the Women's Earth Alliance and Native Youth Sexual Health Network responds to the ways that environmental violence through resource extraction can be linked to sexual and gender violence, from reproductive illnesses to the huge rise in missing and murdered indigenous women and girls (MMIWG) in North America.

However, where women activists are viewed as dangerous by governments and corporations they are also repeatedly put in danger. The organisation Global Witness records the deaths of people killed for defending land, like Berta Cáceres. Their most recent report, *Defending Tomorrow* (published July 2020), states that 212 people were murdered in 2019. One in ten of those killed were women, and the report notes that women faced gender-specific threats such as smear campaigns, threats to their children and sexual violence. Indigenous people were significantly overrepresented among those threatened and killed. While these events might seem far away, they are actually much closer to home. For example, the huge coal-mining project El Cerrejón in Wayúu territory in La Guajira, Colombia, has led to multiple attacks on protestors and land defenders, including threats to the indigenous women-led organisation Fuerza de Mujeres Wayúu (Force of Wayúu Women). The mining project is jointly owned by three mining companies listed on the London Stock Exchange: Anglo American, BHP and Glencore. These dangerous times suggest an urgent need for more intersectional, ecological, feminist work that starts by looking critically from and towards the places we are situated.

Again and again, women activists show that environmental resistance is inseparable from movements for decolonisation and social justice. In 2016 it was a Lakota woman, LaDonna BraveBull Allard, who set up the resistance camp at the Dakota Access Pipeline. Faced with the prospect of the underground oil pipeline that threatened water supplies and ancestral sites near Standing Rock, she explained her reasons for founding the camp: 'Water is life. Water is the centre of everything. Water is female. As females, we must stand up for the water. We have no choice. Without water, we all die. It's common sense to me. We must save the water.' As indigenous feminist scholar Kim TallBear shows in her article 'Badass (Indigenous) Women Caretake

Relations: #NoDAPL, #IdleNoMore, #BlackLivesMatter', this is one of many women-led movements for 'caretaking kin', where kin is understood beyond the narrow terms of the settler colonial nuclear family and includes human and nonhuman communities. TallBear reminds us that caretaking is not the 'sole domain' of women, neither is it exclusive to women: 'men and gender-nonconforming people ... also help caretake our peoples, make relations, and add to our collective strength'. However, she adds, 'the women-led condition of these movements is striking'.

These movements continue to be necessary; in early 2017, then newly elected US President Donald Trump approved the completion of the Dakota Access Pipeline, and above the border in Canada, the Unist'ot'en people from the Wet'suwet'en First Nation are protecting the land from tar sands and fracking gas pipelines. Around the world, activists continue to fight on, including a new generation of school strikers for the climate and grassroots coalitions (such as The Wretched of the Earth in the UK) foregrounding Black, Indigenous and Global South struggles for climate justice. Women and non-binary people are at the forefront of these movements. These ongoing responses to a danger that is at once collective and profoundly uneven reveals what is at stake in climate breakdown after centuries of extraction, exploitation, colonialism and dispossession, and a need to critically examine and dismantle the structures that make it possible.

To remember Berta Cáceres' words, in order to sustain but also to live with each other and the environments in which we are entangled, 'we must shake our conscience free of the rapacious capitalism, racism, and patriarchy that will only assure our own self-destruction'. I dedicate this chapter – in solidarity – to all the dangerous women who are fighting to do just this.

More Information

COPINH @COPINHHONDURAS

Fuerza Mujeres Wayuu @MujeresWayuu

Global Witness @Global_Witness

Idle No More @IdleNoMore4

London Mining Network @londonmining

Native Youth Sexual Health Network @NYSHN

TallBear, K., 2016. 'Badass (Indigenous) Women Caretake Relations: #NoDAPL, #IdleNoMore, #BlackLivesMatter', Society for Cultural Anthropology, 22 December. Available at: culanth.org/fieldsights/badass-indigenous-women-caretake-relations-no-dapl-idle-no-more-black-lives-matter

Unist'ot'en Camp @UnistotenCamp

Women's Earth Alliance @WomensEarthAlly

Wretched of the Earth @wretchedotearth

Women's Labour and Trade Unionism: A Dangerous Combination?

Rebecca Zahn and Nicole Busby

Rebecca Zahn is a Reader in the University of Strathclyde's Law School. Her research interests lie in labour law and European labour law. She has written on socio-legal aspects of European labour law and the history of trade unions in Germany and the UK.

Nicole Busby is Professor in Human Rights, Equality and Justice at the University of Glasgow's Law School. She has undertaken research on the regulation of women's employment, particularly the relationship between paid work and unpaid care.

Women have played a key role in the British trade union movement since its inception. After all, the first strike for equal pay was organised by 1,500 women card-setters in Yorkshire in 1832. However, although trade unionism and the intellectual underpinnings of the labour movement were instigated around and by women – one need only think of the economist and labour historian Beatrice Webb (often referred to as one of 'the

Webbs', i.e. the wife of Sidney), who was a pivotal figure in her own right – as well as men, once institutionalised, the labour movement became focused on the needs and concerns of the 'standard male worker'. Women workers became part of the women's movement – viewed as 'the other' and often subjected to outright hostility – rather than an integral part of the British workers' movement. Women's position outside the mainstream labour movement has continued up to the present day, when gendered occupational segregation and the prevalence of part-time work raise questions concerning the relevance of traditional trade unionism to women's working lives. From their perceived threat to the established organisation of paid work, up to these contemporary challenges to trade unionism, women can be seen as 'dangerous'.

Women workers' early attempts to take collective action against their employers were perceived as a serious threat to social cohesion. A commentator on a female mill workers' strike in 1835 wrote that female militancy was 'more menacing to established institutions even than the education of the lower orders'. Once they ventured beyond work such as spinning and weaving – considered extensions of 'womanly duties' – and into the factories, women workers were considered a real threat to societal order and moral values. In a speech to the Trades Union Congress (TUC) in 1875, the TUC's parliamentary secretary Henry Broadhurst urged Congress to 'bring about a condition where wives and daughters would be in their proper sphere at home, instead of being dragged into competition for livelihood against the great and strong men of the world'.

The strike by women matchworkers at the Bryant & May factory in Bow, east London, in 1888 has only recently been recognised as a vital catalyst for 'new unionism' and as paving the way for the 1889 (male) gasworkers' and dockers' strikes which laid the foundations of the modern labour movement. Rather, women workers were perceived at the time as an all-round danger to employers, the state and society for challenging the status quo; and to the trade union movement too, due to their non-compliance with the normative model of work around which mainstream union activities, including collective bargaining, were based. Women's very participation in paid work threatened the 'family wage' of their fellow male workers and challenged the organisation of workers within specific workplaces.

Between 1888 and 1918, overall trade union membership in the UK grew from 750,000 to 6.5 million. The number of women members also increased during that period. However, by 1910, women made up almost one-third of the workforce but only 10 per cent of union members; over 90 per cent of women workers remained unorganised. Although women were incorporated in mixed unions in sectors such as the cotton and textile industries, where they often outnumbered male operatives (a high proportion of women were also members of teaching, clerical and shop workers unions), for the most part women organised themselves. The Women's Protective and Provident League was founded in 1874 and was replaced by the Women's Trade Union League (WTUL) in 1889. The WTUL's secretary, Clementina Black, moved the first successful equal pay resolution at the TUC's Congress in 1888, despite opposition from the general secretary – although this was a symbolic victory, as the motion was never acted upon – and campaigned widely for the extension of protective legislation for women workers. Other all-female organisations like the Co-operative Women's Guild (1883) and the National Federation of Women Workers (1906) also sprang up around the same time. The WTUL was eventually dissolved in 1921 when the TUC incorporated its functions by forming the Women Workers' Group.

Despite the inroads made in women's collective organisation and the contribution of Beatrice Webb and others to the labour movement more generally, trade union opposition to women workers, and in particular their concerns regarding equal pay and treatment, continued well into the twentieth century. Although female participation in the labour market – and especially in traditionally male-dominated industries – increased during the First World War, this was against the wishes of trade unions. Trade union meetings, strikes and negotiations usually excluded women, and the stereotypical image of the average trade unionist continued to be 'male, pale and stale'.

The 2010 British film *Made in Dagenham* (now a sell-out musical) narrates the strike by women workers at Dagenham's Ford factory in 1968 as marking a turning point in sex equality which eventually led to the passage of the Equal Pay Act 1970. However, the struggle for equal pay actually goes much further back than that. During the Second World War, the expansion in women's employment to fill the gaps left by men fighting at the front was not met by any improvement in pay, with women's average wage sitting at a woeful 53 per cent of that paid to the men they had replaced. Furthermore, the expansion in state-provided nurseries which had enabled mothers to work outside the home was swiftly withdrawn at the end of the war – with the explicit approval of the TUC. In 1944 a Royal Commission on Equal Pay was established, largely in response to the government's resistance to a House of Commons vote to establish equal pay for teachers. However, by the end of the war the campaign for equal pay had lost momentum, as the government and the TUC sought to persuade women to return to their home-making role and to more traditional paid work such as domestic service. The Commission on Equal Pay reported somewhat cautiously in 1946 that women in teaching and certain civil service grades might benefit from equal pay, although it would be the early 1960s before there was any significant progress in either sector. As the following excerpt from the TUC's 1948 annual report shows, the trade union movement continued to hold a traditional view of women's place in society:

> There is little doubt in the minds of the General Council that the home is one of the most important spheres for a woman worker and that it would be doing a great injury to the life of the nation if women were persuaded or forced to neglect their domestic duties in order to enter industry particularly where there are young children to cater for.

Given such systemic opposition to the realisation of women's social and economic emancipation, it is little wonder that the fight for equal pay showed no signs of progress in Britain's post-war reconstruction of the 1950s. However, the rise of the global civil rights movement in the 1960s and the Labour Party's desire to join the European Economic Community cast a spotlight on the entrenched pay inequality, and a new era dawned. The Labour Party's 1964 Manifesto called for a Charter of Rights for all employees to include 'the right to equal pay for equal work', which was supported by a resolution at the TUC Congress. The Wilson Government's application to join the EEC was rejected, and the issue of equal pay was promptly forgotten until 1968, when the actions of the 'Dagenham women' introduced the concept of equal value to the UK. Despite initial union hostility, Ford's women sewing machinists took strike action over regrading. They sought equal pay with men in more highly graded but similarly skilled jobs, as the women were paid 85 per cent of the men's wage. They were awarded 92 per cent, although it took another sixteen years and another strike lasting seven weeks to win the regrading. This prompted other equal pay strikes and the formation by women trade unionists of the National Joint Action Campaign Committee for Women's Equal Rights. However, it was not until 2013, 145 years after the TUC was founded, that Frances O'Grady became the first female secretary general of the organisation. Almost a quarter of TUC affiliates are now led by women.

Despite such progress, we would suggest that women as a group continue to pose a danger to the contemporary trade union movement, although the nature of that danger has shifted. Rather than women posing a (perceived) threat to societal order and to the structure of the trade union movement, trade unions' continuous lack of engagement with women workers now threatens the very existence of such organisations. Union membership has declined rapidly since its peak in the 1980s due, in part, to a rapid deindustrialisation of the economy which deprived unions of their traditional strongholds. In addition, the expansion of service industry jobs and those with 'atypical' arrangements, largely filled by women workers – both difficult for unions to access – have added to the decline in membership. Thus, the proportion of union members in workplaces with more than twenty-five workers fell from 65 per cent in 1980 to 26 per cent in 2011.

As the academic literature suggests, union revitalisation is dependent on the repositioning of unions as representative agents for women and minorities, and it is widely recognised that trade union renewal depends on representative membership which reflects the changing world of work. Women play a pivotal role in this regard. Today, women trade union members outnumber men, and the average British trade unionist is a young, degree-educated, white, professional woman. Trade unions 'talk' all the right language when it comes to perceived 'women's issues' such as equal pay, sexual harassment at work, work–life balance, etc. All TUC affiliates have instituted formal democratic structures and procedures which take women and their concerns into account. However, there are numerous reports and studies which show us that there is a discrepancy within the trade union movement between what is publicly stated and what actually happens. For example, at branch level, women often cannot get their voices heard and their opinions are blocked, their protests and challenges suppressed. The large proportion of women members that make up trade unions is not always reflected in branch officers, workplace representatives and national officers. All of this is despite the fact that some of the most powerful (and successful) labour movement battles in recent years have occurred in sectors dominated by women workers. The 'Justice 4 Cleaners' campaign, which was launched by London Citizens in the early 2000s to demand that cleaners working in the capital are paid the living wage, or the 'Glasgow Women Council Workers' Strike' in 2018 are cases in point.

Unless trade unions are able to reach out to women workers effectively, women will pose a danger to the continued existence of the trade union movement, at least in its current form. Despite their early marginalised position, women no longer dwell in the shadows of the labour movement, but the stubborn persistence of a gendered pay gap and continued discrimination, particularly in relation to pregnancy and childbirth, mean that the modern trade union movement is no longer seen as an effective bastion of protection for all workers – including a new generation of dangerous women.

Dangerously Provocative

Jessica Wolfendale

Jessica Wolfendale is Professor of Philosophy at Marquette University, Milwaukee, Wisconsin. She is co-author of War Crimes: Causes, Excuses, and Blame *(with Matthew Talbert), published by Oxford University Press in 2019; author of* Torture and the Military Profession *(Palgrave, 2007); and co-editor of* New Wars and New Soldiers: Military Ethics in the Contemporary World *(Ashgate, 2011) and* Fashion: Philosophy for Everyone *(Wiley-Blackwell, 2011). She has published numerous articles and book chapters on topics including security, torture, terrorism, bioethics, military ethics and feminist philosophy. Her work has appeared in journals including* Ethics and International Affairs, Journal of Political Philosophy, Georgetown Journal of Gender and the Law, Studies in Conflict and Terrorism *and the* Journal of Military Ethics. *Find her on Twitter @JCWolfendale and at www.marquette.edu/philosophy/directory/jessica-wolfendale.php*

The provocatively dressed woman is dangerous. She is disruptive: a distraction and a temptation. She leads good men to thoughts of infidelity; she distracts men and boys from the important tasks of work and education. She must be monitored and controlled. Schools should ensure that girls don't wear provocative clothing to class, such as tank tops or leggings, so that they don't distract boys and teachers. In the workplace, women should dress conservatively so that men can focus on their work.

But the provocatively dressed woman also poses a danger to herself. Since men are sexually aroused by a provocatively dressed woman, by dressing like a 'slut' a woman runs the risk of sexual harassment and even rape. If she wants to avoid danger, she should make sure that she doesn't wear short skirts or skimpy shorts, just in case her attire provokes the attention of a sexual predator. It is up to her to make sure that she doesn't send the 'wrong message' with her outfits.

This means that, if she is sexually assaulted or harassed, the provocatively dressed woman only has herself to blame. She knew that wearing a provocative outfit could attract unwanted sexual attention, and yet she went ahead and did it anyway. If she sends the invitation, she can't complain if men take her up on it, and men can't be blamed for responding to her invitation.

This narrative of the provocatively dressed woman is persistent and widely held. It is implicit in numerous school and workplace dress codes, in media coverage about sexual assault and harassment, in the advice given to women and girls by police officers, and in depictions of 'sexy' women in advertising.

At first, the narrative of the provocatively dressed woman seems to offer an enticing and uniquely female form of sexual power. Just by wearing skimpy clothing, it appears, a woman can sexually arouse men; she can make them forget their girlfriends or their marriage vows, and she can even threaten their commitment to their work and their education. She is the classic femme fatale: the woman who uses her sexual appeal to control and manipulate men to get what she wants. Men, in this narrative, are hostages to their sexual desire. At the mere sight of a short skirt or tight top, they can't control themselves. Against their better judgement, they can become powerless in the face of a woman's allure.

Perhaps, then, the provocatively dressed woman is a sexually empowered woman: rather than fearing her own sexuality, she embraces and celebrates her sexual power over men. She is dangerous not because she is a threat to sexual morality, but because she knows she is powerful, and she exercises her power when and how she sees fit. If she chooses to wear short, tight-fitting and revealing outfits, like those worn by female celebrities such as the Kardashians, it is not because she thinks that she has to dress like that in order to please men, but because she wants to celebrate her sexuality. She is sexy, cheeky and liberated, and feels no need to hide her sexual appeal. This seems like the very definition of the sexual empowerment that feminists have fought for.

But this empowerment is an illusion. Once we unpack the beliefs and attitudes that are expressed and reinforced through the narrative of the provocatively dressed woman, we see that she is not powerful. She does not have genuine sexual agency. In contrast, her apparent dangerousness and sexual power are embedded in and reinforce disempowering and objectifying conceptions of women's bodies and women's sexuality.

The narrative of the provocatively dressed woman tells us that women are responsible for men's sexual behaviour. In this narrative, male sexual desire is an omnipresent and potentially dangerous force that women must learn to avoid arousing if they don't want trouble. When a man acts on his sexual desire for a woman who is provocatively dressed, it's not only because he's overcome by lust, but because he sees himself as entitled to act on his desire even if she rejects his advances – after all, a woman who wears a provocative outfit is 'asking for it'.

So, the narrative of the provocatively dressed woman privileges male sexual desire over the wishes of the woman who is the object of that desire. Social and cultural attitudes, such as those expressed in media discussions of sexual assault and harassment, reinforce the privileged status of male sexual desire when women's clothing is taken to be relevant. The privileged status of male sexual desire is even reinforced in the law when, as has happened many times, a rape victim's clothing and behaviour are put forward as reasons to mitigate a defendant's responsibility for sexual assault.

This narrative of the provocatively dressed woman also reflects and reinforces the belief that women who wear revealing clothing want sexual attention from all men, not just from men they are attracted to or from whom they would like sexual attention. Thus, the narrative implies that men who sexually harass or assault women aren't fully to blame for their behaviour because women who wear revealing clothing want sexual attention from *any* man. Men's diminished responsibility for their actions towards women is implied by the very use of the word 'provocative' to describe women's clothing. Men's clothing, no matter how revealing or tight-fitting, is never described as provocative. Women's sexual arousal is not depicted as a potentially dangerous force that men must be wary of. Men are not warned against tempting or distracting women, and men are not blamed if a woman sexually harasses or assaults them.

So, the 'power' of the provocatively dressed woman is an illusion. The power attributed to the provocatively dressed woman is based on the belief that women's bodies are inherently sexualised: that clothing that reveals sexualised women's body parts is an open invitation to any man, an invitation that men are entitled to act upon regardless of the intentions and wishes of the women in question. This reveals the insidious message of the narrative of the provocatively dressed woman. When a woman's outfit is described as provocative, she is reduced to a collection of sexually charged body parts (breasts, buttocks, legs). In addition, a specific subjective desire is attributed to her – the desire for sexual attention from men. Because of what she wears, she must want sexual attention, regardless of what she says. Her actual preferences are dismissed, if they are inconsistent with the intentions that men attribute to her, as not reflecting what she 'really wants' – she says 'no', but her outfit says 'yes'. Thus, it is men's interpretations of her desires that are taken as authoritative. His 'you want it' trumps her 'no'. Her so-called empowerment and sexual freedom are truly an illusion if her own desires, preferences and choices are overridden in the face of men's interpretation of her desires. That is not freedom; it is radical disempowerment.

Contrast this with the narrative of the male seducer – the debonair playboy (exemplified in the character of James Bond) who actively seeks sexual attention from women, only to use them and leave them. The playboy figure might wear a dashing tuxedo; he might even emerge from the ocean clad only in skimpy Speedos, as Daniel Craig's Bond does in *Casino Royale*; he might drink and flirt outrageously. But no matter what he wears, how seductive his behaviour, or how many women desire him, he is never accused of sending the 'wrong message'. Nor is he viewed as deserving or 'asking for' unwanted sexual attention. If he rejects a woman's advances, his rejection is taken as authoritative. She cannot then claim that his 'no' means 'yes'. A woman's 'you want it' never trumps a man's 'no'.

But the provocatively dressed woman's supposed sexual power over men can be turned against her at any moment. A woman who embraces provocative dress and decides that she wants sexual attention from men will still be denied her own agency if she chooses to reject a particular man, or objects to certain kinds of sexual attention. Instead, she will be accused of 'sending the wrong message', and the desires of men who sexually approach her will be attributed to her, and her own desires will be denied and overridden.

Thus, women are in a bind. Both women and men sometimes want to be seen as sexually desirable, but for women, the wish to be attractive is tinged with the threat of unwanted sexual attention. Both men and women use clothing to attract others, but only women are punished if they reject men's sexual advances, whatever they are wearing. And only women will be blamed if they are sexually harassed or assaulted. The provocatively dressed woman, it will be said, knew she was playing with fire when she decided to go out dressed like a 'slut'. In this narrative, it's not men's fault if they get 'carried away'. It is the provocatively dressed woman who is to blame for attempting to have it both ways: sending the message that she's 'up for it' but then complaining when men take her up on her invitation.

So, the narrative of the provocatively dressed woman has nothing to do with women's sexual desire and sexual agency. Sexual agency, at a minimum, involves the freedom to refuse or accept sexual invitations from others. It involves the freedom to understand and develop one's own sexual potential, and to have one's sexual desires treated with respect by one's partners and potential partners. But the narrative of the provocatively dressed woman frames female sexual agency purely in terms of male sexual desire and entitlement. Indeed, the satisfaction of female sexual desire plays no role at all in the narrative, since the narrative suggests that arousing men's sexual desire is the sole aim of a woman's choice of outfit. The narrative depicts women as sexualised objects who have the potential to affect and disrupt men (but not vice versa), and the potential to attract sexual violence and aggression. The narrative suggests that men may be entitled to approach a woman sexually if she is wearing a 'sexy outfit', even if she claims she doesn't want such attention. Thus, the narrative of the provocatively dressed woman is dangerous – not because a sexily dressed woman *is* dangerous, but because the narrative reinforces and reflects attitudes about women's responsibility for men's behaviour that privileges male sexual desire and that holds women to blame for sexual assault and harassment.

Research Has Shown: On Gendered Speech Patterns

Laura Waddell

Laura Waddell is a publisher and writer based in Glasgow. Her first book, Exit *(Bloomsbury, 2020), is a short collection of essays exploring the theme of exit. She writes a weekly column for* The Scotsman, *has been published in the* Guardian, TLS, Kinfolk, McSweeneys, *and is a regular cultural commentator for radio.*

Often all it takes to be a dangerous woman is to speak. A wealth of research on gendered speech patterns shows that sometimes the mere act of speaking, that is to voice opinions, to partake in society, to express the self, to take up aural space, to mouth any sound, is to be viewed as disruptive. In this inevitable way, in this simplest of ways, a woman embodying a voice is inherently dangerous – to the status quo. Speak up.

Research has shown that women are interrupted more often than men in conversation.

Refuse to mind the gap. Harden your resolve. Refuse to bunch your words together to fit them in. Point out, when interrupted, that you haven't yet finished what you are saying. Continue speaking regardless, watching the mouths of men moving, talking over you as though oblivious you're still speaking. As though they are goldfish in a bowl of their devising, lips opening and closing in irregular rhythm to yours, thick glass between you and neither hearing the other. Blinking blandly, they expect, upon beginning, that you will stop. So used to and certain of this, they do not notice that you have not stopped for a length of time that can only be described as odd. A length of time that reveals they are not, and were not, listening to you in the first place. When their confusion subsides, and when you have finished what you are saying, possibly repeating for clarity, then others can take their rightful turn. Swim at your own pace. Let him eat fish food!

Research has shown that women speak less often in mixed gender groups.

Refuse to allow the words of others to keep yours in parentheses; be reflected in the minutes. Set the agenda; decide the key. You and your contributions are valid. Tack up on the wall, not on to the end. Choose any instrument that pleases you with its sound and feel; luxuriate in your range. You may agree or disagree with what other women are saying; support their right to speak, as it is your own right. On occasions you are dismissed or interrupted but have not yet finished: change the subject back, and where your notes are reprised to greater acclaim, defend your credit. Pitch up. Pitch. Innovate. Alleviate the drone with your contributions: they are greater than grace notes. Polish your brass until it shines; pass the cloth to others only after you're done with it. Whoever heard of an orchestra with just a tuba?

Research has shown that women are the primary innovators of language.

Refuse to be curtailed in the mode of your expression. Avoid the strain of lifting your words higher, in attempt to carry them above obstacles. Bore through obstacles with your diamonds.

But if skywards is your natural pitch, do not be dissuaded from flying. Fry your vocal in the oil of your choosing. Speak as you would speak uninterrupted. Refuse the legitimacy of others' refusal to adapt. Do not allow the colourful shapes of your language to be put in the toybox by those who resist it. Do not be content to dot his i's and cross his t's. If he speaks an I, let your O stream onwards around it. If he speaks an H, turn cogs with your K. Let his letters tumble onto the carpet until it's his fair turn to pick them up and build with them. Your alphabet letters are magnetised, they will stick: spell with them what you wish.

Other Pieces from the Dangerous Women Project

Hundreds of other pieces can be found on the Dangerous Women Project website at www.dangerouswomenproject.org

A Year of Dangerous Women begins
Dangerous New Year's Resolutions
Reflections on the Dangerous Women Project

Anonymous: *The Silence Around Miscarriage*
Heta Aali: *Merovingian Queens as Dangerous Women in 19th-Century France*
Viccy Adams: *Tonight and for the Rest of My Life*
Esa Aldegheri: *Dangerously Plural: Why Living with Many Languages Is Dangerous*
Swati Ali: *The Dangerous Women of My Family*
Morgan Allan Campbell: *Jessie King: 'Heinous' Child Killer or Vulnerable Victim of Her Times?*
Patricia Allmer: *Lee Miller: Photography, Surrealism, and Beyond*
Maria Alonso Alonso: *Rosalía de Castro: Was She a Dangerous Woman?*
Melissa Álvaro Mutolo: *This Is Your Story*
Sarah Ang: *Dame Gothel Defends Herself*
Naomi Appleton: *Why Is Draupadi a Dangerous Woman? Gender Politics in Ancient Hindu Epic Literature*

Clare Archibald: *Paper Dolls Join Together with Dots of Whispered Steel*
Polly L. Arnold: *A Chemical Imbalance: On Women in Chemistry Careers*
Claire Askew: *Anne Askew – Dangerous Convictions: Three Poems*
Stephanie Aulsebrook: *Hatshepsut: A Female King*

Sim Bajwa: *Shameless*
Debapriya Basu: *Anne Askew: Reforming Dangerous Women*
Pamela Beasant: *Lady Jane Franklin and Kate Rae*
Joanne Bell: *How Yoga Made Me Dangerous*
Meredith Bergmann: *Response to Random Murder III: December 14, 2012, Newtown, CT, 28 Dead (Mother and Child with a Glock)*
Celeste-Marie Bernier: *Visualising Black to the 'Branded, Raped, Beaten' Body in the Life and Works of Maud Sulter (1960–2008)*
Sammy Bishop: *Tilting Gender: Christine and the Queens*
Lynsey Black: *Worst of the Worst: What Did it Mean to Be a 'Dangerous Woman' in Post-Independence Ireland?*
Sharon Blackie: *The Dangerous Women of Irish Mythology*
Anna Błuś: *You May Say I'm a Dreamer: How Dangerous Women Will Save Poland*
Helen Boden: *Joan Eardley: A Woman for all Weathers*
Jasmina Bolfek-Radovani: *Unveiled*
Ruth Boreham: *Mary Somerville: Queen of Science*
Marianne Boruch: *Wonder and Grief, Poetry and Danger: Reflecting on the Life and Work of the 'Other' Wordsworth*
Raquelle K. Bostow: *Hélène Cixous and the Myth of Medusa*
Mary Bownes: *Changing Universities from Within...*
Anna Brazier: *Like a Woman: 'How we move embodies our past and creates our future'*

Robin Brooks: *Beauty and the Breast*
Carly Brown: *Lady Macbeth: Elisabet Ney's Final Sculpture*
Lois Burke: *Dangerous Diarising of 19th-Century Girls*
Catriona Burness: *Mary Barbour – A Dangerous Woman? Beware!*

Sandra Cairncross: *The Alexander Sisters: An Appreciation*
Jenni Calder: *Isabella Bird: Writer, Explorer, Trailblazer*
Jenni Calder: *Naomi Mitchison: A 'Bad and Dangerous' Woman?*
Caroline: *Auld Reekie Roller Girls and the Dangerous World of Roller Derby*
Jan Carson: *How Flannery O'Connor Kicked the Fear out of Me*
Katelynn E. Carver: *This Is Not a Poem*
Shami Chakrabarti: *Human Rights and Dangerous Women*
Annie Chalker: *Dear Boss: A 'Dangerous' Woman's Letter of Resignation*
Deirdre Chapman: *Valda Trevlyn Grieve: What Turned a Cornish Country Girl into a Dangerous Woman?*
Laura Clay: *Dolly Parton: What a Way to Make a Living*
Rachael Cloughton: *Dangerous Mothers*
Jon Coburn: *Dagmar Wilson: Not 'Just' a Housewife*
Beth Cochrane: *Christmas under Construction: A Woman Working in a Male-Dominated Sphere: the Christmas Market*
Michelle Collins: *From the Lookout: A Short Story*
Joanie Conwell: *A Dangerous Woman: An Intertextual Poem*
Emma Cooper: *Dangerously in Love with Plants*
Natasha Cooper: *Not a Princess: Daenerys Targaryen as Dangerous Woman*
Linda Cracknell and Sarah Salway: *Fortunes Large or Small: Nan Shepherd and Jane Austen Compare Notes in a Twitter Chat*
Sarsha Crawley: *The Dawn of Australian Feminism*
SE Craythorne: *Stargazed: A Short Story*

Viv Cree: *'So you're here to provide the glamour are you?': Higher Education, Social Work, and a Career as a Dangerous Woman*

Susanna Crossman: *The Tally*

Verónica Cruz Sánchez: *Danger and Liberty: The Struggle for Women's Rights in Guanajuato, Mexico*

Eithne Cullen: *Slopping Out: What If Holloway Prison Could Reflect on its Closure?*

Arpita Das: *Dissenting and Dangerous*

Isabel Davis: *What's in a Word?*

Shirley Day: *A Short History of Enemies and Friends*

Sasha de Buyl-Pisco: *Speaking Out / Keeping Silent*

Marine Desage-El Murr: *Olympe and Marie: Willfully Oblivious or Truly Dangerous?*

susan c. dessel: *Martha Gruening: 'Brick in a Soft Hat'*

Cara Dobbing: *A Case Study: Dangerous Women and the Nineteenth-Century Lunatic Asylum*

Victoria Duckett: *Sarah Bernhardt: Celebrating Transgressive Celebrity*

Leonie Dunlop: *Bein a Girl: A Poem*

Tessa Dunlop: *An Unlikely Asset: Insight into One of 'The Bletchley Girls'*

Sarah Dyer: *Clover*

Millie Earle-Wright: *Plaits Underneath an Orange Helmet*

Edinburgh Women in Black: *The Power of Silence: Women in Black and the Danger in Peaceful Protest*

Salma El-Wardany: *Cover Up and Shut Up*

Margaret Elphinstone: *Margaret Oliphant*

Athena-Maria Enderstein: *How to Be Dangerous Far From Home*

Jenny Engledow: *Hazel Rennie: Peace and Human Rights Campaigner, Poet and Much-Loved Woman*
Sandra Engstrom: *The Scars on My Heart Make Me a Dangerous Woman*
Mel Evans: *A Woman Alone*

Kate Feld: *Riding with Baba Yaga*
Zuhal Feraidon: *Hide and Seek*
Penny Fielding: *Fanny van de Grift Stevenson and Robert Louis Stevenson: A Dangerous Collaboration*
Nina Fischer: *Ahed Tamimi: A Dangerous Girl?*
Sasha Fisher: *Hotter Than Hell*
Lucy Flannery: *The Empress Matilda*
Gemma Flynn: *On Feminist Stand-Up at the Bottom Rung*
Michelle Frost: *Victoria's Secret*

Elaine Gallagher: *Agendas*
Siris Gallinat: *Eat Them All*
Kathy Galloway: *Helen Steven, 1942–2016: A Radical Peace Activist*
Elizabeth Gasparim: *Being a Dangerous Woman*
Lauren Gawne: *Daisy Bates*
Grace Gelder: *The Dangers of Self-Marriage*
Patricia Gerger: *Dangerous Women in a Café: The Story of a Women-Only Space at a Refugee Camp*
Maddie Godfrey: *Unapologetic Bodybuilders*
Amanda Gouws: *Dangerous Naked Women*
Sotiria Grek: *Dangerous Art: Liubov Popova, Constructivism and Politics as an Artform*
Satdeep Grewal: *Women of Steel*
Jackie Gulland: *Danger in the Kitchen: How Domestic Labour Is Dangerous*

Priya Guns: *Rearguard Action on Neilson Road*

Hazel Hall and Lorna Norgrove: *Dr Linda Norgrove*
Laura Hamilton: *Wifey for Lifey – or Not...*
Catherine Harper: *I Became a Dangerous Woman on Good Friday 1977 When I Got My First Period...*
Claire Harrill: *A Dangerous Saint: St Margaret of Scotland*
Rosemary Harris: *Rosa May Billinghurst*
Frances Hider: *Dangerous Outcast or Town Asset? A Social Paradox: The Unusual Life of Miss Kate Ward*
Kelly Hignett: *Dagmar Šimková: Branded a Threat to Communism*
Hilaire: *Unica Zürn: Creating Art from a Dangerous Place*
Sarah Hilary: *Quietly Dangerous: How My Grandmother Won the War*
Lucy R. Hinnie: *Mary Queen of Scots: Femme Fatale, Martyr, or Tragic Romantic Heroine?*
Catherine Hokin: *Margaret of Anjou: More Sinn'd Against Than Sinning?*
Niki Holzapfel: *Out from the Lost and Found: On Amy Winehouse, Cheryl Strayed, and Finding Yourself*
Irene Hossack: *Obituary: A Poem*
Tingting Hu: *In a Victim's Clothing: The Dangerous Woman Concept in the film* Black Coal, Thin Ice
Lesley Hulonce: *Danger and the Amorous Woman: Prostitution in 19th-Century Britain*
Deb Hunter: *Belle Boyd: 'Cleopatra of the Secession'*

Christine Jacobs: *Diasporic Dangerous Woman: A Story of Survival and Success*
Nadine Aisha Jassat: *Scot-Mid: '...I will always be, always be, to them a dangerous woman'*

Sepideh Jodeyri: *Poetry, Art and 'to dare to talk about my body'*
Alison Jones: *A Cry for the Mothers: A Poem*
Susan Jones: *Conrad's Dangerous Women: The Case of Winnie Verloc*
Alison Joseph: *Its Rider Was Named Death: Agatha Christie as a Dangerous Woman*

Katharina Karcher: *Feminism on Fire: Adrienne Gerhäuser, Corinna Kawaters and the 'Red Zora'*
Megha Katoria: *Ismat Chughtai: An Interrogating Dangerous Voice*
Helen Kay: *Remembering Chrystal Macmillan: Challenging Authority, Championing Equality*
Georgiana Keable: *Wangari Maathai*
Emily M. Keeler: *Tiny Bubbles: The Dangerous Woman Behind Veuve Clicquot*
Janet Kellough: *The Woman Who Stood Up: Letitia Youmans and the Temperance Movement in Canada*
Roisin Kelly: *Persephone No More: A Poem*
Meryl Kenny: *'Dangerous Women' in Politics*
Stella Khachina Busolo: *Divorcing the Culture*
Sarah L. King: *'Whores and Witches': The Women of the Pendle Witch Trials*
Jayde Kirchert: *If a Dangerous Woman You Be*
Angéla Kóczé and Julija Sardelic: *Romani Women – Dangerous Women? Contesting Myths and Struggling Realities*
Ioulia Kolovou: *Anna Komnene: Twelfth-Century Greek Byzantine Princess, Historian, Scholar –and Conspirator?*
Jonatha Kottler: *Guinevere, My First Dangerous Woman*
Tanya Krzywinska: *Dangerous Agencies: Norns, Games and Aesthetics of Emergence*

Stefanie Kurt: *Switzerland: Nation of Brothers with Late Arriving Sisters*

Nicola Lacey: *Dangerous Women in English Law and Literature: From Moll Flanders to Tess of the d'Urbervilles*

Stacey (S.G.) Larner: *'Dangerous Women Take up Public Space': Women and Parkour*

Vanessa Lee: *A Dangerous Woman Is an Ordinary Woman: Lumina Sophie dite Surprise*

Janet Lees: *Madge Saunders: 'Sometimes you have to break certain traditions and laws' – A Pioneer in Intercultural Ministry*

Victoria Leslie: *Woolf's Society of Authors: Where Dangerous Women Swim*

Sue Lloyd-Roberts with Allan Little: *The War on Women: And the Brave Ones Who Fight Back*

Kirsty Logan: *Domestic Magic (Or Things My Wife and I Found Hidden In Our House)*

Marjorie Lotfi Gill: *Gift: A Poem*

Anita MacCallum: *A Picture Tells a Thousand Lies*

Fiona Mackay: *Jane Mansbridge – A Quietly Dangerous Woman (for Dangerous Times)*

Judith Mackay: *Proud to Be a Dangerous Woman: Feminist, Subversive and a Challenge to Big Tobacco*

Audrey Macklin and Zunera Ishaq: *Dangerous to Whom?*

Chloe Maclean: *Fighting Like a Woman: On Being a Female Martial Artist*

Jill Marshall: *Dangerous Women Prophets in the New Testament*

Jill Marshall: *Predicting and Enduring Danger: Women Prophets of the Ancient Mediterranean*

Rachael Martin: *Dangerous Women*

Nkateko Masinga: *The Truth: A Short Story*
Catriona McAra and Lesley McAra: *CALM in the Face of Oppression?*
Eilidh McCabe: *Paper*
Richie McCaffery: *Joan Ure: The Dangers of Fighting to be Heard in Poetry*
Hilary McCollum: *The Elusive Suffragette: Lilian Lenton*
Margot McCuaig: *Honeyballers: Lady Florence Dixie and the Dangerous Women of Scottish Women's Football*
Heather McDaid: *Keeping the Door Open: The 7 Habits of Highly Effective Dangerous Women*
Lesley McDowell: *The Case of Madeleine Smith: 'Lucretia Borgia or only a boarding school miss'?*
Dorothy McMillan: *Fanny Wright: 'Beautiful in bodily shape and gifts of soul'*
Mena: *Eugenics and Feminism: A Brief History*
Jill Menzies: *Dangerous Sisters: The Myth of Procne and Philomela*
Paul Merchant: *Janet Thomson: 'A Woman's Place is in Antarctica'*
Whitney Milam: *Fighting for Digital Justice: The Angry Ones: How Women Speaking out About Abuse and Assault Are Changing the Conversation*
Ali Millar: *Dangerously Thin*
Marianne Moen: *Women in the Viking Age Then and Now*
Hodan Mohammed: *A Self-Proclaimed 'It' Girl*
Laura Moncion: *Marguerite Porete: Fake Woman and Dangerous Mystic*
Eva Moreda Rodríguez: *Amparo Cardenal, the Singing Non-Singer*
Isobel Moulder: *Dangerously Funny: On Women in Comedy*
Katie Munnik: *What the Midwife Taught Me*

Karen Murdarasi: *The Other Ptolemy Girl – Arsinoe IV: Who Was Cleopatra's Younger Sister?*
Gillian Murphy: *Millicent Garrett Fawcett: Dangerous Woman?*

Treasa Nealon: *Her & I*
Nellie, Fiona, Priscilla, Sharon, Polly, Elaine, Brenda, Penny and Marian: *It Gave Me Back My Voice: A Women's Aid Group Contributes a Poem of Strength*
Christina Neuwirth: *I, Dangerous Friendzoner*
Jemma Neville: *Tracing Our She-Lines*
Jane Norman: *Choice in Childbirth: How Can It Be 'Dangerous' for Women to Ask for What They Want?*
Ildiko Nova: *Roma Storyteller*
Ejine Olga Nzeribe and Ebere Okereke: *Flora Nwapa: Pioneering Nigerian Administrator, Academic and Author*

Poppy O'Neill: *Hands of Flesh, Hands of Iron: Remembering History's Midwives*
Ashley Orr: *Nellie Bly: 'A dangerous woman gone mad'*
Jess Orr: *Dare to Be Loud! Interview with Katie Ailes*

Victoria Pagan: *What Does It Mean to Be a Dangerous Woman in the Workplace?*
Margery Palmer McCulloch: *Willa Muir (13 March 1890–22 May 1970)*
Morag Parnell and Máire McCormack: *Theo Colborn: Groundbreaking Scientist and Environmental Activist*
Rosalind Parr: *The Dangerous Career of Vijaya Laksmi Pandit: 'Educated, attractive, charming when she wishes'*
Julia Pascal: *Understanding Men: On Encounters with Martha Gellhorn*

Lorne Patterson: *Anna Akhmatova: 'Enemy of the Soviet People'*
Mary Paulson-Ellis: *Not My Type: A Short Story*
Ana Pavlić: *Marija Jurić Zagorka: Semiotic Power of Her Story*
Eloísa Pérez-Lozano: *Dancing While Married: Can a Wife Only Dance with Her Husband?*
Louise Peskett: *Published and Damned: The Shocking Life of Harriette Wilson*
Alexandra Pierce: *The Case of Alice Bradley Davey Sheldon: A Woman of Many Dangers?*
Wendy Pillar: *Dangerous Woman on Holiday*
Tara Pixley: *Neo-Burlesque's Neo Feminism*
Teresa Phipps: *Law, Violence and the 'Dangerous Women' of Medieval England*
Lucy Popescu: *Anna Politkovskaya*
Lucy Popescu: *Aslı Erdoğan: Day of the Imprisoned Writer*
Lucy Popescu: *Lydia Cacho*
Robyn Pritzker: *Skilled Labourers, Dangerous Rivals: Scottish Women Compositors in the Late Nineteenth Century*
Faith Pullin: *Rebecca West: A Dangerously Honest and Unconventional Writer*

Shazea Quraishi: *The Radical Nude*

Erika Rackley: *Lady Hale*
Harshana Rambukwella and Kanchana N. Ruwanpura: *The Paradox of Sri Lanka's Elite Political Women*
Ru Raynor: *Dangerous Women Refuse to Sit Down, Shut Up, Smile and Shop...*
Elizabeth Reeder: *On Women and Essaying: To Be Genre-Bending Is to Be Dangerous*

Sian Rees: *Lucie Aubrac: The French Resistance Heroine Who Outwitted the Gestapo*

Anna Ridler: *Wikileaks: Saudi Women*

Dame Stella Rimington: *Breaking the Mould as the First Female Director General of MI5*

Natasha Rivett-Carnac: *On Art, Careers and Motherhood: Redefining Danger as a 'Softer but More Durable Quality'*

Rachel Roberts: *Sowing Dangerous Seeds*

Jane Rogers: *Doris Lessing*

Dilys Rose: *Not by Blood Alone: Reflections on the Portrait of Sarah Malcolm*

Brenda Rosete: *Elizabeth Miller: The Maiden of the Sea*

Kim Rubenstein and Larissa Halonkin: *Australian Women Lawyers as Active Citizens*

Frances Ryan: *Dangerous (Young) Widows*

Francine Ryan: *Caroline Norton: The Woman Who Fought for – and Won – Rights for Married Women in England*

Tess Ryan: *'The Chorus of Angry': What Does it Mean to Be a Dangerous (Black) Woman?*

Effie Samara: *Nicola Sturgeon and Jacques Derrida*

Lindsay Sambrooks-Wright: *Upending Convention: How My Mother Taught Me About Bravery, Identity and Human Rights*

J.Y. Saville: *Aspiration in the North: The Bradford Female Educational Institute*

Elif Sazan: *Camille Claudel: The Dangerous French Sculptor*

Kate Schneider: *Alison Smithson: Dangerous Woman*

Savanna Scott Leslie: *An Education*

Abigail Zita Seshie: *The Cultural Premise of Gender-Based Discrimination in Ghana: An Autobiographical Standpoint*

Sea Sharp: *The Biography of Calamity Jane*
Jo Shaw: *'I would be thrilled to be called a dangerous woman': Nancy Fraser interview*
Jo Shaw: *Power, Violence and Voice: The Killing of Jo Cox*
Jo Shaw: *Women at Work*
Molly Sheridan: *Damn Rebel Bitches: Challenging the Way We Think About the Beauty Industry*
Sara Sheridan: *Everyday Dangers*
Meher Shiblee: *Why Do We See Lady Macbeth as a Dangerous Woman? Who Was the Historical Lady Macbeth?*
Juliet Shields: *Flora Annie Steel – the Female Kipling?*
Siobhan Shields: *No Hair, Don't Care*
Victoria Shropshire: *The Inspiration of Josephine Baker: Hips That Changed History*
Catherine Simpson and Nina Mega: *My Daughter Is a Dangerous Woman*
Hannah Simpson: *With Great Power: A Short Story*
Anne-Marie Slaughter: *Insisting on Equality: Still a Dangerous Idea? On Independent Thinking and Honouring Women's Career Priorities in the 21st Century*
Cheryl Smith: *Mrs Martinez*
Rebecca Smith: *She Sells Sea Shells... Mary Anning's Story*
Alia Soliman: *Alifa Rifaat: Writing Women's Desires and Domestic Lives in 20th-Century Egypt*
Heshani Sothiraj Eddleston: *NĀN: Photography*
Jo Spiller: *Sophia Jex-Blake: 'A Fair Field and No Favour'*
Clare Stainthorp: *Constance Naden: A Danger to Herself?*
Shelley Stamp: *Lois Weber, Early Hollywood's Forgotten Pioneer*
Gerda Stevenson: *Horsehead Nebula Speaks... of Williamina Fleming*
Lily Stojcevski: *Unspeakable Nights*
Zoë Strachan: *Muriel Spark*

Liga Strangelove: *The Dominatrix as Marxist Feminist: Dangerous Identities, Dangerous Ideas?*

Alison Swanson: *My Lilac Shed: Planting, Growing, and Garden Politics*

Mari Takayanagi: *A Suffragette 'Dressed as a Man' – Catherine Wilson: A Dangerous Woman in UK Parliament*

Alice Tarbuck: *Kitchen Witch*

Alice Tarbuck: *Nan Shepherd*

Chiew-Siah Tei: *Wu Zetian: She, the Emperor*

Paola Tenconi: *Symbol and Strategy: The Frustrating Ambivalence of Veiled (and Unveiled) Algerian Women in the Decolonisation Struggle*

Law Teng: *Educated, Autonomous and Dangerous*

Wendy Tibbitts: *Fast and Dangerous: An Independent Spirit in an 8-litre Bentley: Carol Mary Langton King*

Gill Thakray: *Sisters in Arms*

Sarah Thomas: *Women at the English Bar: Gender Inequality in the Legal Profession – Distant Past or a Current Concern?*

Sharon Thompson: *4,000 Dangerous Mothers*

Agnes Török: *Reclaim the Internet*

Maria Torres-Quevedo: *Subversive Renegotiations of Identity in Female Coming-of-Age Narratives*

Kerri Turner: *Forgotten: Mathilde Kschessinska Speaks*

Alana Tyson: *Arts vs Crafts? On Resisting Gendered Hierarchies of Practice in the Art World*

Chiamaka Umeasiegbu: *Dangerous Women Know No Sleep: The Story of a Triumphant Non-Conformist Daughter*

Jelena Vasiljević: *Flora Tristan: Utopian Socialist. Dangerous Woman?*

Rebecca Vedavathy: *The Praying Mantis: A Short Story*

Sally Wainwright: *Acts of Audacity*

Jo Walby: *Claiming Their Voices: Tracing a Line from Flappers to Today's Vocal Feminists*

Rachel Walker: *Anne Boleyn: Rebellion or Conformity?*

Aisling Walsh: *Saints, Witches and Whores: We Are Magdalenas and We Are Dangerous*

Lucy Walters: *The Painter*

Penny Wang: *Lady Lugard – Flora Shaw: How Imperialism Endangered the Women's Vote*

Lena Wånggren: *Dangerous Women on Bicycles*

Lynnda Wardle: *You Have Struck Women! You Have Struck a Rock! Celebrating South African National Women's Day*

Ellen Webb: *She Is... Dangerous?*

Amy Williams: *Gin, Short Skirts and the Dangerous Women of the 1920s*

JL Williams: *Dangerous Emotions: Three Poems*

Quentin Wilson and Fiona Wilson: *Elsie Mackay, Pioneering Aviator*

Laura Wise: *Plays Well with Others: Dangerous Women at the Peace Table*

Valerie Wong: *Growing up Dangerous in Conservative Asia*

Ellie Woodbourne: *Danger over the Wires: In Memory of the Wireless Listeners of WWII*

Jo Woolf: *Mary Kingsley: Breaking the Mould*

Talat Yaqoob: *Getting over the Myth of Masculine or Feminine Leadership: Getting Women and Girls into Science*

Acknowledgements

We would like to recognise the work of numerous staff at the University of Edinburgh, first and foremost Peta Freestone, without whom there would simply be no Dangerous Women Project. Peta's incredible work made this book possible and we will always be grateful to her. Thanks also to the many interns who have worked tirelessly on the various stages of the Dangerous Women Project, including Isabelle Gius, Katie Graham, Amy McMonagle, Christina Neuwirth, Jana Phillips, Josephine Teng, Sarah Thew and Shy Zvouloun. Our Advisory Group, consisting of Mary Bownes, Suzanne Ewing, Penny Fielding, Lesley McAra, Fiona Mackay and Mona Siddiqui, has supported us every step of the way with wisdom and insight. The staff at the Institute for Advanced Studies in the Humanities, Donald Ferguson and Pauline Clark, have been invaluable. Dorothy Miell and Steve Yearley steered us superbly and generously helped the book become a reality. We want to acknowledge our original supporters and funders from the beginnings of the project in 2016, including Scottish PEN, especially Jenni Daiches, the Binks Trust and the College of Arts, Humanities and Social Sciences at the University of Edinburgh. Katy Guest, DeAndra Lupu and the team at Unbound have been brilliant partners throughout the campaign and production of this book. Lastly, our heartfelt thanks must go to all our authors from around the world, and all the Dangerous Women who have supported us on the way.

Unbound is the world's first crowdfunding publisher, established in 2011.

We believe that wonderful things can happen when you clear a path for people who share a passion. That's why we've built a platform that brings together readers and authors to crowdfund books they believe in – and give fresh ideas that don't fit the traditional mould the chance they deserve.

This book is in your hands because readers made it possible. Everyone who pledged their support is listed below. Join them by visiting unbound.com and supporting a book today.

Jennifer Adam
Martha Adam-Bushell
Anna M. Adamiak
Angeline B Adams
Katherine Aguirre
Fatemeh Ahmadzadeh
Yasmin Ahmadzadeh
Zoe Aiano
Prof. Lilian-Rita Akudolu
Joan Alderdice
David Allan-Smith
Hazel Allan-Smith
Tom Allbeson
Rhona Allin
Nicola Alloway
Amanda Amos
Ben Anderson
Daisy Anderson
Louise Arbuckle
Charlotte Ashby
Susan Bainbrigge
Emily Bamford
Jools Banwell
Megan Bastick
Kate Baty
Juliet Bawden
Lara Baxter
Vikki Bayman
Nancy Baynes
Joan Beadle

Kelsey Beard
Marc Bechtold
Karen Beggs
Victoria Bennett
Lucy Benton
Lara Bettens
Nikki Bi
Nicola Billington
Caroline Birch
Dagmar Birnbaum
David Black
Cathy Blake
Kerry Blankenship
Elisa Blatteis
Margaret Bluman
Rebecca Boden
Manuela Boghian
Ruth Boreham
Mary Bownes
Richard W H Bray
Adela Briansó
Natasha Briant
Michelle Brock
Christopher Brooke
Sophie Brown
Val Brown
Anne Brundell
Caroline Buckland
Anne Burks
John Burks
Wenjia Cai
Sandra Cairncross
Michele Camarda
Alia, Luke, Zara & Rafay Campbell-Crawford
Xander Cansell
Paul James Cardwell
Livia Carlini Schmidt
Yvonne Carol McCombie
Stefanie Carotenuto
Alison Carroll
Jordan Cartmell
Kay Celtel
Snehan Chakravarthi
Martin Chick
Ailsa Clark
Anna Clarke
Fiona Clarke
Geraldine M A Clayton
Kate Clayton
Philippa Cochrane
Kathryn Cook
Kate Cooper-Owen
Edward Corrie
Kirsten Coull
Elizabeth Coulter
Henrietta Courtauld
Sharon Cowan
Robert Cox
Susan Croft
Kate Cross
Cairelle Crow

Mary R. Crumpton
Krisztina Csortea
Kathrine Cuccuru
Heather Culpin
Billie Custock
Raluca Dana Zoițanu
Raluca David
Helena Davies
Sophie Davisson
Ruth Davy
Joyce de la Guerra
Joanne Deeming
Erin Delaney
Leigh Denton
Susan C Dessel
Hannah Dingwall
Cathy Dixon
Cleo Dobbs
Amy Douglas
Constance Douglass
Darrell Douglass
Noelle Douglass
Natasha Dyer
Joanne Dyson
Astrid Edelman-McCabe
Alison Elliot
Debbie Elliott
Sandra Engstrom
Zoe Ennis
Patricia Erskine
Jenny Everingham
Pegi Eyers
Louise Farquharson
Anne Feltz
Barbara Fernandez Melleda
Penny Fielding
Katherine Firth
Claudia Fischer
Robert Fisher
Maria Fletcher
Ben Fletcher-Watson
Sue Fletcher-Watson
Clare Ford
Kathryn Foston
Lena Frain-Atallah
Bridget Fraser
Kerry Fraser
Milla Fyfe
Luisa Gandolfo
Laurie Garrison
Bärbel Gerdes
Daniele Gibney
Jane Gilchrist
V L Gill
Zara Gilmour
Ed Glass
Sophie Glazik
Caroline Goldsmith
Una Gordon
Rita E. Gould
Claire Grant
Isobel Gray

Lj Gray
Samuel Gray
Shelagh Green
Tim Guenther
Katy Guest
Jackie Gulland
Emma Hadfield-Hudson
Charlotte Haines Lyon
Nicky Haire
Kate Hall
Gretel Hallett
Lisa Hallgarten
Simon Hamilton
Jill Hanson
Sallyannie Harbottle
Alison Hardy
Robin Hargreaves
Ann Harrison
Elizabeth Hart
Nicola Hart
James Hartman
Helen Hartnell
Rachel Hazelwood
Jane Healy
Geraldine Heaney
Samuel Hedley
Ann Henderson
Charlie Henderson-Howat
Adélaïde P. Hersant
Tammy Hervey
Caroline Heycock
Melissa Highton
Catherine Hills
Leslie Hills
Alice Hockey
Theresa M Hoffman
JC Holbrook
Amy Holland
Rachel Holland
Lucy Hollingworth
Holly Holmes
Lisa Holmes
Wei-sheng Hong
Philip Hood
Shirley Horn
Lise Hovik
Bekah Hughes
Tom Hulley
Emma Hunter
Bridget Innes
Vicky Ireland
Lucy Irvine
Angela Jack
Katy Jack
Noor-ud-din Janmohamed
Christian Jeffery
Helen Jeffries
Lisa Jenkins
Susan Jensen
Narinder Jhittay
Colin Johnson
Hannah Johnstone

Jolene Jones
Mary Jordan-Smith
Felix Joseph
Holly Joseph
Renee Joyce
Satu Kapiainen
Helen Kay
Penelope Kay
Sandra Keegan
Stuart Kelly
Meryl Kenny
Jenny Kenyon
Lucie Kettley
Yasmin Keyani
Fozia Khanam
Dan Kieran
Robert Kilbride-Newman
Laura Kilty
Kiersten Kirchdoerfer Douglass
Doreen Knight
Astrid Kopmels
Margaret Korosec
KU Leuven Arts Faculty & Artes Library
Susanne Kuntz
Sarah Kyambi
Jocelyn Kynch
Pierre L'Allier
Anna Lange
Skye Langmuir
Kerry Lavin-Thomson
Victoria Lawrence
Janet Lees
Ruth Leonard
Christine Letter Gregg
Lillian Levy
Anastasia Lewis
Hannah Lewis
Jennifer Lewis
Patricia Lewis
Kate Lewis Hood
Chris Limb
Carly Lockett
Laura Lopes-Buddie
Jenna Ludwig
Fiona Mackay
Susan Mackinlay
Derek MacLeod
Jo Maconnachie
Catherine Makin
Camilla Marie Pallesen
Duncan Marjoribanks
Victoria Marland
Lotte Marley
Anabel Marsh
Carol Marsh
Helen Marsters
Samuel Martin Nye
Wendy Mathison
Lara Matthews
Margaret McAllister

Lauren McAteer
Naomi McAuliffe
Margot McCuaig
Katie McGavigan
Sharon Mchale
Susan McIvor
Fiona McLachlan
Holly Mcleish
Sarah Mcloughlin
Christina McMellon
Dorothy McMillan
Lynn McMillan
Amy McMonagle
Agata McWhirter
Barbara Joan Meier
Ineke Meijer
Stephen Meister
Gillian Mellor
Marie Merillat
Dorothy Miell
Cassiopeia Miles
Karine Millaire
Eve Miller-Hodges
Amanda Mills
John Mitchinson
Yoshimi Miyazaki
Natalina Monteiro
Niamh Moore
Rebecca Moore
Sarah Moore
Vesta Moore
Natalie Moorse
Fionnuala Morris
Maggie Morrison
Lauren Mulville
Ben Murray
Carlo Navato
Josephine Neil
Robert Nelson
John New
Kriss Nichol
Helen Nickerson
Glenda Norquay
Carly North
Karen O'Sullivan
Emily O'Hare
Lorna O'Mahony
Pontus Odmalm
Elsa Osman
Joska Ottjes
Prof Owen
Miranda Owen Wintersgill
Victoria Pagan
Rachel Paine
Nacim Pak-Shiraz
Allie Parker
Mark Parsons
Paul Patras
Aunnie Patton Power
Lampis Pergantis
Audrey Philip
Eileen Phillips

Anita Pilgrim
Frances Pinter
Lydia Plowman
Frances Poet
Justin Pollard
Ivy Pottinger-Glass
Tina Price-Johnson
Laura Pugh
Reda Rackley
Steven Rae
Chaitra Redkar
Marina Remington
Emma Rhind-Tutt
Kristina Richartz
Karen Richmond
Suzanne Richmond Maasland
Nathalie Rivere de Carles
Deb Roberts
Desna Roberts
Hannah Rohde
Michael Romer
Kat Rose
Lizzy Rose
Kirsty Ross
Natalie Ross
Marina Rossi
Lisa Rull
Dan Rutland
Jean Sambrooks
Katharine Samuel
Polly Sands
Christine Sas
Philippa Saunders
Habie Schwarz
Anne-Marie Scott
Sue Scott
Steve Scott-Marshall
Kim Seath
Rhea Selene Enzian
Jayanta Sengupta
Papia Sengupta
Travis Sentell
Penny Sharp
Caroline Shaw
Jo Shaw
Jonathan Shaw
Daisy Sherrington
Karell Sime
Kate Simpson
Holly Sinkinson
Maja Sinn
Hazel Slavin
Joan Smith
Laura Smith
Lorraine Smith
Maria Smith
Martyn Smith
Richard Smith
Kate Snook
Koyeli Solanki
Carmen Soto
Esther Sparrow

Hilary Spiers
Jonathan Spiers
Jo Spiller
Caroline Sproule
Wendy Staden
Clare Stainthorp
Ginger Stampley
Kerry Staples
Hannah Stark
Zoë Stennett-Cox
Courtney Stephenson
Lorraine Stevenson
Stuart Stokeld
Bel Stone
Allison Strachan
Ann Stutz
Georgie Sussman
Cathy Swift
Deborah Swinney
Helen Taylor
Paul Taylor
Susan Taylor
Sena Tèa Laurent Brierley-Belson
Suria Tei
Olivia Thompson
Emily Thompson-Bell
Wendy Tibbitts
Joanna Tindall
Pippa Tolfts
Amie Tolson
Jasmine Tonie
Sabine Tötemeyer
Ian Turnbull
Jon Turner
Deborah Vaile
Astrid Van Den Brink
Heather Ventura
Elinor Vettraino
Alejandro Villalobos
Diana Vladutu
Yvonne Waddell
Karen Waldron
Catherine & David Walker
Rupert Walker
Angela Wallace
Andrew Walsh
Pat Walshe
Lora Waring
Hannah Warwicker
Judy and Michael Watson
Eve Watt
Jill Weinstein
Eva Wewiorski
Alison Wheatley
Bethany Whiteside
Lucy Wilkins
Tess Wilkins
Rae Williams
Catherine Williamson
Shz Williamson
Andrew J. Wilson

Christine Wilson
Keeley Wilson
Rebecca Wilson
Anastasia Winchester
Kimi Winward
Pamela Woods
Steve Woodward
Lara Woolford
Jocelyn Wyburd
Carolyn Yates
J L Yates
Steven Yearley
Jodi Young
Robyn Young
Susan Young
Irmingard Zahn
Verena Zahn
Melissa Zurbriggen